# EXTREME YOU

# EXTREME YOU

## STEP UP.
## STAND OUT.
## KICK ASS.
## REPEAT.

**SARAH ROBB O'HAGAN**
**WITH GREG LICHTENBERG**

piatkus

PIATKUS

First published in the United States in 2017 by HarperBusiness
First published in Great Britain in 2017 by Piatkus
This paperback edition published in 2020 by Piatkus

1 3 5 7 9 10 8 6 4 2

A CIP catalogue record for this book
is available from the British Library.

ISBN 978-0-349-41231-3

Designed by Bonni Leon-Berman
Printed and bound in Great Britain by Clays Ltd, Elcograf S.p.A.

Papers used by Piatkus are from well-managed forests
and other responsible sources.

Piatkus
An imprint of
Little, Brown Book Group
Carmelite House
50 Victoria Embankment
London EC4Y 0DZ

An Hachette UK Company
www.hachette.co.uk

www.improvementzone.co.uk

For Mum and Dad,

Extreme Jenny and Honorable John,

for showing me there were big mountains to climb,

and for letting me figure out how to climb them.


And for Liam, Sam, Joe, and Gabby,

for making the entire journey worthwhile.

It's not the mountain we conquer, but ourselves.

—SIR EDMUND HILLARY

# CONTENTS

# INTRODUCTION

Sitting at the front of the auditorium, waiting to deliver a speech at an undergrad business conference at Harvard, I began to have an uncomfortable feeling. I was to be the keynote speaker, the "opener" at this event, with about a thousand attendees from universities around the world, and my bloody MacBook would not connect to the conference organizer's projection equipment. Yep, that's right—hundreds of young people were streaming through the doors and taking their seats as I stood there with sweat bullets on my forehead wondering what kind of interpretive dance I was going to have to do for them if the damn projector wouldn't connect.

To add a little more pressure, Donna Karan, a business hero of mine and a legend of the business world, was to be the "closer." She wasn't even due to speak for another five hours, yet her "people" had already arrived to make sure her presentation was all set to work. Oh, God—why didn't I have "people" to take care of such issues? This wasn't the first time that the tornado that is Sarah Robb O'Hagan had blown into an auditorium attempting to look perfectly polished and professional when in fact behind the scenes I was anything but.

The young woman who had organized the conference stood up to introduce me. She read out my bio word for word, and of course

I knew what it said. It was the bio used in the promotional materials for the conference, the bio I gladly distributed because it gave the impression that I was a serious success story—a "reinventor of brands" who'd worked at Virgin and Nike, a "workout queen" who "brought an athlete's mind-set to business problems," one of *Fast Company*'s Most Creative People in Business, *Ad Age*'s Women to Watch, a three-time recipient of *SportsBusiness Daily*'s Forty Under 40 Award, and named by *Forbes* as one of the Most Powerful Women in Sports. Many of those accolades had come to me when I had served as global president of Gatorade, one of the world's most iconic sports brands, and led that brand through a major turnaround—a transformational journey from sports drink company to sports performance innovator, returning the once-struggling business to healthy growth. After that I had gone on to be president of Equinox, the world's premier fitness lifestyle company, named by *Fast Company* as one of 2015's Most Innovative Companies in Fitness, and now I am the CEO of Flywheel Sports—the awesome, fast-growing indoor cycling company.

But as I listened to this aspiring young businesswoman describe me, something felt very wrong. What bothered me was not what she said but what she left out. My bio made it sound as if I were this polished, perfect business fem-bot. It certainly didn't mention what most of my colleagues see in me—the wild storm of enthusiasm and determination, tempered by plenty of embarrassing trip-ups as I work hard to try to hold it all together.

My bio also neglected to mention that for much of my life the results I had delivered had been, at best, average. Sometimes I'd not quite "made the team." Other times I'd been a disappointment. At still other times, I'd been what I can only describe as an epic fail. Yep, I'm that person who got fired not just once but *twice* in my twenties. The first time I was singled out as a rabble-rouser and nearly deported from the United States back to my home country of New Zealand because I didn't have an employer and a work visa to keep me here. The second job ended when I was laid off as part of a larger restructuring. Three years of what I fondly refer to as my "canyon of career despair"—hardly a picture-perfect journey.

On the job, too, I've had plenty of seriously embarrassing screw-ups—ideas that seemed huge in my mind but shriveled to nothing in the marketplace. Despite all of that, though, by my late thirties, I was giving speeches at conferences where audience members would line up to meet me, asking, "How do you do it? Tell us your secret."

My secret, if you really want to know, is that I'm about as far from perfect as you can get—but in my experience perfection is overrated. Yes, I made it to president of a $5 billion global sports brand at a pretty early age. But I think all that happened exactly because I wasn't scared of my imperfections, contradictions, and attitude. Listen: I'm a big, bold, over-the-top, laugh-till-ya-snort, opinionated, don't-sit-on-the-sidelines, mega-enthusiastic kinda gal. Simple things such as my giant, man-sized feet were an early clue that I was never going to be perfect the way society defines it for us. But I figured that if I kept trying and experimenting to find where I was great and where I sucked, if I kept believing that I could excel somewhere, somehow, eventually I'd find my own path to my own kind of greatness. I chose the path of living my personality to its fullest to get where I wanted to go. And I've come to realize that I'm not alone.

Angela Ahrendts. Bode Miller. Condoleezza Rice. Mister Cartoon. Angela Lee Duckworth. Sam Kass. Casey Wasserman. Bozoma Saint John. You might wonder what a business leader, a downhill skier, a former secretary of state, a tattoo artist, a psychologist, a chef, a sports business founder, and a music executive have in common. They just happen to be the best in the world at what they do, but none of them started their careers knowing exactly where their true greatness would lie.

One of the great benefits of my career journey is the amazing opportunity I have had to meet and work with so many successful people from many different walks of life. I've had the chance to observe how they do what they do. Behind the accolades and the glowing media articles that say how awesome they are, you'll find that they have had an extraordinary impact by embracing every aspect of themselves—the good and the bad—because they took risks and worked through the sometimes tough negative consequences. They didn't expect their greatness to just happen; instead they worked their asses off to outperform everyone around them with a potent mix of drive and humility. They are *Extremers*, those who reach the summit of their potential by developing their unique mix of abilities in their own personal way.

Anyone can do this. I call it developing Extreme You—becoming the best you can be as only you can. Extreme You is not one fixed goal. It doesn't depend on the typical early indicators of success (high test scores, star turns in sports or the arts, membership in elite social and professional networks) or on flashy short-term achievements. The fact is, most of us don't make a big splash early, and most achievements, as the world judges them, soon fade. Nor is Extreme You just a style or an attitude. Extremers have a ton of attitude—do we ever!—but it goes far beyond surface dazzle.

Extreme You is a lifelong method for discovering and making the most of what's in you, starting from wherever you are with your own diverse mix of interests, skills, and experiences—and yes, that includes setbacks, losses, weaknesses, and failures. Extremers discover that the more they develop themselves, the more new potential they find. They learn to embrace the support of others in making their Extreme efforts and to collaborate by bringing out the Extreme in others. They are successful, yes, but on their own terms, almost as a by-product of developing Extreme You.

Are you a dreamer? I know I was. As a kid growing up in New Zealand, I imagined I could have a big impact on the world. I was constantly searching for my calling, trying on different visions of my future. I dreamed I could be a famous tennis player, but then I had the small problem that I never won any tournaments. I thought I could win an Olympic swimming medal, but my parents weren't "those" kind of parents—they showed no interest in taking me to a pool at five every morning. I wanted to sing as beautifully as Dame Kiri Te Kanawa at the royal wedding (though I still don't think we should forgive Diana for that dress choice . . . ), but the choir director never picked me for solos. I thought I could be a famous actress, and I was certain my moment was coming when I tried out to play Sandy in our high school production of *Grease*. But—you guessed it—I didn't even get picked to be one of the Pink Ladies. I was in the section of the chorus for people who don't belong on the stage.

Now, don't get me wrong. I think I was considered "bright," and my personality definitely stood out as bold and bossy. (Oh, if I had a dollar for every time in high school I heard the line, "Sarah and company, would you please *stop talking*!") But no one ever found me reading chapter books in my crib or playing chess in my high chair. And despite what felt to me like herculean efforts, if I'm going to be honest, I never really excelled at anything. I never made the top team in any sport or won a scholarship to university. I barely scraped by with "B"-level grades. I wasn't a jock or a homecoming queen or singled out as most likely to succeed. I definitely wasn't model beautiful—big feet, rugby-player thighs. Thanks, Dad! I didn't have any well-connected uncles to help me skip over the line to a great internship. I never even earned an MBA.

By now you may be wondering, "Who is this crazy New Zealander lady? Why is she talking to me?" I'm writing this book because it's high time someone talks about a different, more fun, and more uniquely ownable path to making the most of our potential, a path open to most everyone. That day at Harvard, my own bio with its list of accomplishments proceeding logically, one to the next, made me feel uncomfortable because, like so many of the success stories people tell, it left out the most important part. Those stories so often make it sound as if the successful are the ones whose gifts and advantages become clear early and lead them to early, inevitable victories. Then they step confidently from one triumph to the next, building on those early wins. But that's definitely not how it happened for me or for the many Extremers I have talked to.

I know there is another way.

It was exactly because I *didn't* have one clear, natural gift, because I was bold and loud and no one's stereotype of a perfect petite female, and because I lacked dramatic early successes that I had to watch others win their accolades from the sidelines and feel, so strongly, *I want some of that*. Because success didn't come easily, and because I kept bumping into authority figures telling me that I was too loud, too talkative, too mischievous, too bossy, I gained the hunger and the determination to fuel my inner drive. With that magic drive as my engine, I pressed on, and as an adult I discovered that I actually did have a unique combination of characteristics, experiences, and skills that was distinctly and extremely *me*, and because I honed and developed them as my unique formula I was able to overcome my average start and become world class. I created my own special way of finding success.

The secret I found, after my early disappointments, was that when you aim for oversized achievement, you must make a choice. Every challenging situation, personal or professional, that comes with the possibility of serious success or failure will also come with pressure from others and from yourself. Pressure to conform to the accepted norms. Edit yourself down. Fit in. Do what is usual and comfortable and in so doing make yourself seem more average, more expected, and less threatening to the status quo—*less of yourself.* If you make that choice, you may find that you are well rewarded in the short run because you don't make anyone around you feel nervous or look bad. But it's also like playing a game of tennis on the defense, putting all your effort into not making mistakes and not losing points. It becomes very hard to break through and win because you're not playing your own game.

The other choice is to embrace what I call Extreme You, to confidently put all that is distinctive and relevant about yourself into everything you do. I bring a huge amount of passion to my work—and I have very little patience for those who don't. I show up intense. I give my all. *I care.* And although you might say that not everyone is wired that way, I would answer that many people, from colleagues to friends, have said the same thing to me: "I never in a million years would have done ____, but now that you've encouraged and pushed me to do it"—try harder, push further, *care more*—"I'm doing it!" And that's not only a good thing when you win; it's a good thing, period. Because in the end, playing the game your way, full steam ahead, means that you have a much greater chance to live your full self at work and at home, in everything you do. That's a whole lot more fun and more satisfying than pretending to be something you're not.

## WHAT EXTREME YOU IS NOT

Extreme You is definitely not about being a reckless loudmouth. It's not about being persistent to the point of harassment, and it's definitely not about "my way or the highway." I remember when I was five years into my Air New Zealand career. Now based out of Los Angeles, I got some great news during a performance review: I was getting a big promotion! For the first time in my life, I was going to hire people to report directly to me. My boss told me about my new position, my new salary, and it all seemed good. Then he said, "You've got real talent, Sarah. But—you need to start presenting yourself in a more mature, more respectable way. You just don't dress well enough."

I was *mortified*. I mean, to be clear, this dude was hardly a fashion icon, and in my mind he had absolutely zero idea what was hip and happening in the world of popular culture. But dammit, his comments were also familiar. Even back on high school choir trips, I had always been the one getting into trouble because I was too immature—not respectful enough, too loud, talking too much. And now the same embarrassment had followed me into my performance review. As if it weren't bad enough to be told publicly that my appearance was unprofessional, my boss went on to suggest a solution: his "partner"—that is, his girlfriend—would take me shopping and help me pick out clothes.

Of course, I wanted the promotion and the new responsibility.

He even offered me a onetime clothing stipend to help "clean myself up." For about a week, I was smarting in my corner, planning my perfect comeback to tell him how wrong he was. But though that might have qualified as a kind of Extreme Me, it would also have been Extreme Unemployed. So after I had a chance to think it over, I decided, *All right. I'm going to man up and look at Ann Taylor suits with this lady.* They were giving me a clothing stipend, so in my mind there was money to be spent on clothes, and, Lord knows, I love clothes. (Nothing like a bit of retail therapy to get the party started!) But no one could make me buy anything I didn't want. They weren't going to dumb me down or turn me into someone I was not, but my boss had given me advice for a reason and I knew I needed to acknowledge that reason. So the right question was: How can I mash it up and make it into something that will still be me?

His lady friend was actually pretty cool about the whole crazy situation. Can you imagine being told, "Honey, go take this misguided young thing shopping for some decent clothes?" We met and we looked at the "appropriate" suits, from the midlevel heels—not too high or too low!—to the match-matchy suit and skirt that announced to the world, "Yes, I am boring." I would rather have shot myself than look as conservative and as expected as that. But I thanked the lady friend and received the message my boss had sent. I committed in my mind to upping my game and acting more like a manager.

In the end, on my own and at boutiques of my choosing, I bought myself some business suits (blazer and pants) but with a far more *me* kind of look. Clothes that said, "I have a point of view. I am wearing bold black boots because I am about to kick some ass, and I give a shit about styling myself in a way that makes me stand out from the crowd." I went back to the office with new clothes to show that yes, I had listened—but I had taken the advice in a way that was Extremely Me.

Extreme You has been my approach all the way, and in this book I'll explain how what worked for me and the awesome Extremers I've interviewed from all walks of life can work just as powerfully for you. In the first half of this book, I'll show you how to develop the five essential qualities of Extreme You. You'll learn to Check Yourself Out, to discover your own unique mix of Extreme skills and interests. Then you'll Ignite Your Magic Drive to build the stamina and the confidence to power you through any challenge that comes your way. I'll show you the importance of knowing when to Get Out of Line, to put your Extreme qualities to use even when others around you don't appreciate them, and the equal importance of learning to Get Over Yourself, so your Extreme strengths don't become liabilities. Finally, I'll reveal the secrets of Pain Training, which can turn even your biggest failures into an awesome personal trainer guiding you to future success.

In the second half of the book, once you've developed your Extreme nature, I'll guide Extreme You to meet and crush challenges alone and with others, making use of what I call the Extremer Cycle. I'll share my own stories of learning by trial and error to develop Extreme Me, and I'll share the epic stories and insights of Extremers I've interviewed. Then I'll end each chapter with a section called Extreme Moves, to give you practical insights and action-oriented advice to help you step up your game.

Along the way, I'll reveal some secret weapons. One is to look for examples not just in other individual Extremers, but in the Extreme brands and organizations and teams you most admire. To me, the questions of how to make the most of what's in you and how to make the world recognize what you've got are a lot like the questions that great leaders grapple with when figuring out how to build the best teams, brands, and businesses. In this era of social media, people talk a lot about "personal branding"—building your profile out in the world so people know who you are. But to me it's so much deeper than that. Personal branding is less about attracting legions of followers on Facebook and more about knowing who you are and what you stand for, and I'll share many lessons from great brands and businesses that apply to Extreme individuals.

Another Extreme secret weapon is support. Again and again, in my stories and those of others I will share, the Extremer has succeeded only because someone else was providing support, air cover, coaching, mentoring, or lead parenting. In today's media-driven era, we tend to focus on individuals instead of celebrating the team of supporters necessary to bring out the Extreme in an individual. But extreme success depends on extreme support from those around you.

Here's an awesome example. Being a New Zealander, I am enormously proud to come from the country that boasts the first man to summit Mount Everest. It speaks to the adventurous and pioneering spirit of our country that is observed in Kiwis the world over. But Sir Edmund Hillary's epic climb to the top of the mountain is even more relevant today because there are no photos of him at the summit. When he reached this pinnacle of human exploration, his Sherpa, Tenzing Norgay, didn't know how to work the camera to take a photo. And Sir Ed was just fine with that because in his mind they had reached the summit together. He took photos of the majestic brilliant views in front of him so that he could share an experience that no human in the world had ever seen. He didn't need a selfie.

You might still be wondering why I take the risks of disruptively, unabashedly being Extreme Me. If my story says anything, it's that this approach has enabled me to overcome my own average level of talent and my history of average results to unlock unique but unrecognized inner potential. It also says that on the day I gave that speech at Harvard, even with the technical issues with my MacBook and the sweat bullets on my forehead, I knew that even if I didn't get my presentation on the screen, I would still give those young business students an inspiring, unforgettable speech.

Why? Because I know in my heart what I believe so deeply, and no technological glitch will ever stop me from sharing it passionately. In every company where I have ever worked, and in organizations of every type around the world that I have visited, there have been employees with extraordinary potential who went to the office each day and put their best efforts not toward making the most of their gifts and knowledge, not toward reaching their personal best in the service of what was best for the organization, but toward fitting in and not getting fired. The Gallup organization's 2016 "State of the American Workplace" report confirmed this, finding that a truly scary seven out of ten American workers are either "not engaged" in or "actively disengaged" from their work.

There are so many managers and leaders out there who are capable of developing creative ideas and performing remarkably, but that potential is not being realized. Even for aspiring entrepreneurs, as I have seen in my own business experiences, there's a lot less real innovation than meets the eye. I've experienced what feels like a gazillion young whiz kids try to get meetings with me because they believe they can partner with my company. They think they have invented the next Fitbit, the next Jawbone, the next Facebook, the next Uber, the next Lululemon—but so many of their "innovations" are really just copycat products, and a big reason many of those entrepreneurs are even in business is that there has been so much cheap capital funding available. When I speak at business schools, I'm amazed by how many of the students reveal that their life plan is simply to walk the safest path that their parents can find for them. When I speak to middle managers, I hear them reveal in a thousand different ways how they believe that their real job is just to please the boss, never mind realizing their potential or improving their company's results.

I'm so passionate about the approach I call Extreme You because investing all of our distinctive selves in everything we do is the only way to unlock our untapped resources of innovation, energy, and potential reinvention. Any person, any team, any company, and any country will reach a higher level of performance if it stands on its own unique foundation.

I have written this book for believers who want more—for those who are at the start of their career journey, choosing a life path and a way to walk it, and for those who are stuck in a rut in the middle, feeling constantly pressured by the mantra "Don't take risks for big wins; just make sure you don't lose." I write for anyone who wants to find the courage and the means to get out of the middle of the road, to go for it—and own the consequences.

That's Extreme You.

# EXTREME YOU

# ONE
## CHECK YOURSELF OUT

Sam Kass is a badass. You might know him as the White House chef—the guy that cooked for the Obama family and all of their high-rolling guests—but I've come to know him as a wicked Extremer who explored many corners of the world (including New Zealand . . . yeah!) on his way to one of the coolest jobs on the planet. Sam's served as assistant White House chef and as the White House food initiative coordinator, helping First Lady Michelle Obama to grow the first substantial White House vegetable garden in more than a hundred years. He was also part of the First Lady's Policy Office, working with the Departments of Agriculture and Education and the White House Domestic Policy Council in their efforts to reduce childhood obesity. I bonded with him when we had our first lunch together, riffing on how we must end this obesity crisis once and for all, and my Extreme radar went on high alert. In my mind Sam had an incredible gig, but not one that I can remember the guidance counselors at my high school putting on the list of "things you could be." I simply had to know: how had he figured out it was in him to become chef to the most powerful man in the world, and how had he developed the knowledge and skills to do it?

I wondered if he was one of these people who had known where he would wind up from the day he could sit up and look around. Nope. "Growing up," Sam told me, "all I dreamed of was becoming a professional baseball player." He played ball at the private school where his father was a teacher. Many of his classmates went on to big-name universities to pursue professional careers, but Sam went to community college in Kansas City, Kansas, in the hope of getting drafted by a baseball team, taking courses such as Techniques in Baseball and Sprint Practice. (BTW—who knew you could study baseball in college?) But after a couple of years of effort, he said, "I realized I was a good player but not better than everybody else. At the same time, I realized I could probably use an education, as my mom had been telling me the whole time."

Sam transferred to the University of Chicago, where he studied history. One summer, he worked at an Italian American restaurant, 312 Chicago, which had a focus on local agriculture and organic ingredients. He loved food, but he felt no wish to become a chef. With no idea what he wanted to do besides baseball, he followed a desire to see the world and spent his final semester of college studying abroad in Vienna, Austria. While there, he mentioned his enthusiasm for food to someone who introduced him to the sous chef in one of the top restaurants in the city. Sam told the chef that he had thought at times of studying cooking just to learn to cook for his family, when he had one. "The chef said, 'Don't be a fool and go to culinary school and waste all that money! Just come into the kitchen and hang out.' So on my third day in Vienna I was in this Michelin-starred restaurant kitchen. There's a wonderful ethic in kitchens where if you're young and you show a strong work ethic and willingness to learn and show some promise, they're willing to tolerate you messing up a lot of stuff. So they let me do a little bit and I had fun, and at the end of the night they said, 'You're welcome back anytime.' I said, 'Be careful, I'm the kind of guy who will take you up on that. I'm the kind of guy who will keep showing up.'"

Now, here's the really cool part. It turns out that the way the kitchen staff works together in a restaurant is just like the intense team dynamics of a baseball team. "It's a team sport, and nothing happens if everyone doesn't work together, but it's fundamentally individual. If you burn something and mess up the order or you're late, everyone knows who made the mistake. It doesn't get lost in the flow." It was also like baseball in that there were many at-bats, many "plays," and no matter what mistakes he made on one dish, he had to turn around and keep cooking for the rest of the night. And it was hard work: "You're moving fast for hours, like you're sprinting, and you're cutting yourself, burning yourself, and your back hurts. It's brutally, brutally hard work, physically and mentally, and that's what sports teach you: to work your ass off. I was definitely ready to work hard." As I said—Sam is a badass!

He worked in the kitchen for free, getting "paid" in the form of a free room in the chef's apartment and meals in the restaurant. "They threw me a little pocket money, but basically I got paid in knowledge." He couldn't get a work permit, and the authorities eventually made him leave, but by then the ball was rolling. Through boatloads of hard work he'd discovered a passion and a talent in himself that he hadn't known he had—and he'd started developing it into the skill that would shape his entire career.

## WHAT BLOWS YOUR HAIR BACK?

If you are going to live Extreme You, you need to know what that looks like for you, but let's be real: for most people, it's not that obvious. In hindsight, Sam's years of baseball training were perfect preparation for a restaurant kitchen, but who knew? His enthusiasm for food and his summer job at a Chicago restaurant had nurtured his passion to be a chef, but he hadn't been aware of it; he had even told the chef in Vienna that he wanted to learn to cook only so his family could eat well at home. He discovered his Extreme Chef over time, by allowing his curiosity to be his guide, by following what grabbed him, and by working his ass off at the opportunities he chose to pursue. He took off the baseball uniform, and then, just because the opportunity came along and it spoke to him somehow, he tried on the chef's apron. Then he checked himself out—took a fresh look in the existential mirror—and what he saw was someone who fit into the high-pressure team environment of the kitchen and loved the "game" of gourmet cooking.

For Sam, checking himself out revealed new skills and a possible career path. But sometimes, for some people, it reveals not a formal skill but rather a new way of approaching situations, a different way of bringing one's personality into the world. For me, one critical moment came when I was fresh out of university. Working our first full-time jobs, my girlfriends and I grew tired of the typical Friday-night grubby gathering at the pub. We dreamed of dressing up in sexy evening dresses and going to a glamorous dance party.

I could picture the night in my head: the hot guys in tuxes, some decent champagne to kick the night off instead of the "Marquee Spew" that we had become accustomed to drinking in college, and of course some bloody good fun on the dance floor. Now that we were out of university, though, we hit an obstacle: there were no formal social events being organized for us anymore. Still, I couldn't let go of the mental picture I had of my friends and me dressed up in our fab dresses at a ball.

Finally I thought, *What the hell are we waiting for? Nobody else is going to do this for us. Let's friggin' make it happen for ourselves!* I started drawing up a project plan. Some people, I figured, would buy tickets for a glam event, but it would be more broadly appealing if we were raising money for, let's say, a charity supporting cancer research. Then I put out the word to my friends and asked who would pitch in.

I still have a scrapbook of all the planning memos. I deputized ten friends as ticket sellers, with a free ticket offered as a prize to whoever sold the most, and I sent out frequent email updates on the sales standings. I found someone to help us hire a band, someone else to take photographs that we could offer for sale, and others with more event experience to hire coat check attendants and a bouncer. We had to be sure not to trash the rented room! I printed up tickets and receipts and convinced my bank to let me open a separate account just for the event. A friend had a friend who would handle the decorations (lots of balloons!). And to keep it all moving forward, I scheduled and ran the meetings—always including plenty of beers for motivation—and cheered everyone on.

Sample email from twenty-one-year-old me: "Hi there all budding ticket sellers!! The decision has been made and there's no stopping us now. The ball is going ahead so we have one hell of a lot of work to do to sell those 200 tickets. Enclosed is your ticket selling kit and expectations for sales by week." Looking back, it's amazing that my friends could deal with how bossy I was. But it worked! Together we put on a fund-raising ball, and we had one of the most epic nights of our young lives. And all this despite the fact that the afternoon of the event I discovered a zit on my forehead that made me look like fucking Cyclops!

I did it for fun. And except that I made generous use of the Air New Zealand marketing department photocopy machine to print posters and tickets, to me it had nothing to do with my career. No one had ever said about me, "Oh, yes, this Sarah is a future business leader. This is a young woman who could one day run an international company with tens of thousands of employees." Or even two employees. Believe me, the thought was in no one's mind, not even mine. But in my future job interviews and in early discussions with supervisors, if the question of organizational leadership experience came up, I had something to talk about: I had organized a charity ball.

It wasn't just that I now had a little management experience; I had begun to discover a talent that I'd never really known mattered, because it certainly did not appear on my university transcript or my résumé: and that was my own rather unique style of collaborative and imaginative leadership. I had imagined a goal and a way to reach it, then inspired and prodded and cheered others along to pitch in and make it happen together. That approach would turn out to be one of my lifelong specialties, but I first found it, as I would find other key skills and areas of special expertise, by being open to whatever floated toward me during new experiences. (OK, if I'm honest—because I had the selfish goal of wanting to go to a hot dance party with some good champagne and great-looking guys!)

My discoveries, and the successes they led to, were made possible by a fair amount of randomness. I went for the dance party, but I came away with the discovery of the start of a lifelong talent. Who could have predicted? No one. So we need to rely less on predicting our Extreme path and more on trying out new experiences and observing the results. Franz Johansson, the author of *The Click Moment: Seizing Opportunity in an Unpredictable World*, analyzed breakthrough success stories in business and found that success depends much more on serendipity and surprise than we might want to think. "When it comes to our career or developing a strategy for a business," he says, "we think we can circumvent this notion of randomness by analyzing or strategizing, and that's a mistake. If you scratch underneath the glossy exterior of success stories, you're going to find behind those things an unexpected meeting, a surprising insight. . . . It follows then that we should court those types of things, we should try to get unexpected meetings, we should try to find unexpected insights." Again, developing Extreme You is like matchmaking: you can't predict who will fall in love with whom, but it helps to throw a party and show up.

## YOUR PERSONAL MOON SHOT

Here's the thing that gets me so fired up. It's not as if people who don't check themselves out walk around knowing what they missed. The fact is, some of the most accomplished people in the world are people who stumbled onto their Extreme areas of skill—and until they did, all signs suggested that there was nothing remarkable about them. I think of Angela Ahrendts, who told me, "I thought I wasn't smart." Now, if you know her reputation, you're probably

thinking, *What the freaking frock? Are you kidding me?* In 2016, Angela was ranked fifteenth on *Forbes*'s list of the World's Most Powerful Women. She was the CEO of Burberry from 2006 to 2013,
during which time the company's value increased over 300 percent
to £7billion. Then she joined Apple, becoming one of its highest-
ranking executives, charged with leading its entire retail business—
the single most valuable retail business of any company in the world.
You don't get much more accomplished than that! Which is why it
still blows me away that Angela took time out of her insanely busy
schedule back in 2012 to return my email. You heard me right.
There I was, just stepping into my role at Equinox and desperately
looking for some advice about the technology transformation that
I was embarking on at the company, and Angela not only got back
to me but took the time to sit with me for a good hour or two
to give me her candid insights and learnings from the technology
transformation she had led at Burberry. OK—I'll be honest—I did
send a flattering email and play the woman president–to–woman
CEO card, but that one single meeting with Angela gave me more
confidence to meet the challenge ahead than months of listening
to external consultants. It was a pivotal time for me both professionally and personally. In Angela, I had found my first ever female
CEO mentor.

How could that person have ever assumed she wasn't smart? I for
one assumed that she had been a superstar from the day she was
born. But she told me, "In a left-brain, analytically oriented school
system, I was a rock-solid B student no matter how hard I worked.
My mind was not wired to think in a linear way, not wired to pick up
all those patterns or algorithms. Nor could I conquer languages—so
even though I took French for three years, I struggled to correctly
structure a decent sentence. When you have this experience year

after year in school, you get a little insecure. So I was incredibly blessed to stumble on fashion. All of a sudden things made sense to me and my entire right, creative brain became unlocked. For the first time I could use my whole mind and everything connected to it."

Moving to New York City to work in the fashion industry, she wound up eventually working for the luxury brand Donna Karan. There she developed not just her "right-brain" fashion and leadership skills but her "left-brain" strategy and business skills, which led her to Fifth & Pacific Companies, then Liz Claiborne, where she helped acquire and oversee more than twenty brands, including Juicy Couture, Laundry by Shelli Segal, Lucky Brand Dungarees, and DKNY jeans. With each step, she checked herself out and dramatically broadened her Extreme skills and knowledge, excelling like never before. "I moved from loving fashion to the business of fashion, to the marketing of fashion, to creating great global brands. I don't think it's any different from a great athlete discovering she was in the wrong sport. I tell kids when I interview them: *Know who you are.* What do you *love* to do every morning when you wake up? Don't let someone else tell you what success is. Success is understanding who you are, how you are naturally wired, and what moves you. That's the lane we need to get you in. If we do, and you work hard, you'll go to the moon!" Checking Yourself Out is what makes the difference between getting into the moon shot lane and just puttering around town, wrongly imagining that you aren't that smart.

## GET READY TO RECEIVE THE BALL

There's a pattern here. Not once but several times, Angela was able to Check Herself Out, apply her drive to what she had freshly discovered in herself, and then, as if on cue, a new opportunity popped up right in front of her. For Sam Kass, too, checking himself out was not a onetime fix but a recurring process with the unexpected power to coax opportunity out of even the most barren situations. Checking himself out in Vienna, Sam discovered that within the disappointed ballplayer was an up-and-coming chef. His turning point came during his study abroad semester when he was working as a volunteer at the restaurant, showing up every night and trying to learn everything he could. The chef responsible for all the sauces suddenly needed surgery, and the executive chef was forced to do his work because no one else knew how. "He was really unhappy about having to do all that prep," Sam told me, "so he pulled me over to teach me how to do it as fast as possible. I got great training really fast. When you put yourself in the right position and start doing the work, then the opportunities start to manifest." So watch for them. As my field hockey coach told me all those years ago, if you expect someone to pass you the ball, you better get into position to receive it.

Sam spent much of the next five years living his dream of traveling the world, funding his travels by working as a private chef. Most of us would expect that at the end of his travels he might have returned to the United States to work in a restaurant he admired or start one of his own. Right? Nope! Not Extreme Sam. While he was cooking and traveling around the world, he was also continuing to check himself out. He was finished with school, which for most people means no more studying, but he found that his interest in history and politics, especially the politics of how we get what we eat, only grew stronger. He wondered: What were the political implications of what he was cooking? How does the way we cook affect the land, the people who grow the food, the health of those who eat it? So school or no school, he kept on studying. That was before you could load a portable device with as many book titles as you like, and so, he said, "Two-thirds of my bag was packed with food-policy books that I lugged all over the world."

After five years of travel, feeling "a little lost" and aware that his former classmates were establishing careers and moving on with their lives, he returned to Chicago. A family he had cooked for in New Zealand turned out to know the family of Senator Barack Obama, and because of the work he'd been doing as a private chef and the political reading that had been shaping his thoughts, he saw the chance to cook for a political family as his big moment. "I saw the opportunity quite clearly," he told me, "because I'd done the hard work and the research. If I hadn't done the work, it wouldn't have seemed like an opportunity." He was in position to receive the ball and he grabbed it, eventually becoming not just the White House chef but a strategist and policy maker on health. Why? Because the last six years of learning to cook and studying the politics of food had made him the perfect candidate. With that Extreme combination, he was better qualified than any other chef they might have considered.

Sam cooked for the Obamas for a year and a half, and when Barack Obama won the election he naturally followed them to the White House. By checking himself out repeatedly, working hard to develop his new skills and areas of knowledge, he found not just a new skill set or a new trade but a career that was extremely him. Transitioning from a baseball player to a chef seems like a pretty big leap to me, but moving from a chef to a lifetime of influencing and driving policy on health and nutrition is huge. I love Sam's story so much for the fact that it proves that when you follow the stuff you're passionate about, you just never know the places you might land—places you probably didn't even know existed when you started.

## A RANDOM WALK TOWARD AN ARCTIC ENEMA!

Because checking yourself out requires an openness to surprise and a sensitivity to whatever intrigues and grabs you, it can often happen unexpectedly on a vacation or a break from the formal world of work. Like my story of planning the charity ball, it may sound like a goof-off and a big party. But it's just as possible to check yourself out by design, with practical goals in mind. Either way, buckle your seat belt because it may well involve uncertainty and painful self-examination. That was the case for Will Dean, the founder of the Tough Mudder obstacle course events. If you don't know Tough Mudder, it's a ten-to-twelve-mile event involving bizarre obstacles such as jumping into giant Dumpsters full of ice cubes or sliding through a ring of fire, and let me tell you it's the most crazy fun you can ever have with a bunch of mates. I'm one of the more than two million people who have participated in a Tough Mudder challenge, and I just had to track down and meet the guy who came up with the thing. With hindsight, the idea seems like a clear winner, but I think we can all imagine that proposing an obstacle course with names such as "Electroshock Therapy" or "Arctic Enema" would have been met with more than a few naysayers.

Before he checked himself out, Will Dean hardly seemed like the person who could make it succeed. A British citizen who completed university and then joined the prestigious UK Foreign Service, he worked as a counterterrorism officer, working as far afield as Washington, DC, and New Delhi, India. But as he told me, "Although I had some success and won some plaudits, in other ways I irritated people. It seemed to me that they say they want people who are going to be 'entrepreneurial in mind'—until you say something that doesn't fit in. Then they say, 'You've got a lot of growing up to do, young man!'"

Feeling that he would never fully fit in, he left his job and enrolled in the Harvard Business School. His goal was to use the two years of the MBA program to conceive and launch a business that would be more meaningful to him and a better fit with his nature. Essentially, he was telling himself: *You've got two years—go check yourself out.*

Looking back, he can say that the experiment worked. "Harvard treated me well," he told me. He came up with the plan for Tough Mudder, which was a semifinalist in the school's annual business plan competition. He made friends and even met his future wife. But like the boarding school he had attended in England, which had almost convinced him never to go to university, business school struck him as rigid, conformist, and expensive. The constant emphasis on head-to-head competition for student rankings (so unlike the approach he had known in England, where schools compete but individual students do not) spoiled the working atmosphere. "I wanted something that would be less of a rat race, something to force people to laugh at themselves and be more collaborative." Maybe for those reasons, his search for the right business idea proved harder and more uncomfortable than he had imagined. "It was quite a painful personal journey, looking under lots of rocks and not quite finding the thing I wanted. Many days I thought, my gosh, maybe I'm never going to find it."

By leaving the job where he didn't belong and checking himself out at an American business school, you might say, Will discovered that he didn't belong in B-school, either. The formal, structured educational environment was even less like the entrepreneurial culture he yearned for than the Foreign Service job he had left. But over time, seeing all the ways he did not fit helped him to imagine Tough Mudder. In a Tough Mudder the obstacles on the course are seriously challenging, but they are also outrageous and funny. Teams can't complete the course unless the teammates work together, and the atmosphere is one of camaraderie, humor, and mud in places you did not know could get muddy. "I wanted to build something with a clear set of values around teamwork, camaraderie—and, yes, something kind of countercultural." The business he dreamed up was like an answer or an antidote to the rigid, isolating world he had wanted to leave since boyhood.

But Will pointed out to me that this "answer" had not come in any bolt of inspirational lightning. "If one day someone makes a TV movie about Tough Mudder, I'm sure they will create a scene where there is an 'Ah-ha moment,'" he said. "But the reality is, getting brought onto a mission and internalizing it, knowing that it makes sense and believing in it—that all takes time. It isn't like picking from a menu. Getting to Tough Mudder took a lot of introspection, a lot of asking myself who I am, what I engage with, and what fulfills me. It was a painful and lonely process, with huge moments of self-doubt." His mother would remind him that William Hague, the former foreign secretary and former leader of the Conservative Party, had come from their part of England and had used business school to launch a career in management consulting. Why, she would ask, couldn't Will do that? As he told me, "There are days when you feel, 'Oh, I'm going to screw this up. Should I do something that would be easier?'"

Checking yourself out takes time and patience. There is a lot of ground to cover, and the route rarely runs straight. This is no mistake. The alternative to taking the winding path is never getting there at all. As Will told me, "They have a phrase for this in economics. They call it a 'random walk'—steps along the way seem missteps, but they aren't missteps, they are key to getting where you ultimately need to be." The term "random walk" comes from probability theory, and it describes a kind of movement that has so much randomness in it, no one could ever predict it. Short-term changes in stock prices are thought to be random walks. So are the weaving and stumbling of a drunk person. The only way to find out where a random walk will take you is to follow along and discover it as it happens. Checking Yourself Out is a random walk you need to take now and then, even though you don't know—in fact, exactly because you don't know—where you're going.

## YOU'RE CRAZY

As unpredictable as it can be, there is one thing you can count on. For you, it may feel confusing to take the time and maintain the openness to Check Yourself Out, but some of the people around you will think you're a total nut job. Sam felt like the failure among his high school classmates, endlessly bumming around Europe while they were home establishing professional credentials and careers. Will's own mother said he was making a mistake. And in my own career, as I'll describe, I left several excellent companies where I might have stayed for the rest of my working life, and at every one people struggled to understand my choices. The society around us and even the people we care about often don't see the full extent of our Extreme Selves. How can they when they are not us?

## CHECK YOURSELF OUT FOR A LIFETIME

I love stories of Extremers reimagining themselves. But in the course of a lifetime, we don't just need massive new realizations; we also need to adjust to the shifting demands and opportunities we face as one life era gives way to the next. We need to balance love and career, private time and time with loved ones, short-term goals and longer-term ones. I received an unexpected lesson about this on an airplane when I identified the passenger next to me, Laura Wolf Stein, as a fellow Extremer. What I loved in her life story was the reminder that checking yourself out is also a way of making the most of what you've got. Laura sees the elements of drive as being like the cylinders of a car engine: they often fire separately, not all at once. She told me, "In the years before I met my husband, I ran my first marathon, biked across Massachusetts, took up yoga, and really focused on my career. I had time to do all that. Later, when I found love, got married, and had my first child, I found myself days into maternity leave letting thoughts about my professional life and to-do lists take focus away from my newborn. I had to quickly say to myself, *Stop stressing about your career. This is the time to enjoy becoming a mom and take care of you and your family—don't waste this time feeling anxious about your job.* I quickly focused on my baby, my husband, and being active and outside as much as possible.

"Now, instead of dwelling on what feels unresolved, what I'm not doing, or what feels too hectic or chaotic, I try not to get down about the imbalance and instead ask a practical question: Am I inspired in the different parts of my life? And if not, what can I do to change that? Can I dial something up and something down? I know that if I have too many days of not being physically active, I don't perform at anything at a high level. So if a few days go by, I have to make fitness a priority. Or if I'm staying late at work and I really miss my kids, I'll say to myself, OK, tonight I won't get to see them, but I know I'll get to binge on them all weekend long. And over time I get moments when I'm energized more by my kids and my husband and moments when I'm energized more by my job."

Love that!


## EXTREME MOVES


There's no choice at times but to go it alone, trusting to the process of discovering and getting comfortable with ourselves so that we can live that personality out loud. Ultimately, Checking Yourself Out is a solo journey, but though no one else can tell you what you'll find on your own random walks, there are techniques to help you make the most of them.


### 1. Get In on the Action

Checking Yourself Out begins with trying on heaps of things, both in your imagination and in the real world. I started in early childhood, I see now, when I fantasized many possible careers (hugely successful, naturally). When I was a teenager, I took various jobs to discover what felt like a fit. Let me tell you that working in a fashion retail store where we spent half our slow days playing loud cheesy music that was so not within the store's standard operating procedures and trying on the merchandise in our own private fashion shows was more fun than preparing shipping invoices for my dad's meat-exporting company. (OMG—if I never see a bill of lading again as long as I live, I will be a happy woman.)

But the point is to learn by trying, and to try a lot of things, often because there is no way to see the outcome in advance. Nate Silver, a political poll analyst and expert on gambling, suggests that life and success always contain a large random element, but that we humans have trouble seeing it. In his book *The Signal and the Noise*, he wrote, "Our brains, wired to detect patterns, are always looking for a signal, when instead we should appreciate how noisy the data is." If we can't receive a clear signal, we can't predict what will be useful and what won't, so we have no choice but to try a lot of different things for ourselves and see what happens. Franz Johansson summarized it this way: "If we could predict what would work, we would never ever do anything that doesn't work. If success is random, it follows that you need to roll the dice frequently."

Had my attempts to organize a ball been a disastrous failure, I might have thought, *Hmm, yeah, that organizing thing . . . not so much.* Instead I discovered that organizing a group to reach a shared goal seemed to be something I was really good at. It brought out something awesome in me, and slowly I realized that organizing and energizing people—leadership—might be my greatest talent.

So let your imagination run wild. Let it wander to the places you want to be, and make some moves that will allow you to experience those places and learn from them. I want to make clear to my millennial friends that I am not just talking about checking boxes to add things to your résumé so that you appear perfectly "rounded." I feel you are all under so much pressure these days to build an impossibly perfect profile of wide extracurricular experiences. But it's no use going to a foreign country if all you do is sit on a tour bus and then come home again. It's also a bad idea to fall into the crazy trap of doing things just because your friends did them. You need to follow your own intuition to find the kind of experiences that are right for you. Every new experience is an opportunity to be surprised by what compels you and gives you energy, and by what the experience brings out of you.

A friend of mine tells the story of a morning that his wife unexpectedly asked him to take their daughter to school. In the classroom, another parent urged him to attend a PTA meeting, something he had never done. A vote was scheduled on whether to use the money from a recent fund-raiser as originally planned or to divert it to buy a new high-tech video security system. Compelled by the issue, Woodie surprised himself by raising his hand to speak at the meeting, at length and with feeling. The vote turned out to be very close, and the result was the one he wanted. Several parents spoke to him afterward, saying that he had helped to change their minds, and it seemed that his speech had swung the vote. That sort of activism was far from his usual work, but it reminded him that there was a side of himself that had once enjoyed public speaking and especially advocating for a cause. He had not planned to check himself out at that PTA meeting—he hadn't planned to go at all!— but now he began to think about how to participate more in that way, and whether his next job might include a more public, activist role.

Now, some of you may be sitting reading this thinking "Yeah—I totally check myself out because I am super open to new experiences." But are you? Take an inventory of your average year, and look at the activities you choose to do. Do you always vacation in the same place, with the same friends? Do you tend to eat at the same spot for lunch every day or stick to the same favorite workout routine with the same fitness instructor week in and week out? If so, that's a sure sign that you have more to experience out there—so go ahead, change it up!

### 2. Be Ready to Catch the Ball—Whatever Direction It Comes From

Which new experiences will make the difference? How will they fit together as part of your Extreme Self? You simply can't know. And you won't need to know, for a while. To begin with, it's enough to be open to whatever experiences suggest themselves to you—the more varied and diverse, the better.

Sometimes, checking yourself out may lead you to identify a very specific skill or goal you want to pursue, as it did for Sam Kass when he discovered he was a chef. It happened that way for my dear friend Gordon Thompson, one of the "legends" of Nike, who helped put that brand on the map. Gordon is one of the most talented designers in the world, but his story started with the struggle of not fitting into his family's expectations for him. Rather than pursue a legal career like his father and brothers, he focused on design and won the Knoll Internship while he was in graduate school. As he described it:

"This huge, glamorama furniture company brought one kid a year to become part of their design team for four months. I came to New York and worked on Wooster Street in their old studio, where Jeffrey Osborne was creative director. He seemed like a god to me, walking around with these big foulard ties. On my first job, we were reviewing someone's work and he arrived a little late. All he did in the meeting was point. 'I like this, I don't like this. If you do this, change that.' And I thought, *That's the job I want! I want Pointer*

*Guy! The guy who says 'I like it!' or 'I don't!'* He was the creative director of Knoll. And that's what I became at Nike." At the time, Gordon didn't even know there was such a job, let alone that it was his dream. But on that first day as an intern, he checked himself out and set himself a new goal.

Other times, checking yourself out will lead you to discover a general area that's worth your while to explore—not a skill or a goal but an area of expertise to develop or an aspect of your personality, previously unappreciated, that turns out to be a hidden strength. "Food politics." "Competitive creative teamwork." For me, the discovery was that although I would never be a sports champion, I was wired like an athlete, and playing on a team energized me and inspired a fierce competitiveness that has helped me excel in sports environments ever since. What's more, my love of Mozart was an important clue to my love of creativity and using my imagination. Years later, you would find me taking the lead in imagining new strategies, products, and services with amazing teams of people for sports and fitness brands to which I felt a deep loyalty. It's been one of the keys to my entire Extreme career. By checking myself out, I found an unseen and unappreciated quality that showed me how I could succeed.

The trick is to be willing to retune your peripheral vision, so you have your eyes open for opportunity balls that might be flying your way. A great exercise is to list opportunities you think you really want. They might include a dream job, a perfect spouse or partner, a dream role in a play, or being selected for the sports team you've always dreamed of. Now imagine if you ended up taking an opportunity that was totally opposite to the one you are dreaming of. Try that opportunity on in your mind's eye, and see what parts of it might actually be a fun fit for you. I know this sounds weird, but

I gotta say it's worked for me in some of the most important decisions of my life, such as, for example, picking a life partner. When I was younger, I always used to think that my dream husband was going to be a jock, an extroverted captain of the team, a business magnate whom everyone took direction from—certainly the guys I dated earlier in life seemed to fit that pattern. It was only after my friend Sam pointed out that I might find an even better match by looking for an unexpected and more cerebral trailblazer, someone who might complement me in different and unexpected ways, that I opened my mind to something else.

### 3. Don't Half-Ass It

In New Zealand, the ultimate put-down is saying that someone is making only a half-ass effort. If you're serious about checking yourself out, know that half-ass efforts won't get you to the discoveries and opportunities you need. Just as Sam Kass worked in a kitchen until his back was aching and Will walked for months through the desert of indecision, you will need to keep going until you discover and develop the Extreme capabilities inside you. So promise yourself this: when you discover something that captures your imagination, you will go *all in* to develop it. Too often today I hear stories of young people quitting jobs too quickly because they don't meet their perfect picture of what a first job should be—there's too much menial work, or it's too corporate or too hierarchical or whatever the case may be. But if you don't stick around long enough and experience some of the less exciting aspects of a job, you might miss the opportunity for your Extreme Self to unlock your own unique perspective on the role. Finding something you're passionate about generally takes time and effort—so beware of giving up too soon.

As a young executive at Air New Zealand, I remember a few years into my career when my boss entered into a major sponsorship with a proposed college football bowl game. For a number of reasons the project was fraught with problems, and it would have been easy to sit on the sidelines and watch things fall apart, but instead I offered my nights and weekends to work with the company organizing the event to help salvage it. Essentially I ended up taking on almost a second full-time job because I knew how important it was to my boss. As it turned out, the project ended up being a colossal failure (oh, yes—a story that could be told over many beers because of its ins and outs), and though you might think I'd be disappointed after completely giving up my social life for months on end and getting no success out of it, in reality that act of checking myself out gave me my first big experience in the sports industry. I didn't know it at the time, but I could never have joined Nike years later if I hadn't been able to put some sports experience on my résumé by going all in for that opportunity.

So as you come upon new areas that compel you, take a moment now and then to consider your level of engagement and commitment—in other words, where you are at on the "assing it" scale. Think about a time when you know you were mailing it in—just checking the boxes, putting in as little effort as possible. Reflect on how fulfilling that experience was for you. Now compare that to a time when you went all in. Make a commitment to participate only in experiences where you go all in. Quality over quantity is always the way to go when checking yourself out.

When you let yourself be surprised at what appeals to you or brings out a hidden strength, you are on the road to becoming an Extremer. When you pursue that opportunity, going all in to develop that part of yourself or combination of traits you never valued before, you're making serious progress. But as an Extremer, you need more than discovery and commitment. You need boatloads of drive—the commitment and the energy to get you there. In the next chapter, I'll show how I overcame my own tendency to half-ass it and tapped into a degree of drive I didn't know I had.

# TWO
# IGNITE
# YOUR
# MAGIC
# DRIVE

Some Extreme Moves seem to come naturally. Others . . . not so much. When it came to teenage me starting to Check Myself Out, the trying-on part, feeling what blew my hair back, was no problem. I love trying things on! But going all in? Back then, I was a lot less consistent. I had a whole lot of areas of interest and enthusiasm, but too often I half-assed them and wound up with little to show for my efforts. I remember one day in high school, complaining to my field hockey coach about the unfairness of keeping me on the B team. Why couldn't he put me on the starting team, the First IX?

"You're lazy," he told me.

He wasn't trying to be insulting; he was simply pointing out that while I was standing still on the field, dry heaving after I scored a goal, the rest of my teammates were racing back to get on defense, having barely broken a sweat. I didn't seem to have the drive for the fitness it took. Was that a flaw in my nature, a debilitating laziness? I refused to believe that. And I think it was then that it came to me: maybe to succeed at sports, I actually needed to *work harder.*

I decided to have a crack at jogging in the early morning. To be honest, when I'd first tried running, I'd absolutely hated it. We had a compulsory schoolwide cross-country race every year, and I was the kid who conked out after the first mile and ended up walking the next five, getting to the finish line when everyone else had gone home. There had to be a way to make running feel less like torture. Luckily for me, it was the height of the eighties, so Sony Walkmans were all the rage. My runs became a great opportunity to scream out Pat Benatar's "Love Is a Battlefield." I started slowly, increasing my distances until I could do 5K without stopping.

*Huh,* I thought, *look at that. That actually felt great. So . . . could I run 10K?*

I increased the distance of my runs a little more, and a little more, with my eye on that next goal. Sure, it was kind of intimidating, but by now I'd already done five kilometers. Couldn't I do five more? And in time, when I was able to run a 10K, I felt, *Wow, this kind of rocks!*

If this were a fairy tale, you could guess the ending. The little girl learns an important lesson about hard work and goes on to win her hockey championship and maybe at the end a hot-looking man on the sideline as well. Yeah, no. It wasn't quite like that. I never made the First IX. But I did score more goals, I covered more of the field, and frankly I had heaps more fun because I wasn't spending half of the game wheezing and looking for a vomit bucket. Pushing myself to work hard and then feeling and seeing the progress, including my greater range and success as a player, felt amazingly fulfilling. New confidence coursed through me. I was working harder *and* liking it more. Who knew?

As I kept up my running, year after year, I continued to hear that audacious wee voice in my head. One day, now into adulthood, it said: *If I could run a 10K . . . how bad could a half marathon possibly be?* And wouldn't you know, once I'd run a half marathon, I started to think about a friggin' marathon! It seemed impossible that the loser girl who couldn't finish the high school cross-country was now seriously and enthusiastically (if still a little nervously) considering a marathon, but that kind of progressive success, stretching for one goal and then stretching a little more for the next, is addictive. It gives you more confidence and drive.

So I started training for a marathon, plodding along one step at a time, learning to push myself further and drink up more of the addictive joy of accomplishment and self-improvement. To my enormous satisfaction, at the age of twenty-five I checked "marathon" off my bucket list, too. These days, in my forties, I am participating in everything from triathlons to Tough Mudder obstacle courses.

What happened to the "lazy" girl who finished last? How had I received what seemed like a magical infusion of drive? By increasing my goals to build my momentum, step by step. I felt so energized after climbing one mountain (to me, anyway, that first 5K felt like a freakin' mountain!) that I was inspired to look for a bigger one.

That's the first magical aspect of drive. I discovered that the secret to working hard is to find the satisfaction in hard work. Throughout my early years, though I was a champion at nothing, what kept stoking my drive was my joy in the progress I made. This is an example of what Teresa M. Amabile, a business professor, and

Steven J. Kramer, a developmental psychologist, call the power of "small wins." When they asked hundreds of professionals working on long-term projects to keep diaries of their experience, they found little mention of external rewards such as salary or bonus. Instead, the feeling of making progress was what spurred the big increases in creativity and productivity. As Amabile explained in an interview, "This is good news! Big breakthroughs at work are really rare. But small wins are something people can experience pretty regularly if the work is chunked down to manageable pieces." By doing the hard yards one "chunk" at a time, you get to experience for yourself the highs of achievement and the pleasure of personal mastery. That can keep you energized when there is no obvious win or loss on the horizon, by tapping into what runners term their *personal record*—enjoying the private feeling of improvement. Then, by stretching yourself to meet manageable challenges, one after another, a little mountain, another that's a little bigger, another even bigger, you keep strengthening your determination and feeding your drive, until you're doing things you never thought possible.

## NOT EVERYONE IS A WINNER

Too many people get this backward. They look at a challenge, a mountain peak way up in the clouds, and they think, "That's too hard. I don't have the energy/commitment/stamina to do *that*!" They make the mistake of first measuring the distance to the goal— wow, that mountain peak looks pretty bloody high!—and then checking within themselves to see if they have the drive to meet it. And what do they find? They don't have it. They have no idea how they'd do it. But they've misunderstood how drive works. You don't get a fixed amount of it, like gas in a tank. Or, I should say, it might be fixed on any given day, but over time, unlike a car's gas tank, your "tank" will grow in proportion to where you are trying to go if you keep pushing and challenging yourself.

That's one of the most valuable things I know. Magic Drive is a resource I have returned to over and over again throughout my life, and it has propelled me to achieve things I never would have thought possible. So it breaks my heart to realize that these days the cultivation of this resource is endangered. It was a shock to me when I was fortunate enough to start a family in America to discover the widespread belief that kids shouldn't experience losing. "Everyone's a winner," they're told. Every kid gets a trophy. I have seen this with all three of my kids—two boys and one girl—when they started playing soccer. Don't get me wrong, my kids are all energetic young soccer players, and I don't think they'd be upset to hear me say that none of them ever appeared destined for professional soccer greatness. Yet in all three cases they were placed on teams whose organizers went to great lengths to "cover up" which kids were playing at a higher level than others. The team names—like "Black Wolves" or "Tsunamis"—didn't reveal it. Back when I was a field hockey player, I had understood that I was on the B team. When I played tennis, I knew I was at the C level for interclub play. But my kids didn't know, and when we tried to tell them that they needed to train to get to a better level, they didn't have much motivation. Weren't they already Tsunamis? So why look for higher mountains to climb?

This is a national trend. As Ashley Merryman pointed out in the *New York Times*, local branches of the American Youth Soccer Organization spend up to 12 percent of their yearly budgets on trophies alone, and the trophy and award industry overall is worth roughly $3 billion a year in the United States and Canada. Did you hear that? Holy shit balls! An entire industry dedicated to suppressing our kids' potential by rewarding them before they've even won anything.

Now, I know it's nice to see your kid with a trophy. But for the kids, I'm afraid it can be very confusing. After reviewing the psychological literature on telling everyone he or she is a winner, Merryman concluded, "Nonstop recognition does not inspire children to succeed. Instead, it can cause them to underachieve." Kids as young as four or five have been shown to know very well who played better and who played worse. When everyone gets a trophy, those who played better feel cheated and those who played worse realize that they didn't deserve it, which makes the reward lose its power. Over time, all those trophies make it *harder* to succeed, because they sap motivation and give a false sense that life will be easy. As the psychology professor Jean Twenge put it, "You're going to lose more often than you win, even if you're good at something. You've got to get used to that to keep going."

Plenty of kids on the junior soccer fields of America are dreaming of being pro athletes. But if they're going to pursue such a difficult career, surely they need a chance to discover the competitive challenges they will face. They need to begin to unleash their own Extreme Selves to meet those challenges, setting a goal, succeeding or failing, and then setting another goal. None of that is going to happen as long as they believe that they are already winners. And though I don't believe in telling my children what to be when they grow up, I refuse to stand by while they miss the chance to develop an essential aspect of Magic Drive. It doesn't seem fair to them—especially because it doesn't end in childhood. We're starting to reap the fruits of this "everyone's a winner" culture, and it's not pretty. Jumping from childhood sports to college, we find, according to a recent study reported in *U.S. News & World Report*, that in two hundred top colleges and universities, more than 40 percent of all grades awarded were in the A range. Every college student's a winner! And guess what? Millennials are more likely than any other age group to have a fear of failure (40%) in comparison with Generation Xers (31%) and baby boomers (23%), as reported by Linkagoal's Fear Factor Index 2015. What difference does that make? One sign comes from a survey out of Babson College last year: almost 30 percent of twenty-five-to-thirty-four-year-olds who saw an opportunity to start a new business said that fear of failing at it would hold them back from the entrepreneur route. That number is up from 23.9 percent in 2001. That sounds to me like a whole lot more trophies on shelves and too many potential Extremers missing their chance.

This shit fires me up! I call it the woossifying of the Western world! Why did we decide that our young people should not be inspired to seek excellence? I hear so many managers, leaders, investors, and others in my generation complain about "entitled Millennials"—but in my view, we're the ones who created this cultural shift and raised young people within it. So for my part I am all in. Let's provide the tools, knowledge, and inspiration to inoculate all aspiring Extremers against the participation trophy plague!

## WHEN IT'S YOUR DREAM, YOU'RE UNSTOPPABLE

Our drive will strengthen or weaken based on the mountains we choose or choose not to climb, the momentum we build or fail to build, and that's as true of professionals at the very top of their game as it is of kids. I was completely blown away when I heard the amazing example of what Magic Drive can achieve—and how it can die if the momentum fails—when I got to speak with Janet Shamlian, a national correspondent for the NBC *Today* show and NBC *Nightly News*, but only after—wait for it!—she had her fifth child. Talk about drive and persistence.

I met Janet when we were seated together a few years ago at the *Fortune* magazine "Most Powerful Women" annual dinner. Given that Janet was someone I watched on my TV multiple times a week, I was quite chuffed to be able to hear firsthand the epic story of her career greatness.

Janet keeps a picture of herself as a little girl holding a can of corn in her hand as a pretend microphone, playing at being a TV reporter. Unlike many of the other Extremers you'll meet, she knew what she wanted early in life, and once she was out of school she spent her twenties working her way up, first as a reporter at a local news station in Grand Rapids, Michigan, and then in bigger markets in Houston and then Chicago. Slowly she won the chance to cover some of the more thoughtful human interest types of news stories that had inspired her to become a reporter, not just the daily headlines that news people call the "wheel of death," meaning who died where and how. She scaled increasingly higher media heights, building her drive as she went, always with the awareness of what for her was the ultimate summit: to become a national correspondent for the *Today* show.

But like so many of us, she felt the conflicting pulls of career and family. Pregnant with her first child, she moved back to Houston, where her husband had business interests. There the new mom continued working as a weekend anchor and a three-day-a-week reporter, but she had to content herself with covering less compelling stories. "It was car accidents again," she told me. Comparing the job she'd left in Chicago to the more family-friendly one she'd taken in Houston "was like comparing diamond with zirconia."

No network even maintained an office in Houston, so after the birth of her second child, acknowledging how her life had changed, she told me, "I threw in the towel. I had stepped off the career track, and I thought it was over, completely over." Drive grows in stages and dies in stages, too. It was as if Janet had run her first half marathon but then all she could find as a follow-up was a 5K. So she did less, it felt less satisfying, and her commitment and energy ebbed. Having completed her 5K, she was then offered the chance to do a little Fun Run—but really, for her, what was the point? By then her momentum had faded away.

Meanwhile, she'd discovered a new area in which her drive could grow. "I'd fallen in love with having children," she told me. "Being the A type personality that I am, I figured that if I couldn't do the TV stress test, I would do the children stress test! We had five kids in seven years, five kids I loved." Did you hear that? I mean, talk about Extreme—on any scale that is an amazing accomplishment. Janet was now an Extreme Mom, and she was done with Extreme Reporter.

Or was she?

As much as she loved her kids, she couldn't quite let go of her dreams of broadcast news. Every morning, at home with her kids, she watched the *Today* show. Every evening, in her kitchen with a little TV on the counter, she watched the NBC *Nightly News*. "I did not miss it ever, ever, ever. And each time as I watched, I felt: *I can do that better*." She constantly evaluated the work of other correspondents: this story was not well composed, that reporter needed grammar corrections. "I was starting to critique their wardrobe choices! It was not about them, it was about me; I was starting to become someone I didn't want to be.

"Then one night I was making mac and cheese—I had little kids, so we ate mac and cheese—and as I was standing there by the kitchen counter, I felt: *Is this all there is? To live with this nagging sense that I gave up on the dream? Screw it. Even after five kids, I'm going back.*"

Boooooom! I mean, how freakin' badass is that?

Janet still had friends among her former colleagues, and she told them she wanted to return to her television career. "Of course, almost everyone told me it couldn't be done. Here in Houston, they said it with love: 'Janet, you haven't even had a job in six years!' I knew what they meant. There were a zillion people at the top of their careers in local news who wanted to move up to national— people who were younger, more attractive, probably better writers. And they didn't have—I say this with all love—the ball and chain. They could work anywhere. I was committed to Houston. *Janet, how are you going to do this? What are you thinking?*"

But Janet had a few Extremer secret weapons to draw on. The girl who used to hold that can of corn as a pretend reporter's microphone had the support of a husband who knew how much that had meant to her. "He was of the mind-set that 'I want to stay married to you forever, and I really don't want you to have regrets twenty years from now. No woulda-coulda-shoulda. And this is what you want.'"

With his support, Janet responded to all the warnings with an amazing show of drive. Taking everything she had learned about the television industry and tapping all the old connections she could muster, she tried everything she could think of, all at once. Two arms weren't enough, she imagined herself having eight. "I try to be a spider with my arms," she said. "Every avenue I see, I ask myself: How is this going to work for me, how is it going to help make it happen?"

She wrote to the heads of several networks, telling them why she thought she could be a strong correspondent, but she had been out of the game so long that nobody knew who she was. Her greatest hope lay with one network head she had worked with years prior, but when she followed up after his lack of response, she was told he didn't work there anymore. She reached out to her former agent, but she couldn't even get past his new assistant. "I tried to explain to the assistant that he had found me when I was working in Grand Rapids, that he helped me make the moves to Houston and Chicago— but I'd been in my twenties then. It literally took weeks of persistent phone calls to finally get past her.

"Meanwhile, it felt like the networks put up every hurdle they could. Eventually NBC invited me to interview in New York, but I had to pay own way. They asked me to bring a résumé and a tape of my work, but mine was six years old, so I didn't bring it." Finally she got to New York and aced a writing test, and they took her on as a freelance hire. It wasn't the job she was dreaming of, by any means, but she had climbed the first mountain. BOOM! Her momentum was building again. And what's more, it was not lost on Janet that NBC had made a huge bet on her—it had made a move that absolutely no other network was willing to make. That very act made Janet more determined than ever to deliver and prove that the people there had made the right decision.

## WHEN YOU START YOUR CLIMB, THE ONLY WAY IS UP

For Janet, coming back after starting a family, the "mountains" were even higher than before. They took more effort to climb and came at a greater emotional cost. Yet the same magic took hold, and her drive grew to match the increasing challenges she faced. As a freelance reporter, she would wait for a phone call saying that a big story had come up and the network needed her to get on a plane immediately. "When you go on these stories as a day hire, you don't get to say, 'I'm sorry, I need to go home first' or 'It's the preschool meeting today' or 'It's the pediatrician checkup.' They called and I dropped everything, ran to day care, and then headed to the airport." Her arrival on the TV set would free another reporter to go cover the breaking "marquee" story, and she would stay behind, providing hourly updates on camera.

"One year I was on the road 175 days," she told me. "It was rough on my husband the first two times, at home with five kids. But then the hard part of this was really that their lives continued without me. We agreed that if he was going to be what you might call the lead parent, then I had to hand over a lot of decision making. My children all told me, at some point, that they felt closer to him than to me. That has been the price that I paid."

Once, returning with her family from a vacation, she was on an airplane in Paris when she got a call to go to London to cover terror bombings in the London Underground. Before she got off the airplane, she said, "I had to convince the pilot and flight crew that I myself wasn't a terrorist who was going to disembark and leave a bomb behind to kill the rest of my family. Then I went into London with only a diaper bag for my things and a credit card. I bought a wardrobe that the network funded, and I stayed for three weeks covering the story. They were grateful and shocked that I would do it."

On the strength of that kind of effort and dedication, she was offered a regular staff position, but based out of Chicago, far from her home. Now she was starting to appear occasionally on the *Today* show, as she'd dreamed. The promise of that ultimate win fueled her drive, but there was something else reenergizing her day after day. "On stories," she said, "I was a sponge." She absorbed everything the other correspondents did and threw herself into every aspect of her work. She was putting in the hard yards and thriving on extreme work, upping her game in ways that only the most intense experience can do. "My writing improved. I developed the ability to take on anything as a reporter." She just kept reaching her goals, looking around, and asking, "Well, what else could I do? And what after that?"

That brings us to another magical aspect of drive: when you can do the hard work for the satisfaction it gives you, it leads to objective improvement. Janet found that working so many long days on the news set, the network began to notice that she could take on stories and succeed with them in ways that some reporters could not. "NBC realized that especially for an emotional story, I had more sensitivity as a mom than the twenty-six-year-old man they could have put on the story. I could help get emotion out of an interview subject. I was performing at a very high level, and I represented their demographic—the show was watched by women with children, but the only women with children appearing on the show were sitting at the anchor desk," not reporting stories as a correspondent as Janet was doing. Of course, she hadn't decided to have kids or grow older in order to distinguish herself as a journalist. She'd built up her drive and ridden her momentum and in doing so had developed the skills she needed along the way.

For a year, she flew from Houston to Chicago on Mondays and returned to her family on Fridays. How did she cope with that commute? "There were trips for stories when I cried every night. But my most honest answer is that I was making the drive toward the touchdown and I was all in. I was committed. It's almost harder now looking back at the sacrifices I made, particularly being away from my children, than it was at the time. Because I saw the goal in sight. The dream was going to happen."

After a year of commuting from Houston to Chicago, NBC made a very family-friendly decision to enable Janet to work out of Houston as her home base. It even installed a small broadcast studio in her home office so she could report stories and still be close to her family. As Janet summed it up, "I got back to Texas and I didn't have to commute anymore because I was a harder worker." The challenges had ignited her drive, and with enough drive she had become a reporter the network couldn't do without. Her drive had been strong enough to get her home again—with her dream achieved.

## SELF-DISCIPLINE ISN'T ENOUGH

If building drive is a matter of Extremers setting increasingly difficult goals, I have to say right away: the goals can't be just any goals. The mountain has to *really* matter to you. I had the chance to discuss this with Professor Angela Duckworth, a leading psychologist who studies "grit," the passion for a goal combined with the motivation to achieve it. How did I meet her? you ask. Well, I guess I should fess up: I basically stalked her. As I was researching for this book, all roads kept taking me back to her fascinating work. When I read an article about her that said she is comfortable dropping the occasional F bomb, I just knew I had to meet her. So our good mutual friend Adam Grant made the introduction—almost terrified, he said, at the energy explosion that he predicted might happen when Angela and I connected. And, wow, he was right. This woman is a power source unto herself.

She told me she felt that one of the biggest misconceptions about grit is that it's only about discipline. Many parents and teachers go wrong, she said, because they think that "what's really important is to get kids to work hard and be disciplined as if it doesn't matter what the kids wants. That's a deep mistake. The point about grit is to find something that you love and then do it. Not just to make kids practice piano or be a doctor if they don't like those things. Grit is not just the hard work, but hard work in service of something you find interesting and meaningful."

Here's what I love: Angela hasn't just studied this with more rigor than almost anyone in the world; her own personal journey embodies this same insight. She began on a fairly expected career path as a management consultant, but she knew that wasn't going to be her lifelong career because she'd always had a personal interest in kids and education. And so, just as many of her class peers from Harvard were charting increasingly impressive business careers, she did what all great Extremers do and Checked Herself Out, leading to a courageous decision to teach math in the New York City public school system. She quickly felt the change in status—everyone from her father to an officer at passport control seemed to go from "Wow, that's impressive" to "Oh, that's nice." At a moment like that, anyone would feel the pressure to go back to the higher-status work. And as she told me, "It did bother me a little to have that drop in status—I like to be impressive, I guess—but I don't think people who persist in things are invulnerable to insecurities. I thought to myself, okay, that is a part of this decision that I don't love. But I was also overwhelmingly convinced that the status thing was part of what I want to work on. It's ridiculous—people shouldn't look down on teachers! And in a way that kind of fueled me."

In those words you can hear that a more intense drive was kicking in, and it kept growing as she worked to help her students achieve better results and began to explore her options for helping kids achieve on a larger scale. Remain a teacher? Start a charter school? In time she became a psychologist studying grit, and as her ideas gained renown she added, on top of a full-time career, a nonprofit "character lab" to show people outside academia how grit could be taught. With each step, her drive grew stronger. "If you had asked me years ago, 'When you're forty-six years old with two kids and a husband, will you work eighty hours a week?' I'd have said, 'Probably not.' But my interest is so deep, I wish I didn't have to sleep. I wish I could just read articles and talk to people about grit."

That fits with my experience. You can't build momentum toward climbing some great mountain if you hate the mountain or if the work of climbing it bores you. That's why I say first Check Yourself Out, *then* build Magic Drive. Find something you care about and *then* go all in, increasing the challenges to build your drive.


## IT'S YOUR MOUNTAIN, SO FIND YOUR OWN PATH

It amazes me how many Extremers attribute their successes to setting subjective goals. Will Dean, the founder of Tough Mudder whom we met in chapter 1, told me, "When I have tried to do something other people tell me is important, it generally doesn't go as well as it should. My performance suffers. Where I have been successful is where I have said, 'It may be that the goal looks arbitrary to the outside world, but it's one I have chosen myself and I believe in it.'"

But there's a danger: I've seen too many people choose a long-term goal for themselves—choose their own mountain to climb for their own reasons—but then hand their choices about how to reach that goal over to someone else, perhaps an expert, a boss or coach, or even a parent or older sibling. They resist "fitting in" as far as their objectives—go, Team Extreme!—but they succumb to the pressure to pursue those goals in ways that others have prescribed for them. That tends to sap their motivation.

That was one of the key lessons I learned from Bode Miller, the most accomplished alpine ski racer in American history. I had the awesome experience of getting to work with Bode as he prepared for and competed in the 2006 Winter Olympics. Talk about an epic Extremer. Holy shit, I love everything about the guy! I learned so much from observing his utter self-discipline combined with his extraordinary self-knowledge—his determination to set the terms of his success for himself. As he explained, "The way I trained, I was outside the model that sports science was providing at the time, but I was more successful in my specific sport than guys who fit the model of sports science." Bode relied instead on setting his own subjective goals and learning from people who could help him pursue them his way.

The first of those, in his small community in rural New Hampshire, was his grandmother, whom he described as "a risk taker, a gambler, someone who swore a lot, a skier—kind of a badass."

When he was little, he would ask her about the sports heroes he saw on television. "She said they were born, they had diapers, but had the right opportunity and the right drive. I asked, 'Do you think I have that stuff?' She said, 'Yeah. You come from a very athletic family, you come from an environment where you're exposed to a lot of sports, and you're mentally really tough because of growing up in the woods.'"

Bode set out to pick a sport in which he could be a winner. His grandparents ran a tennis camp, so the obvious choice was tennis, but in time he realized that his tennis game was going to depend on the quality of the opponents and the coaches he could find, and in the mountains of New Hampshire that quality wouldn't be high enough. Skiing, though, was something he could do on his own. "I liked how much in skiing I controlled my own destiny. You had to go from point A to point B as fast as you could, and no one could tell you anything different. When I started off, I had no ability. My biggest asset has been my ability to assess, to be cognizant of the different challenges I faced and then think solutions through. I would just look at a race course and ask, 'What would it take to win if you were me? And am I willing to do that? Yeah, I am.'"

Bode told me that when he was establishing himself in the early part of his career, "I didn't set objective goals. They were all subjective goals." Even after races, which would seem to provide an objective result—first place, second place, third place—he pushed himself to interpret the objective facts in terms of his own subjective understanding. If he finished third rather than first, that could be a great accomplishment, relative to other more experienced skiers. If he'd put in more effort and skied more skillfully, a third-place finish might mean more than first place in some other race. Or it might be that he had performed poorly but others had done even worse, and a first-place finish meant only that he hadn't made the biggest mistakes of the day. The race standings and the praise or criticism he received were not what made him conclude that he had done well or badly; he measured himself by his own subjective and uniquely informed standards. "People get so worried about everyone else that when other people tell them they did a great job, they may disregard the fact that they know they performed shitty or could have done much more—they believe it just because somebody else pumps their tires."

Did his commitment to his own subjective judgment mean he sometimes missed out on good advice? Yep. He was known as a defiant kid who argued with coaches. Once he pissed off a coach so much that the man lied to the judges about his performance in a race and got his results disqualified, costing him in the overall standings and in sponsorships. Sometimes he would have to tell his coaches, "In hindsight, I screwed up. I was wrong. I should have listened to you." But he also came to feel that standing up for himself built what he called "self-belief," a quality he found essential to a solo sport such as skiing. "You have to have self-reliance and self-belief to shoulder that burden and not shy from risk. Most people rely on coaches and teams and infrastructure to support them, and then when the actual race starts and the shit hits the fan, their hundred percent becomes seventy percent. I realized I needed to be able to be independent, because when you're in the start gate you're by yourself. Things get awful quiet."

Can't any Extremer relate to that? I sure as hell can. If you're going to climb your own mountains in your own way, ultimately you're alone. You have to trust yourself to do it your way.

Bode's focus on subjective goals reminds me of what the psychologist Robert J. Vallerand called "harmonious passion," the feeling people get about their work when they have "freely accepted the activity as important for them without any contingencies attached to it"—in other words, doing something because it feels important to you, not because you will be excluded or shamed by others if you don't meet their standards. It's the difference between doing your work because you can't afford to get fired and doing it because you feel it adds something worthwhile to the world. In Vallerand's studies, "harmonious passion was associated with positive emotions, concentration, and flow," leading to greater success. Its opposite, "obsessive passion," doing something because of the negative consequences that may come from not doing it, creates negative emotions that can interfere with your performance. There is now a large body of research, spanning several decades, which suggests that although setting "mastery goals" (mastering a new skill or body of knowledge) makes you more motivated, performance goals (winning recognition, a pay raise, an academic degree) generally undermine people's persistence and pleasure, and that "performance-avoidance goals," where you try hard not to do something wrong, undermine motivation the most. (If you're just doing your job so that the boss won't humiliate you, you're not going to want to do it at all.) Bode was giving himself mastery goals that he freely chose as part of his own larger ambition. That's an approach that builds championship performance.

## COME OUT OF THE EXTREME CLOSET

So much has been written about drive, and much of it harmonizes with what I've said so far. In his book *Drive: The Surprising Truth About What Motivates Us*, Daniel Pink reviewed studies of motivation going back to the 1940s and concluded that three things motivate us effectively in the long run: *not* rewards or punishments but what he calls autonomy, mastery, and purpose—the chance to direct our own lives while getting better at something that serves others as well as ourselves. But for Extremers, there's another source of drive that's less well known, almost like a secret extra gear.

You can fire it up only when you're already pursuing that next, higher mountain in your own subjective ways. You're scaling that peak, and you realize that your goal is going to ask more of you, and more publicly, than you had planned. Extreme You is all about putting more of yourself into whatever you do, but there will come times when you realize that, honestly, you've been holding something back, partly because of what other people might think. Then you face a choice: Should you hide Extreme You or should you bring it out in the open, and what should you do with other people's responses—good, bad, or indifferent?

I hit that nerve-wracking moment when I was applying for my first job out of college. One job seemed just perfect: to become a "graduate trainee" at my country's national airline. As part of my application, I was given a written aptitude test. It was multiple choice, and I totally fucked it up. I failed the test. The company didn't even offer me an interview and I was *gutted*. (That's Kiwi for "so disappointed you want to throw your laptop against the wall.")

Air New Zealand had turned me down, but Mobil Oil had offered me a position, a solid job that would pay my rent. The Mobil job was something that I could write home about to Mum and Dad and say, "Yay, I got a job and it's respectable." I might have settled for that. I could have let the system tell me, based on its supposedly objective testing, what was best for me. But I couldn't. I deeply, passionately wanted to work for Air New Zealand, and in my own mind I was without question the perfect candidate for the job, almost from birth. Three months after I was born, my family relocated to London, and to this day my mum proudly tells the story of how I was the twenty-eighth piece of luggage on a trip to the other side of the world. I knew the romance of flying on a jumbo jet, and I knew there was a much bigger world beyond our small island nation. My early formative experiences were of global exploration and travel on Air New Zealand. To me, for all those reasons, the chance to work for Air New Zealand represented the beginning of an adventure that was meant to be, one that would take me all over the world as a glamorous business executive (albeit one whose large feet don't really look that good in Louboutins). And had Air New Zealand even met me? NO! How could they possibly miss out on this dynamic, globally aware, awesome personality to represent their company around the world? I mean, what were they thinking?!

I simply couldn't accept being remembered only as a name and a bad mark in some applicant file. Deep down, Extreme You is a form of matchmaking, and I felt inside that although I could have "dated" Mobil Oil for a while, I could fall in love with Air NZ. So I faced a choice—an awkward, uncomfortable, "put yourself out there and probably make a total ass of yourself" choice: I could hide what I felt about myself inside and take the job that was objectively correct for me, or I could take the much bigger emotional risk and try to show the people at the airline who I was and what I was all about—and hope that when they got to know me, they would want me. My choice was either to try to pass as a young oil company executive or to step out of the Extreme closet.

I managed to get on the phone with Vicki Lodge, the woman in Human Resources who led the hiring process at Air New Zealand. I told her some of my story and why I felt so strongly that I was better equipped than anyone else for the job. In other words, I regaled her with my witty repartee, and along the way I reframed the airline's hiring process, shifting it from a left-brain, analytical evaluation, where I was relatively weaker (can you answer the multiple-choice questions correctly?), to a more right-brain, personality-driven evaluation. It was enough to convince her to set up an interview for me with the hiring manager. Then I studied like crazy to understand what the airline was doing so that I could go in and dazzle him not just with my fabulous personality but also with my focused and relevant ideas for the business. Talk about igniting my Magic Drive! The Mobil job was already mine for the taking, but instead of going out to celebrate, I stayed in, working even harder than I had before, to show Air NZ just who I was and what I could offer it. By that time, it had already hired the graduate trainees it was seeking, but after my interview it created an additional position for me. I was the seventh graduate trainee hired for a group of six.

But of course, once you reveal yourself, you're revealed. Everyone knew that I was the extra hire, the unexpected add-on who hadn't followed the usual process. With a start like that, from my first day on the job, I felt I had to prove that I was worthy of being there. We all knew I didn't have the same qualifications on paper as the others. And ultimately I believe that's why I went on to outperform some of my peers at the company—exactly because my success there had *not* come easily, because I had to show them why Extreme Sarah deserved a spot. The pressure to overcome their skepticism triggered a new level of drive and determination to succeed. I had faced the choice between hiding myself away or bringing out more of myself, and I'd chosen to show up Extreme, which took my drive to a whole new level.

I think it's true that if you're doing something only because you don't want to be penalized or humiliated for not doing it, that can interfere with your drive. But when Extremers set out to do things that they believe in, climbing their own subjective mountain in their own subjective ways, then putting their self-esteem on the line— coming out of the Extreme closet, no matter what people think—in my experience it intensifies their drive even more.

## SUPPORT OR NO SUPPORT?

That was true for the designer Gordon Thompson, who stepped out of multiple "closets" to build the drive that fueled his awesome career. A natural artist, his design work was discovered by Nike, where he rose to become head of all design and research and development, one of the key people that made Nike the giant global brand we know today. In all my years at Nike, Gordie was one of those iconic names that people talked about all the time, but I never actually got to meet him. It wasn't until years later, when I was undertaking my work at Gatorade and seeking a brilliant design mind to partner with, that our paths happened to cross. Not only did Gordie open my eyes and teach me so much about the world of design, but he is without question the most self-motivated, driven human being I know. I had to understand where his drive came from.

Gordon was the third son in a family of hugely accomplished California lawyers and judges. Named for his father and grandfather, he was expected to continue the family traditions: attend USC, support the USC football team, study law, and contribute to California legal history. But Gordon was different. I asked him: Where did he get the drive to do something his family did not expect or support, when there was arguably such a clear and relatively easy path laid out in front of him for a successful life?

"At five or six," he said, "I started drawing. My first job, at age eleven, was at Pat Platt's Puppet Playhouse, where you had your birthday parties. I was chief set designer and costume designer. This was fantastic! Then, when I was twelve or thirteen, I started a greeting card company. It was the seventies, so I drew lots of rainbows, lots of trees, pen and ink. My parents' friends would commission me to do Christmas cards or custom birthday cards or their stationery. I got a bank account and rode to the bank on my bike to deposit checks. I got into sales and making money—it was fascinating.

"Then, around thirteen, I started decorating Christmas ornaments. I would dip silver balls in white paint, decorate them, and personalize them. My family is a big boating family, so we always had lots of cans of varnish. In the detached garage, my dad made us all these enormous train boards, HO gauge. They were suspended from the rafters in the garage. I put teacup holders in the undersides of the boards in rows, and that was where I'd hang my ornaments. One day I'd be a little engineer guy driving my trains, and the next I'd be the guy painting ornaments. I called them Gordaments. This was big business—twenty-five bones apiece. I was raking it in! Many years later, at my dad's funeral, people told me, 'We still have your Christmas ornaments.'"

Gordon's gift for art gave him a special kind of confidence, what he thought of as his "Wonder Woman cuffs—those gold bracelets she wore to block the bad guys' bullets. But my mother seemed to feel equal embarrassment and pride about my success with art. Bad enough that I was never going to be a lawyer. (I remember even when I graduated from architecture school, my mom said, 'You know, you can get to law school from architecture school.') On top of that, being an artist was 'different,' and being different in my family was not well received. I knew that they thought that if you were an artist, you were going to be poor and live in a garret—and we were a very success-driven family.

"Then it became clear I was also the homo of the family. The Puppet Playhouse was just the first domino to fall! And in my family's eyes, if you were a gay guy, then you were likely to only ever be a florist or a hair dresser or something cliché like that. Most gay guys will tell you there is that drive to prove your self-worth, and I think with all those little businesses I was trying to prove to my parents that I had something. To prove there was something there."

Someone different might have chosen to hide himself, to try to make a life as a lawyer and to pass as a heterosexual, upholding the family expectations. But Gordon was never going to live in a closet. "I was strong enough and knew myself well enough to know that my destiny was design and I just happened to be gay." He put his Extreme Self out there, firing up his drive to make his family recognize him for what he was. "I look back at my career, and I see at every opportunity, I just hammered it into my family. You love sports? Oh, yeah? I'm going to work at Nike! Here I am in meetings with Michael Jordan and Andre Agassi and everybody else! My brothers were dying with jealousy that I got to do all that. You watch TV? Really? I'm going to be on *Oprah*! I'll show you! I'm going to hit you over the head until you recognize me."

Some Extremers, such as Janet Shamlian, are fortunate to have as their secret weapon a close family member who supports their Extreme efforts no matter how outrageous they may seem. But many of us, like Gordon, don't. My parents didn't fight my choices, but honestly there was a side of my conservative old dad who expected me to find a nice man in New Zealand and settle down to be a lead parent. Some of my drive has come from wanting to succeed so big that he'd have to notice me all the way over here, running businesses in America. But that's Extremers in a nutshell: whatever feedback they get, whatever others think of them, they let it push them to do even more.

## EXTREME MOVES

Have you had a success? Let it inspire you to find a bigger mountain. Does someone close to you support you completely? Give that person a big hug—and then let him or her help push you even harder. And if others don't support you, if they don't understand you? Fight even harder to prove they were wrong *not* to recognize Extreme You.

And whatever they understand or don't understand, whatever they say or fail to say, let it fuel your Magic Drive. Here are some ways to keep it going.

### 1. Keep Finding Higher Mountains to Climb

It's up to you to keep finding that next mountain—the one that calls to you, challenges you, and is the right size for you. No new challenge? Your drive will plateau, or worse. Too big a challenge? Frustration, exhaustion, discouragement. You have to keep looking for that next mountain to climb, the one that will bring out more of your personal best.

In my more recent life, I've run half marathons with a group of women friends who are all significantly faster than me. The truth is that as a runner I'm about as slow as an ocean liner. These years, I'm not even trying to run the best personal time of my life—once, I could run a two-hour half marathon, but after I had my babies that stretched to 2:20. Now it might be 2:07 at the absolute best. So my girlfriends all reach the finish line way ahead of me, then text me to make sure I'm still alive, "Where are you??? We're at the finish line!" And I text back, "Seriously? Shut it, you annoying fast friggin track stars! I'm on my way!" And I feel just fine about it. I'm on a journey of my own improvement; I'm not comparing myself to anyone else. Could I ever get back to a two-hour finish? I don't know, but when I get even a step closer on my time, it feels good. And that's not just me. Dan and Chip Heath, brothers and coauthors of *Made to Stick: Why Some Ideas Survive and Others Die*, have suggested that even "whisker goals" (a hairsbreadth from the status quo) motivate greater long-term accomplishment. Even one second improvement on my time helps me feel how far I've come since my 2:20 finish, even compared to the teenage me who couldn't keep up in field hockey or finish the 5K in school.

So if you're looking for a good challenge, your best bet might be to start with a physical challenge. It's the easiest way to get your engine turning over, so you can quickly feel the addictive fulfillment that comes from succeeding and finding a bigger mountain to climb. Your physical challenge can be small or big, but it's got to be something that stretches you beyond what you've achieved before. It doesn't matter what it is—just set the goal, come up with a training plan, and post it on Facebook. Once you've declared it to the world, you're so much more likely to achieve it and feel the awesome beginnings of your Magic Drive momentum engine kicking in. And it's amazing how starting with a physical goal quickly fires up drive that can be applied to other life challenges.

## 2. Make Your Goals and Methods Your Own

It's so easy, and potentially so costly, to drift into accepting the goals that other people or indeed society in general pick out for us, or to limit ourselves to the usual and expected ways of reaching the goals that matter. That to me is one of the things that makes Bode Miller so inspiring. He became, objectively, the best American alpine skier in history, but at every step, from the decision about what sport to take up to the little decisions about what to require of himself, day by day, as he worked up serious competition, he set his own goals and judged his own results on his own terms. As he explained to me, back when he was first making a name, "Even making the Junior Olympics was not a goal of mine. Sure, I wanted to be there, I knew that I should be there if I was performing the way that I could, but I looked at the things I could control. Am I being vigilant on my training? Am I paying attention to my equipment? Those were things that only I could judge. Did I tune my skis the night before? Goal met. That was what mattered to me." His goals, his methods, his personal integrity were what kept it all working. Others may have trained as many hours as Bode or had as much personal grit, but they didn't set Bode's training goals, didn't do it Bode's way, and didn't get Bode's results. Individuality matters: Extremers using their Extreme gifts in their own Extreme ways.

And for me, meeting my own goals in my own way isn't just a method of achieving big objectives; it's a way to make each day go better. Setting and then meeting goals I set and judge for myself makes me feel a degree of focus and inner harmony that carries through my day, even into the areas where I have to meet other people's sometimes harsh expectations. You don't always get to set your own goals or do things in your own way, but having some goals that are your own makes it easier to swallow the ones that are out of your control or just flat-out unpleasant. It's like my morning run: no one is making me get up early and put in those five miles, but I know that when I do, no matter who or what I have to face later in the day, even on the worst, toughest day, I can walk in, look at anyone, and think, "You know what? You may think you know more than me and you're going to push me around in this meeting, but I ran five miles this morning while you were still sleeping—and you can't take that away from me."

How do you think you fare when it comes to setting your own goals? The best way to find out is to go back to your list of dream opportunities from the previous chapter—both your dream opportunities as well as the new ones you discovered in your peripheral vision. Now pick the biggest, most important dream opportunity on your list and assess your current plan for achieving it. Are the steps you are taking and the goals you are setting objective (need to land the job) or subjective (need to take an online skills course to prepare me to get the job)? Make sure you have your subjective goals plan put together, and get ready for action!

### 3. Put Your Balls on the Line

Every kid has at least some experiences of feeling like the oddball who doesn't belong. Every adult has the fear that we might just fail, humiliatingly, in front of our peers. It's tempting to try to hide our differences and potential setbacks, but there's nothing like coming right out and owning it to fire up your drive. You will be questioned, doubted, told you're making a mistake, so you might as well expect the blowback and accept, even welcome, the chance to put your balls on the line. The more *you* are on the line, the more you will go to extremes to succeed. That's when your drive will go to eleven.

I've talked about the amazing support Janet Shamlian got from her husband, but Janet, like most Extremers, also ran into serious doubt and criticism as she scaled her personal mountains. Some of the other moms in her community had a lot to say about her choice to leave her family so often and for so long. "One of the hardest things," she told me, "was people questioning my decision: 'You left the kids? Who's taking care of them?' Society would not have said this to a man. There was so much criticism, so many little comments about it—the moms at school who say, 'Oh! So nice of you to come in person today! So great to see you here!' Those backhanded compliments. It wasn't *that* hurtful, but I got plenty of it.

"The teachers got used to seeing my husband at the parent conferences. They got used to dealing with him. It pained me, but does it mean I'm a bad mom?" Encountering resistance and doubt about her choices as an Extreme Working Mom, Janet could have scaled back. Perhaps because of that resistance, she found a way to both fight for her own dreams and serve her family. She told me, "Sure, I had this really cool job before the girls were born, but they were never going to know it. What was I going to do, haul out old pictures and videotapes from before they were born? Today I have three teenage daughters who see that you can make your dreams come true—and having kids doesn't have to stop you.

"Now my daughter is at college. She's got a different last name, my married name, and shortly after she got there a senior came up to her and said, 'Hey, do you know Janet Shamlian? I saw she posted on your Facebook page, and she's my favorite correspondent on NBC news! How do you know her?' And Jennifer said, 'That's my mom!' Then she called me immediately. She said, 'Mom, I'm so proud of you!'"

Though in some people's eyes, Janet was letting the team down by pursuing her career goals, for her it was an Extreme opportunity to prepare her daughters for a better future. That was another essential part of her remarkable drive.

Janet's story is so powerful because of the important people who were relying on her to succeed; she was putting everything on the line for both her husband and her family. But often for younger people, it's easier to seek and find the kind of safety nets that have the effect of diminishing this special kind of drive. Beware of the shortcuts that might be provided to you if someone else is bearing the risk or doing the work for you. I know that a huge part of my drive to succeed in the United States was that it was my dream, funded by my own savings. I'm sure if I'd had a financial safety net to call on for the days when I literally ran out of money and could not afford to eat between paychecks, I would not have had anything like the same drive to rise up from the toughest challenges. The first time I lived in New York—when I went from a weekend of near starvation to triumphantly leaving with some savings in my account to go on to my next job—I remember listening to the brilliant Frank Sinatra—"If I can make it there, I'll make it anywhere"—and knowing that I'd made it. Would I have carried the same kind of confidence forward if my parents had bailed me out when I needed it? No way—that hunger was a huge ingredient in my Magic Drive.

So now back to you—it's time for some serious honesty. Think about your experiences to date—your approach to your big dreams. Have you truly put yourself out there, telling your loved ones, your bosses, or your friends what you aim to achieve and how you're planning to go about it? Or have you backed away from the stuff that really fires you up because there are too many naysayers who don't get your dream? Are you working at a job that your parents wanted you to take instead of putting your own balls on the line? It's easy to cast blame when you are following the decision that someone else made for you. Promise yourself to go all in and leave the safety net behind.

When you ladder up from one challenge to the next and those challenges come from your own Extreme interests, skills, and passion, you can develop the drive to climb farther than you would have thought possible. But even the most skillful, driven player can wind up getting left on the sidelines. In the next chapter, I describe how to Get Out of Line, so you can make yourself noticed and get into the game.

# THREE
# GET OUT
# OF LINE

After six years with Air New Zealand, first in Auckland and then in Los Angeles, I was ready to let it rip. I'd worked for that one company since college and I'd loved it, learning a ton by working alongside people who had become like family to me, but now I was ready to unleash my new skills on the world. It was time to make my move into a different industry, time to broaden my experience and move into the big leagues working for a major global brand. But when I put calls in to recruiting firms, they didn't get it.

"You don't have the right skill set," they told me. "You're an airline person."

I tried to explain that I knew honest-to-God airline specialists because I worked with them—folks who got high from the smell of jet fuel. And that wasn't me. But to the headhunters, I came to realize, it was more convenient and tidy to put me in a nice little conceptual box marked "airline" and expect me to stay there, waiting in line for my next promotion. My non-airline experiences and my talents and ambitions beyond marketing were not in the least bit interesting to them. I was hearing the conventional approach to career building: do something once, get a little experience, trim yourself down, do that thing some more, repeat, repeat, retire. It was like a one-way ticket to an average, hellaciously predictable life.

I realized that if I waited around to be noticed for my unique potential, I would probably be waiting forever. That's a challenge every Extremer will face: you may have developed a powerful combination of Extreme interests, knowledge, and skills, but how to win the chance to use them? It was time to take my ambitions into my own hands and find other people and other places where Extreme Me could be appreciated and rewarded. I needed to figure out a way to leverage my résumé in the airlines to start navigating toward new and broader experiences.

One airline seemed different from the rest. Ever since I'd studied marketing at university, I'd been fascinated by the Virgin Atlantic story and the charismatic founder behind the airline, Richard Branson. He didn't come from money, and he didn't have Ivy League qualifications—in fact, he was dyslexic—but what he did have was a larger-than-life personality and a huge vision for a business with a new style of swagger. I loved the look and feel of the Virgin brand—its bold logo in red, which happened to have been my favorite color since childhood. I loved the brilliant company name that spoke to naïveté, sexiness, femininity, and liberation. Its anti-establishment approach had won the loyalty of some of the hippest travelers: the old dudes were snoring on British Airways, but the cool media moguls were hanging at the in-flight bar on Virgin. This airline acted as if it were in the entertainment business. So if it had to be airlines for now, I decided, Virgin was the airline for me.

While researching the company's key players, I read up on its head of marketing. She had to be a daring, fun kind of gal, I thought, to have a job like she did. Then, by coincidence, a brochure arrived in the mail inviting me to attend a conference called the Marketing Forum, held on a cruise ship, of all places. It claimed to bring together the best and brightest minds of the industry in a three-day networking and learning event, and Virgin Atlantic's head of marketing was among the industry stars headlining the event. I felt a flutter of excitement, followed by the realization that I was going to have to ask my boss for three days out of the office to attend. But I knew I just had to go—if necessary, I would take personal vacation time. Everything I had read about Virgin made me feel that it was the perfect next place for me to work; I just had to figure out a way to get in the door. So when I saw a chance to meet its head of marketing, I had to make it happen.

As I walked up the gangplank of the *Queen Elizabeth II*, I could tell that this was going to be a once-in-a-lifetime experience. After dinner the first night of the cruise, a small group of attendees headed off to the bar. No surprise, I was among them, hoping to stumble upon my future boss. Yes, I'd definitely do well as a professional stalker, it seemed, because my plan worked like magic. Not only was I introduced to my heroine from Virgin, but by some awesome miracle we legitimately really hit it off. By the end of the cruise, I felt that we'd struck up a genuine friendship. When we said good-bye, it didn't even feel awkward to say that if Virgin had any openings, I'd just kill to come and work for her.

A few weeks later, I received an email asking me to give her a call. The role of promotions manager had opened up, and she wanted to know if I would do a phone interview with HR. Hmmm—I thought about it for possibly three seconds . . . Yes! The role was more junior than what I held at Air New Zealand, but as I saw it, Virgin was a bigger airline, so I would be getting exposed to bigger challenges, and if I proved myself I would surely move up once I got there.

All went well, and I was offered the job. After a trip to Connecticut to meet the team, I accepted the offer. *For reals!* I'd Gotten Out of Line—gotten noticed and taken myself somewhere I could showcase my Extreme Self to better effect. Virgin and me—a match meant to be. I couldn't wait to get started.

## NOT SO FAST

In retrospect, I see I'd gotten a bit ahead of myself. I'd thought getting the job would be the hard part. It turned out that actually getting to do the job was even harder. Getting Out of Line, I was discovering, isn't a onetime fix—it's more like a way of life.

Before I could quit Air New Zealand and leave Los Angeles to start my new job in New York, Virgin had to apply for and receive my US work visa. Thinking that it would take only a matter of weeks for the paperwork to be completed, I moved out of my apartment and sold my car to save money. But then months went by while I waited. Every day, without the paperwork in hand, I grew increasingly freaked out that my entire plan might fall apart. What if Virgin lost patience and withdrew the offer?

Without an apartment, I slept on the couch of my dear friend James and continued to work at Air New Zealand. When I couldn't hitch a ride to work with a colleague, I used my only remaining mode of transportation: a red triathlon bike. To be clear, back in the late 1990s, *nobody* biked in LA, let alone a ninety-minute bike commute, so everything from my sweaty entrances at work to my serious helmet hair made me look like a freak.

Waiting was hard, but waiting without being able to control the outcome was really hard. I've always been described as impatient—ask my mother or any of the multiple bosses who have told me to relaaaaaax and slow down—but after so many years developing my drive and taking satisfaction from the forward motion and a steady stream of wins, this kind of waiting was hell on wheels for me. I felt like a sailboat with no wind. As the weeks passed, I got so wound up physically that I slept poorly and began to act grumpy and down. I ate badly and then beat myself up for it. If I didn't do something with all the energy and frustration that was building up inside me, I knew I could lose my Magic Drive.

I found my goal in training for a triathlon called the Half Iron-man. I had run a marathon, but this would be by far the toughest physical challenge I had ever undertaken: a 1.2-mile swim, 56-mile bike ride, and 13.1-mile run, all in less than eight and a half hours. I just knew completing it would be an awesome outlet for my pent-up energy and a great way to maintain my drive.

The training consisted of working out twice a day, several days a week, to cover multiple disciplines, and then once every other day except rest day. I might swim an hour in the morning, go to work, and then bike for an hour or two at night. On the weekends I had to do really long sessions putting pieces of the triathlon together—for example, swim for an hour and then bike two hours back to back. Because it's such hard training, you feel physically knackered at night—and really satisfied, actually. You go to bed feeling as though you had one hell of a great day and accomplished way more than anyone around you.

Just a couple of weeks before my race, the moment I had been desperately waiting for finally came. My visa application to work for Virgin Atlantic had been approved! Suddenly my life in neutral moved into high gear. Finally, I was hopping on a plane to New York (and maxing out my credit cards) to find myself an apartment share and get my East Coast life organized, all while finishing my training. The Half Ironman took place on a Saturday, and, wow, it was for sure one of the most grueling days of my life, but in just over seven hours (complete with wasp stings and one hell of a sore bum from the bike ride, plus blisters from the run) I was able to reflect with satisfaction that I'd knocked this big-ass Half Ironman off. I even had a medal to show for it. Afterward I drove back to James's apartment, slept one last night on his couch, and flew to New York Sunday morning to get ready for my first big day at Virgin Atlantic on Monday.

Before the race, the organizers had written our ID numbers in thick black marker on our calf muscles and upper arm, so if we had any injuries or if the course photographers took photos, we could be quickly identified. Once the race was over, I could have scrubbed those numbers really hard in the shower, but they were like my battle scars—there was no way I was going to lose them that fast. I wanted to show up at my new job with my race number in bold black ink because I felt fully badass for what I had just accomplished. And sure enough, my new colleagues asked, "Wow—what's that?" When I think about it, that choice to leave the numbers on my arm was itself a way of Getting Out of Line. I showed up on my first day looking different, standing out from the crowd, with a conversation starter that introduced me as a Half Ironman finisher. Using my career downtime to set a physical goal and achieve it didn't just raise my spirits and keep my drive strong; it also bolstered my confidence for the new job and helped me show my new team I was ready to succeed—and willing to go to extremes to do it.

## HOW NOT TO BE PATIENT

Even so, when I finally did arrive at Virgin's headquarters in Connecticut that first day, I had major butterflies. At the reception, I asked for the head of marketing who had hired me. The receptionist gave her computer a few taps—kind of like the gate agent at an airport—lifted her head, applied her perfect Virgin smile, and said, "I'm sorry, but she doesn't work here anymore. She left last Friday."

Wait. Whaaaaaaaat? You have to be shitting me. This was the moment I had spent literally months preparing for—and it was suddenly in jeopardy? I felt the adrenaline pumping through my veins. Here I was, knowing no one at Virgin or in the entire state of New York, for that matter, down to my last dime, and the person who'd hired me had left without a word. Faaaaarck! Did I even have a job?

Pointed in the direction of the restrooms, I rushed into the first open stall, hyperventilating as the tears rolled down my cheeks. Was my big Virgin dream blowing up in front of me? No, no, no! As a kid, when I'd tried hard and failed, I'd thrown tantrums, throwing my tennis racquet onto the court. I'd since learned to restrain that anger, but I'd also learned to value it. If you rage at people indiscriminately, they will leave you alone. If you rage against yourself, you can wind up curled into the fetal position with the blinds lowered on every window. But there's nothing wrong at raging inwardly at the world when it fails to recognize Extreme You. That rage is power. It's energy. It's the motivation and the courage to get back up and Get Out of Line and insist the world recognize you for the best that you are. My mum had always said to me when I was a child, "Every dog has its day." This was my day, dammit!

The butterflies in my stomach were gone. I felt like William Wallace, the rebel leader in the movie *Braveheart*—complete with bright blue face paint, of course. I stepped up to the mirror and threw cold water on my face to hide the tears. Then I marched myself back up to the front-desk receptionist.

"Could I please trouble you to have the head of Human Resources come down to meet me? I am the new promotions manager, and I need my paperwork completed."

An HR manager found me a desk and asked that I be "patient" as the organizational structure and roles were sorted out after the head of marketing's departure. It seemed that for now, at least, I had a job. But with the marketing boss gone, would the company be downsizing? Would I be the victim of the LIFO inventory method— Last In, First Out? I needed some way to get noticed and secure my position. Yep, some way, somehow, I would have to Get Out of Line once again.

Those first couple of weeks, I got to know the team. They seemed to be exceptionally nice and smart people, and they showed empathy for my situation, but so many complained about a lack of leadership in their department. No one seemed certain where it was headed. And where was *I* headed? Had the entire move to Virgin been a mistake?

After all, I'd moved from an awesome lifestyle in LA to a small, exceptionally sweaty non-air-conditioned apartment in Manhattan that I shared with a much older roommate, recently divorced—not exactly someone I was going to hang out with. It was the only living option I could afford, and often I had to lie in a cold bath as my only way of cooling down on a hot August night. My commute turned out to be far more grueling than I'd imagined: two hours door to door, looking like a packhorse, with my work bags hitched on my shoulders as I went from bus to subway to Metro North train to shuttle bus to the office.

Facing a trip like that every morning, I was tempted to say: forget it, I can't fit working out into my day. But most mornings in my new Manhattan life, I started with a five-mile run along the East River. That morning run was the anchor that held everything in place. On my runs I felt fully myself. I also knew that running was when I did some of my best thinking.

So I got up before dawn each morning and ran, and as I ran I kept thinking about all of the one-on-one interviews I was having with my new colleagues. What I had found was that the marketing department didn't seem to have a clear overall strategy. The people there spent the day reacting to what potential marketing and advertising partners pitched: "Virgin should be advertising on my media platform." "Virgin should be sponsoring my event." "Virgin should be partnering with my movie." We had no clear road map, just a lot of smart individual marketing people reacting to different pitches. As I had meetings and lunches with different members of the team, I would ask how they coordinated their efforts, but all I got in response was variations on "We don't work like that; we each focus on our own areas."

I remember thinking *We may as well take our multimillion-dollar marketing budget up in a Virgin plane and dump it out the door. All those dollars would scatter in the wind, just like these marketing efforts.*

Soon I was consciously reviewing my notes before I went to bed in the evenings, so I could think about them in an organized way when I was running in the mornings. Little by little I realized there was a gaping hole in the organization. The voice in my head kept growing louder. *This department has a great brand, a clear point of view, and great people. But where is the vision for where we are going? Where's the road map? Imagine how much more successful they could be if they all started focusing on bigger, better market-moving initiatives, with everyone lined up behind the same plan.*

I kept trying to silence my audacious thoughts. I was the newcomer, I reminded myself, lucky to have any job at all. But the more I tried to silence that voice, the louder it got. One Friday night, about a month into my new job, I opened my laptop in my tiny Manhattan apartment and began writing. And writing. My fingers ran like lightning over the keyboard as all the crazy ideas that had been rattling around in my head started to come together on the screen in front of me. What emerged that weekend amid the sweat, the Ben & Jerry's breaks, and the ice-cold baths was a complete marketing plan for Virgin Atlantic Airways and a new organizational structure and team approach. I felt so freakin' pumped up to have gotten the ideas out of my head, and I *knew* they were good—some of the best strategic thinking I had ever done. Yet I felt equally terrified. What to do with it all?

I didn't have a friend at Virgin. I didn't have a mentor or an ally. My credit cards were maxed out from my cross-country move and my pricey new Manhattan life. On one occasion, I'd had to make it through a three-day weekend without spending any money, even for food, as I waited for my next paycheck. (I was saved by the good fortune of a Sunday-night business dinner at which I inhaled the entire bread basket before my host even had a chance to ask me how I was getting on in New York.) I was literally counting pennies to make sure I could afford the commuter train to work. Was this really the time to Get Way Out of Line?

One possibility was to keep my marketing plan to myself as a sort of private mission statement. Another was to show it to one colleague in my department and test whether my ideas would be welcome. But what would more experienced Virgin Atlantic executives think of some newbie upstart telling them how to fix their marketing team? Might that be the perfect excuse to toss me off the boat? No question, sharing this document would be a risky move. I had to ask myself: Honestly, am I just being impatient? Pushy? Arrogant?

No. I realized that it wasn't enough to be driven or to possess unique skills and specialties. You can't just wait around for others to notice your potential. My choice was either to stay in my expected place and hope not to get fired—to play not to lose—or to take the risk of Getting Waaaay Out of Line: to play to win.

On my next morning run, I hatched a plan: I would give my marketing ideas directly to the president of the airline. But did I have the cojones? Honestly, it was my morning runs that filled me with the courage I needed. When I am running and thinking about something scary that I have to do, it never feels as scary because I am physically firing it up. I can feel my strength, my momentum. And that gives me courage.

I printed my plan and put it in a large envelope with a handwritten note to the president of the US division of the airline. I said I hoped he might find some of my thoughts helpful. I signed the note and then slipped the envelope under his office door.

The next few days were excruciating. More waiting. No word from the corner office. Had he liked what I had to say? Had I pissed him off? Even worse—after all that work, had he just not gotten around to reading the plan? All those thoughts were going through my mind at the moment his secretary called and asked me to come up to his office. Deep breaths . . . this was it. I was nervous as hell but ready to hear his reaction.

He told me that he was willing to go with my plan. *Holy shit!* He liked it! Not only that, he liked it far beyond anything I had expected. He said how hugely impressed he had been not only with my thinking but also with the balls it had taken to put my thinking down on paper. Then he told me he knew he was taking a big bet on me, promoting me to director of marketing, with the rest of the marketing department reporting to me, in order to get my plan under way.

To some people, a result like this—a newbie Getting Out of Line, taking on a major big challenge, and winning big—might sound like a freak accident, reckless but lucky. But there's research to suggest that, done right, it's both wise and repeatable. While researching her book *Rookie Smarts*, the leadership expert Liz Wiseman found that people new to a pursuit often perform surprisingly well. Her advice to new hires—regardless of their age—is to try to "contribute big on day one." She gave the example of a program at eBay where recent college grads were encouraged to submit ideas for patents even though they were young and new to the company. The new recruits submitted 25 percent more ideas for patents on average than their colleagues did, and more of their ideas became submissions for formal patents. Wiseman even suggested that new hires try to identify the biggest issue confronting their boss and then offer a solution. Hmm . . . I think she's onto something! (But be sure to read the next chapter, "Get Over Yourself," to make sure that when you Get Out of Line, you're doing it with the preparation, knowledge, and humility it takes to keep from making a total ass of yourself. Believe me—I've gotten it wrong, too!)

## WARNING! WARNING! THE DANGERS OF HARD-PARTYING KIWIS

As the new director of marketing for Virgin Atlantic, I reported directly to the vice president of sales, who now also took marketing under his purview and became the VP of sales and marketing. This was awesome news for me because I had really hit it off with this guy and was absolutely stoked at the idea of working for him. And given the big bet that he and the president were placing on me, I was absolutely determined not to let them down. I promised myself I was going to work eight hundred times harder than anyone else, if that was what it took to ensure that my team and I delivered spectacular results. When my new boss sent me home that evening, I hopped on the train back to Manhattan in the best mood I could imagine—just so pumped that I had been promoted. After almost a year from the time of that fateful boat cruise, of waiting, hoping, trying to get the big break, finally it had happened. Wasn't this what Getting Out of Line was all about? The promotion was the win, the biggest of my career, and a win is for celebrating!

By chance, that night was the annual Kiwi Club of New York Christmas party. The Kiwi Club of New York was about one hundred people strong, believe it or not—and this year we were joining forces with the Aussies for a booze cruise on the Hudson River. Let's just say that Kiwis love to party. I remember the sauvignon blanc flowing freely. I remember all of us getting up to some mischief (it's possible there were Christmas trees involved . . . ). Was I worried that I needed to be up at six to catch my train to be at the office for my big kickoff meeting with my new boss and the new team? I wasn't worried. It's fair to say that I do like to party, but I'm a responsible girl. I'm usually very good at knowing my limits. By midnight, I will usually start remembering that big things need to happen tomorrow and I have to be sure I'm there to get it done. Or if I'm still going strong at, say, two a.m., I'll look at my watch and think, *OK, so waking up tomorrow is going to be painful as all getup, but it's all about endurance, I got this . . . I will push through it, and then I'll sleep like crazy tomorrow night.*

That night, as I finally crawled into my bed around five, I had a plan: catch one hour of sleep, and then get up at six for work.

I fell asleep before I even set my alarm. When I awoke, I turned over to look at my alarm clock and realized that it was not six in the morning but eleven. Holy shiiiiit. Career Armageddon!

I had just slept through the biggest meeting of my professional life.

I hadn't even called in to say where I was.

But now I didn't have a second to think about what I had done. I needed to get on the first train up to the office in Norwalk and somehow explain my way out of this. Bear in mind—the kickoff meeting with my new boss had been scheduled for nine a.m., it was already eleven a.m., and my commute to the office was a minimum of two hours. This was baaaad. Really bad. On the train—shocked, sweating, head pounding—I kept trying to come up with a reasonable explanation to excuse my absence, but short of having lost both of my legs in a car crash, what excuse would have done it? I had nothing. I flashed back to childhood, and suddenly I could see my dad's face before my eyes, reminding me to "Never let the side down." Where was my concern for the side in a stunt like the one I had just pulled? I had Gotten Out of Line to try to show the airline president what I could do for the company, but had I now done the opposite? Would he hear about this shameful oversight and now think that I was only in it for myself, that I thought the "win" was standing out just to glorify myself? Never in my life had I felt more ashamed.

As I shuffled into the office, I saw my new boss sitting calmly behind his desk. He didn't say anything. Not one word. He just waited for me to explain myself. And as I stood there, I knew that there was only one thing to be said: the truth.

"Umm, I don't even know how to begin telling you what happened to me this morning. I am beyond mortified, and I am all too aware that on my first day, in a new and important job, I have deeply let you down. I wish that I could say there was a decent reason for my absence today but there isn't." *Deep breaths . . . sweat bullets on forehead beginning to roll down . . .* "The reason I didn't make it this morning is because I slept through my alarm. And the reason I slept through my alarm is because I got carried away celebrating last night at the Kiwis in New York Christmas party. I don't know what came over me. I've *never* done anything like this in my life before . . . Well—I don't mean the partying part, but the oversleeping and missing the biggest meeting of my life part. Truly, I can assure you I am not irresponsible even though I look it. I just hadn't heard a familiar voice in weeks, and, well, it wasn't even just Kiwis—there were Ozzies too—and we were on a cruise—and the wine was free . . . and . . . and . . . I'm sorry. I'm really, really sorry."

And then did he ever make me sweat. Silence. He just sat there for what was probably only a matter of seconds but felt like an hour. Saying nothing. Staring at me. Giving me that "parental" look of disappointment. Eventually he talked. He told me, rightfully, that I had destroyed his trust in my reliability. Fuck fuck fuckety fuck. I was just waiting for the hammer to come down: the dreaded news that he was taking the promotion away from me. But those words didn't come. Instead, as I turned toward the door, ready to retreat to my trusty bathroom stall and cry my eyes out, he called me back.

"Sarah, you definitely let me down this morning," he said. "But I wouldn't be honest if I didn't tell you . . . I think it's pretty hilarious—and it's *very* Virgin!" He explained that if I were to make one more move like that, I would absolutely have to be demoted. But he was giving me another chance to show what I could do— not just to get noticed or win a promotion but to get results for the company.

I didn't waste that chance. As director of marketing, I didn't wait for ideas to come to us. With the support of my team and our fantastic advertising agency, we went looking for a pop-culture tie-in that would help explain to the American market what our airline was all about, and we landed on the Austin Powers movies. I found myself in the amazing position of pitching Richard Branson the idea of branding the airline "Virgin Shaglantic" for the duration of the campaign. (Imagine giant billboards in New York and LA with Austin Powers standing next to a Virgin 747 saying, "Five Times a Day . . . Yeah, baby!") This was unconventional for an airline marketing campaign, and it led to complaints from those it offended— and love from our core consumer, who couldn't get enough of it. The campaign was a huge breakthrough in that the viral buzz and the PR around it far exceeded our marketing budgets.

I had made some ballsy, attention-getting moves for myself with that campaign, but all for the sake of using my Extreme Self to help the company succeed by being truer to its own Extreme Virgin Atlantic self. I had Gotten Out of Line so we could all succeed. That was the real win.

## YOUR BEST CHANCE IS THE CHANCE
## YOU CREATE

When you take action, today, on your own, to try to get results you want in the future, psychologists call it "proactivity." And wow, does it make a difference. According to a number of studies summarized in the *Journal of Occupational and Organizational Psychology*, including a meta-analysis of more than 30,000 participants, proactive employees rock. They perform better on core tasks, have more entrepreneurial success, receive more favorable evaluations, receive higher salaries and more promotions, and show more commitment to their organization. When they are fired, they find new jobs faster. Yowza! Sign me up now!

But I would have to add that it's easy to miss out on all of those benefits because they start out hidden in the future. I suspect that a lot of people who don't Get Out of Line miss their chances because it's hard to see up ahead to what they might miss. I know that when I first arrived at Virgin, I was worried about a downsizing, but at the time I was only making a guess about the future, trusting a hunch. If I had not put that marketing plan under my boss's door, maybe I wouldn't have lost my job. Maybe the company would have hired someone else to be its new director of marketing and continued to let each marketing person work separately, and I would have worked for that person and things would have continued on that way, which for some people would be predictable and reliable and satisfying enough. It's not necessarily the case that people who don't Get Out of Line are unhappy.

But if I hadn't Gotten Out of Line, I doubt I would ever have pitched Richard Branson on that wild Virgin Shaglantic idea or driven that concept all the way to a big success. I might never even have known the opportunity could exist for me—after all, when I was hired, no one was expecting that I would become director and lead a team to achieve what we did. Not Getting Out of Line might have meant that my achievements stayed small and quiet. I might never have made for myself the chance to succeed in such a big way.

The costs for you of *not* Getting Out of Line may depend in part on the advantages you already have. In this era of increasing income equality, according to research that Matt O'Brien summarized in the *Washington Post*, "America is the land of opportunity, just for some more than others. . . . Even poor kids who do everything right don't do much better than rich kids who do everything wrong. Advantages and disadvantages, in other words, tend to perpetuate themselves." For the very privileged, it may be possible to get along quite well without taking the kind of bold, creative risks I'm describing. But for everyone else, it's a lot harder than it used to be to succeed on the basis of talent and hard work. It takes some Extreme Moves just to create a chance for yourself.

But the fact is, no matter what your situation, Getting Out of Line in the service of your own personal hopes and dreams gets you so much farther ahead than playing it safe and coasting in environments or roles that feel secure but limit your ability to grow. A great example is my friend Dan Keyserling, whom I met a few years ago at a conference. You never know when an Extremer is going to pop into your life, but when we got chatting and Dan told me the epic story of how he'd landed such a blow-away job at such a young age, I knew we were going to be friends for life. Just a few months after graduation from a prestigious college, Dan stepped off the expected path. He had secured an excellent job at the *New York Times*—what most aspiring journalism grads would kill for—but he knew in his gut that he was looking for something different, something more than straight journalism. He was lucky enough to navigate his way into working for Google. Even with a job at a different kind of dream company, though, he discovered it was up to him to Get Out of Line, to create his own chance for Extreme Dan to find what he was best at, so he could build his own Extreme kind of success.

"I was hugely excited to be recruited by Google," he told me. (Um, yeah! You think?) "I felt like I was around the people who were inventing the future, so I was willing to scrub the floors to get in the door—and that's more or less what they offered me, an entry-level position as an administrative assistant for two engineering teams.

"When you get hired to Google, there's a period when you can't believe your luck. There was all this free food—you could easily spend half the day congratulating yourself. (Hey, I'm having lobster for lunch!) But while I knew I was in the right place, I still felt out of my element. If you've spent time around software engineers, you know it's like they speak another language. In engineering meetings, I thought I'd had a stroke—I couldn't understand what people were staying. Even the words they used were completely foreign to me, and there was nothing I could do to fix it. I was frustrated that my contributions to this band of noble nerds was so limited."

Fortunate as he was, Dan was quickly discovering the limits of a job that has no need of Extreme You. "There is only so long you can stay jazzed about what's going on in other parts of your office building. Ultimately you need to find some satisfaction in the tasks you do yourself, because the tasks you do are your job—not your title or how you describe it or what you tell people at dinner parties.

"Meanwhile, Eric Schmidt, the CEO, hired this young wonder kid, Jared Cohen, away from the State Department. He'd given Jared the title director of Google ideas. Almost no one seemed to understand what that meant, but although they didn't understand it, they were pretty sure it was going to fail. Still, I thought: what an interesting character. He had worked for both Condoleezza Rice and Hillary Clinton and made a name for himself around the world when he asked Twitter to delay scheduled maintenance in Iran so that the dissidents there would not lose a crucial new communications tool. I wanted to meet him. In college, I had studied political and social thought. I was executive editor of the school newspaper, and I worked for Hillary Clinton's presidential campaign. I had thought that the politics of public policy or journalism would be my career."

Do you hear the suspenseful music starting to play? Can you spot the Extreme opportunity coming into sight? Dan had checked himself out in college and knew what interested him most. Now among the engineers he'd discovered someone else compelled by Extreme politics.

"I found this Jared Cohen working in a windowless office on the fourth floor, with just an assistant, a researcher, and one other employee who hadn't started yet. I introduced myself, and he started to talk to me about his vision. He talked for maybe an hour, and it all made sense. What makes Google important is its power to organize information and make it universally accessible, and that's political whether you want it to be or not. He was asking: What was the Internet going to be? Was access to information basically a human right?

"I was so inspired by what Jared was setting out to accomplish. It was as if we shared the same vocabulary about the way the world works, the same sense of how technology could affect geopolitical issues and security issues. He was talking about tackling the problems that I already thought about and read about for fun, what I wanted to hear on the news—what had animated me to study what I had studied. I felt: *He may be crazy, but he's my kind of crazy. I want to work for him.*

"But Jared had no budget yet, no head count. He couldn't hire anyone. He said, 'I guess I wouldn't mind if you helped out with stuff.' So I said, 'Yeah. No problem. I'll just . . . hang around!'

"Of course, I already had a job. But one advantage of being part of a two-hundred-person team is that no one notices when you're not in the room. Google is a big building, and everyone works on their laptops anyway, so I did my paying job from random places in the building, and, after listening and learning, I started to help Jared out with odd projects—anything to prove my value as a member of the team. At first it was kind of awkward—he would tell his assistant something, and I would just be sitting there next to her, smiling and trying to learn. And I would be lying if I said that I didn't neglect a little bit the responsibilities of my nine-to-five."

Dan was Getting Out of Line—and taking a risk. "Google does not suffer fools," he told me. "You have to perform." Friends at the company warned him that he was making a mistake. Google was organized by product areas, which meant that even if a boss got fired, those responsible for the product still had a role to play. But Google Ideas wasn't a product. "Google Ideas was created as Jared Cohen, and if he left, I realized, it wouldn't exist."

Dan had Gotten Out of Line to volunteer his services, but he came to feel he would have to go further to make his gamble pay off. The chance came in the form of a request he didn't think he could honor.

"One day, sitting at my actual desk on the eleventh floor, Jared pinged me with an IM that said: 'Hey, I know this is a little awkward, but my assistant is not available and the former president of Brazil is coming. I need you to take notes.'

"I can't," I messaged back. "I'm in shorts and flip-flops."

"It will be fine," Jared said.

"So when I met the visiting head of state I said, 'Hello, Mr. President. I'm so sorry I'm dressed so casually.'

"He said, 'Oh! You have Brazilian flip-flops on!'

"After that meeting, I went back to Jared's office and said, 'Look, you're going to hire me. Maybe not today, maybe not tomorrow, but soon. In the meantime, I'll work from here.' I moved my desk into Jared's office, and my bosses saw the writing on the wall. It's not like I was the most superstar assistant anyway, and they had known when they hired me that I was political. When they heard what I was doing, they said, 'That makes perfect sense.'"

Boom boom ka-boom! Jared made it official, and Dan joined the Google Ideas team. And I can say, as someone who gets to work with Jared, Dan, and the team (now known as Jigsaw within the broader company known as Alphabet), that Dan's big move has propelled him way further than even he could probably have imagined. Jared is now known as one of the most prominent and important political thought leaders in the world and Dan has risen through the ranks to become the chief of staff—traveling around the world meeting major world leaders and working on issues that have huge potential impact. By Google standards, he has become a veteran— more than 90 percent of the company was hired after he arrived. Did Getting Out of Line help him find his true calling? "I'm not sure that people have callings that endure for their entire lives, but I'm so compelled by what we're doing at Google Ideas—this promise that my kids could grow up in a world where the Internet is free and open to everyone—that I'm not sure I could do anything else. This may be the most noble thing I can contribute with the skills that I have."

Dan had come to Google with a deep interest and skills around politics and journalism, and he had been lucky to get an entry-level job at a great company, but he would never have found this opportunity, this career so well tailored to Extreme Dan, if he hadn't found the courage to Get Out of Line. He took a risk to pursue an opportunity that no one around him saw or believed in. He found a career and a calling for Extreme Dan.

## EXTREME MOVES

So many people seem to be asleep at the wheel. It astonishes me how often people miss an opportunity to leap forward because they don't take the chance that is right there in front of them. I suppose that's because Getting Out of Line requires balancing such opposite extremes. Here are some approaches to making sure you get the balance right.

### 1. Show Respect as Big as Your Balls

It takes cojones, yes—that's the part that requires courage and gets all the attention—but it also takes understanding, caution, and respect. We have all met arrogant, self-absorbed loudmouths who push themselves in front of their work mates or major in brownnosing, and there is always a risk in Getting Out of Line that it won't seem as though you're doing it to match your Extreme Self with situations where it will be valuable and appreciated. It might just seem like arrogance and self-serving recklessness—showing off how cocky you are and what you can get away with, without any plan or regard for the impact it has on your colleagues.

A study by Donald Campbell described what he called the "initiative paradox": as much as employers reward employees who take the initiative—those who Get Out of Line for the right reasons—they may punish those who try to take the initiative but don't seem to serve the company's values and interests. So the more you're going to Get Out of Line and stand out, the more you need to show the other people involved that you respect them and your shared interests.

As someone who's been in a number of public leadership positions, I'm amazed at how many of the people who are bold enough to break through to me and ask for my time and attention seem *not* to be able to show me how it's in my interest—in fact, they often seem not to know what they would do with my attention if they got it. They're all balls and no respect. I'm thinking now of a young man with a personal connection to someone close to me, someone I felt I owed a phone call and an open mind. When I took his call he told me, out of the blue, "I have to work for you. I'm in America, I have a US passport, and I'll do anything!"

Hearing that, I wished I could say, "Kid, I don't know you from a bar of soap. Why do you think it's so urgent to work for me?" What I actually said was "Why don't you get together a plan for what you want your career to be, what you can do for my company, and how working for us would help get you there. Send me that, and we can talk again." In my view, I was giving him exactly what he needed, but I wasn't really surprised that he never sent me his plan. Instead, he left me way too many voice mails, tweetstalked me, and offered to babysit my kids. (I'm sorry, but that's just creepy.) He was plenty aggressive, plenty bold, but in the service of nothing.

So yes—the opportunities to Get Out of Line are all around you, and to succeed, it's likely that you will need to step up and stand out in a way that you have never done before. But don't be reckless; it requires having essential people around you who will support and understand your move if you're going to pull it off.

### 2. Scan for Opportunities—and Look for Support

War stories about great proactive moves that crushed it tend to feature one gifted rebel goin' it alone against all odds. But the reality is that I couldn't have done what I did at Virgin Atlantic if my boss hadn't recognized and supported me, even when I screwed up. Studies of proactivity show that although some people are wired to Get Out of Line, having a supportive boss or a workplace environment that encourages autonomy can also bring out people's proactive side. So if you're an Extremer looking to make a mark, seek out environments where you'll be encouraged and supported.

Opportunities to practice Getting Out of Line are all around you. A student who raises a hand when the teacher hasn't asked a question is Getting Out of Line. So is a person who rallies for a cause by helping those in need or working to right a wrong. Often, what motivates me in the moment is the simple worry that other people will think of what I have thought of, too, and that they will act first and beat me. To this day, at the end of meetings I want to be the one to say, "I'll take the follow-up" or "Let me pull together what I think we are talking about." Even if it's just making notes from the meeting, I leap for it so that no one else will step up and take away my opportunity to lead and get a new experience or understanding.

The trick is to make it a habit to scan for opportunities going to waste. Often the chance will reveal itself first as a gut feeling of either frustration or worry. *Why can't I move up faster? What if I get fired? Why is everyone around here just sitting and waiting for someone else to take the initiative?* Those unpleasant feelings could lead you to complain or distract yourself with more tangible tasks, but they could also be signals that there's an opportunity for you to do more and get bigger results. So start looking around. Where is the opportunity? What's standing in your way? How could you Get Out of Line and beat that obstacle?

### 3. Proper Planning Prevents Piss-Poor Performance

I remember a great saying I heard from a most awesome football coach whom I met during my time at Gatorade: Whether you're trying to create the break or to jump into a gap that has opened up, the most important thing is not the opportunity that you make or discover, it's your *preparation.* Before you make your move out of line, you'd better be really sure you've done your homework.

Getting a meeting is nothing if you don't have a plan for what to do in it.

Presenting your ideas is nothing if you haven't thought through how to execute them.

Brilliant planning won't deliver results unless you have support from other people. Have you gathered their input? Are you aware of what they are looking for and what will motivate them? And can you show how your bold move will benefit the person you're talking to and not just bold you?

Like a star Formula 1 driver who may trail the car ahead for a hundred laps or more before moving to take the lead, you must work at the extremes of both daring and responsibility, doing something that is unexpected by others but from a place of your own thorough strategic understanding, not just of your needs but of theirs.

If you wait around for others to notice Extreme You, you're always going to be disappointed with the results. But Getting Out of Line can backfire. As you plan, take time to think through not just how Getting Out of Line will help you reach your goal but whether you can live with falling short. That kind of emotional planning will make you better prepared and more ready to get seriously, extremely bold.

Getting Out of Line is an absolute necessity for Extremers, because we are always works in progress, putting together new skills and personalized areas of knowledge in ways the world is probably not expecting. It's up to us to make sure our Extreme skills and knowledge are noticed where they will have the biggest impact—but at the same time, that's our biggest weakness: it's all too easy to get carried away with developing and demonstrating our strengths, and fall into the trap of thinking that as Extremers we can do it all and on our own. In the next chapter, I'll show you why it's so important as an Extremer to Get Over Yourself.

# FOUR
# GET OVER
# YOURSELF

**A**t twenty-six years old, I felt I had this whole Extreme You thing down—as if I were a fully formed Extremer and it would be smooth sailing from now on. Maybe that overconfidence was a warning sign, but did I notice? I'd just spent my birthday at an intimate team dinner with Virgin founder Sir Richard Branson, sitting on the Croisette at the Cannes Film Festival. Yes, you heard me right. I mean, never had this crazy Kiwi kid imagined herself in the middle of *that* scene. And it just kept getting better. Our success with the Virgin "Shaglantic" marketing campaign had helped me get noticed by the team at our sister company Virgin Megastores, which recruited me back to LA to be its director of marketing. Finally I was making my big move out of airlines and into the sexy, fun world of entertainment. Yeah, baby!

I felt as though I had everything I needed, that I could fly solo and succeed by myself on my own terms. I'd even more or less given up on finding Mr. Right, ever since I'd gotten my heart smashed when the supposed love of my life had run off with a flight attendant.

But my brother, Olly, had found love, and much to my excitement he had asked me to be one of his groomsmen. I realize that sounds a bit odd, but fear not: the plan was for me to wear a bridesmaid dress but stand on Ol's side of the aisle. Of course I had to ask if, as a groomsman, I was allowed to attend the stag night (the bachelor party, as Americans call it). I was fully expecting him to want no lady folk present, but he said, "Sissy! Of course you have to be there!"

That got my mother's attention. She told me, "You must go. It will be you and thirty-five men. If you don't score one of them, there's no hope for you!" Yep—always the loving, encouraging type, my mum. Then, referring to one of my brother's geeky friends—someone I had known growing up by the name of Fleece on account of his childhood hair—my mother said, "Sissy—I must tell you that I ran into Liam O'Hagan the other day. Well . . . the years have been good to him—he's *quite* the dish these days!"

*Really, Mum?* I thought. *Fuckin' really? Does any normal female on the planet want a guy her mother calls a "dish"?*

My invite to the stag party led to mucho smack talking, with me telling the other groomsmen that I could drink a big game and they better watch out, etc. WTF was I thinking? I've always liked a good wine, but as a drinker, I've got to be honest, I'm a lightweight. So flash forward: it's the stag party, and there I am in a bathroom stall, violently ill. My brother's friend, the geek formerly known as Fleece (but now this tall, dark, insanely good-looking guy I was flirting with until I got sick) swoops into the ladies' room, pulls my head out of the toilet bowl, and tells the rest of the blokes he's going to take me home. Which he does, and like a complete gentleman. Yes, that's right—the night I met the love of my life, I puked all over his shoes.

But the next night, more sober, I saw him again at the wedding and we more "appropriately" got together. He was the one who took me to the airport when I headed back to the States, and once I got home, we started emailing at all hours of the day and having big phone marathons at night. For years, I'd thought I had no time for a relationship, but I quickly made time for him!

Within three months, I'd begun to feel that Liam (oddly enough, he no longer answered to Fleece) would be the one to take me off "the shelf" that Mum continued to remind me about. I was for going slow, but Liam had a different idea. He decided it was time for one of us to find the courage to explore whether *this* was *It*. He quit his job as a hiking guide in New Zealand and bought a one-way ticket to come live with me in Los Angeles. Really!

At that point I was about a year into my new role at Virgin Megastores. The day before Liam was supposed to arrive, I arrived at the office expecting the usual. I had just set my coffee cup and laptop down on my desk when my phone rang. It was the chief operating officer's assistant, asking me to pop over. No problem, I thought as I grabbed my coffee and notepad and headed over to the executive waiting area. In the COO's office, I saw my boss. He was sitting with someone from Human Resources. Suddenly my breakfast started rumbling in my tummy.

Most of the next ten minutes is still a blur. I recall being told that my "role had been terminated." The HR person put some paperwork in front of me and asked me to sign it. I remember the rush of blood to my face and the feeling of absolute panic. This didn't happen to people like me! I was—in my own mind, anyway—an unstoppable rising rock star. Now I felt as if I were having an out-of-body experience. I waited for my bosses to return to their normal, friendly selves, but they didn't.

I was getting fired. Painfully, crushingly, embarrassingly *fired*.

Escorted back to my desk by the HR representative, I felt like a criminal. I could see out of the corner of my eye everyone popping up from their cubes like little prairie dogs, wondering what had happened to the loser girl from the side office. It seemed the whole building was staring at me, knowing everything that had just gone down and thinking I was a smartass who had gotten her comeuppance. My office with my pictures all over the wall had suddenly gone from my own personal sanctuary to someone else's space. I threw everything into a box and got out fast.

What would gnaw at me for a long time was that I had never heard or understood a reason for my firing. It felt like an injustice. I was owed an answer, dammit! I'd been brought there to put Virgin Megastores on the map, and that was just what I'd been doing. In those years it was the beginning of what we still called the "information superhighway," and I had put together a strategic plan like nothing Virgin had ever seen, combining digital advertising and direct response tactics. I was even assembling the bones of a customer loyalty program that would curate new musical choices for Virgin shoppers based on what they had bought with us before—all this, years before Spotify and its musical competitors. When I briefed market research and communications agencies on my plan for the future, again and again I heard, "This is the most well-thought-through strategy for a brand that we've ever seen." Even today, I would stand by the quality of that work.

But none of that mattered because there was one big problem

that I had completely overlooked: my boss and his boss had never fully bought into all I was doing. Perhaps they didn't understand it? I remember when the COO who would eventually fire me first took me to "walk the stores" with her. I wanted to talk about the future of marketing, but she couldn't stop complaining about the signage in the stores, signage I was now responsible for. She said the signs looked like "little postage stamps" instead of big, bold signs that customers could easily read. She was very clear that she wanted me to spend heaps of time on this signage kind of stuff.

I walked along the store aisles with her, silently critiquing her heavily dyed helmet of hair and her work history with a clothing retailer for middle-aged women. *This lady dresses really badly,* I thought, *and she came from a stodgy old retailer. She can't possibly get the Virgin brand the way I do.*

So instead of taking her suggestions and learning all that I could from her, I blindly kept my head down and focused on myself and my strengths. I felt I had a great strategic vision for the future of the company, and I devoted most of my time to developing it. What I overlooked was that Virgin Megastores was a retailer, and the retail business, no matter what category or brand, is a tactical day-in-and-day-out grind. It requires a lot of quick and dirty practical work to keep the inventory moving. Most of our marketing budget was spent on in-store signage and window promotions with the record labels—not big, bold branding ideas.

I also overlooked the important fact that our industry was in distress. Napster had made possible free online music downloading, and the Internet was decimating traditional music sales. In a few years, our stores in North America would begin to close, and by 2009 they would all be gone. I couldn't have seen that coming, but I could have understood that we were, first of all, a bricks-and-mortar retailer, and the retail tactics and details our COO wanted to focus on were the things that would motivate a shopper to spend an extra five dollars at the checkout. That might have helped keep us in business long enough to build the future.

Truth be told, I knew in my heart that I was not spending enough time where my bosses wanted it—maybe 20 percent? But I wasn't fully honest with myself about the reasons. I felt intimidated by tactical retail work because it wasn't an area I knew well. I hadn't grown up in retail, understanding the business from the ground up. What's more, my natural orientation in life is to see the forest, not the trees. I'm a big-picture thinker, and I thrive when I'm given major strategic challenges to solve; but in the weeds, I have a tendency to tune out when I'm feeling lost. So I just kept focusing on my Extreme You strengths and areas of expertise. I believed that those proven strengths could carry me, to the point of not really bothering with my weaknesses. And when I felt doubt, I would start bitching and moaning about our bosses—their complete lack of alignment, their confusing directions, and their inability to see the bigger opportunities in front of us.

When you're the one leading the bitching and moaning sessions instead of just participating in them, though, you're going to become known as a troublemaker. When you don't understand the needs of your boss or show that you care enough to learn from others more experienced than you, your boss won't show much interest in trying your new and different approach. Today, as a business leader, I understand that when you are leading a company, as our bosses at Virgin Megastores were, you need new talent and disruptive thinking, but you also need institutional knowledge and experience with a close eye on the "day to day." And that when you see the world only through your own lenses instead of listening to, and learning from, the perspectives of your colleagues, you can grow very lopsided in your skills and understanding.

## EXTREME STRENGTHS—AND
## EXTREME WEAKNESSES

One could look at my Virgin "suicide" in two ways. From one point of view, when I accepted that job I got my Extreme matchmaking wrong. You might say I should have done a better job of checking myself out and realizing I didn't exactly belong there. Virgin Megastores required more tactical retail skills than big strategic Sarah-style vision of the future of the brand. But I'd argue that it takes a long time to find a perfect match between Extreme You and your job description. It's a long journey, and even if you get it perfect, the market will continue to change and you will need to change with it. So I would say instead that the matchmaking is never truly perfect and that my problem was that I was so focused on my strengths, I developed a blind spot for my weaknesses. Those included my un-developed "retail tactical" skills—which the COO, whom I was so busy criticizing, could have helped me learn. But I couldn't Get Over Myself, and so, instead of acknowledging that Extreme Me was only a partial fit for the situation, I kept trying to use the approach I felt comfortable with and ignoring the need to learn and to grow and to do what didn't feel so comfortable. My Extreme strengths became Extreme liabilities.

In other words, even if I did have a brilliant strategic plan, as an employee I could be a nightmare. I was a rogue force on the Virgin Megastores team, and though at the time it seemed a terrible injustice, in hindsight it's clear: I needed to be fired. It would take a few years of both anger and career setbacks, though, for me to be able to see that truth and learn what to do about it. In this chapter, I'll talk about how Extremers can get over themselves and learn to acknowledge and compensate for their weaknesses. Then, in the next chapter, I'll look at the mess I made of my career—and how Extremers can recover from serious failure.

## WHEN STRENGTHS BECOME LIMITATIONS

When you Check Yourself Out to discover your unique advantages, Ignite Your Magic Drive to power your use of them, and find opportunities to Get Out of Line and get attention for your powerful new knowledge and skills, you develop parts of yourself to the extreme—*but only parts*. Living Extreme is the *opposite* of being well rounded. You will have some rough edges, to put it mildly, and big areas you haven't developed at all. You have to understand that your Extreme side, awesome as it may be, can't do everything. Not even close. And if you try to do everything solo, relying on only your personal strengths, no matter how awesome they may be, you'll fail.

Why? Because, as Tom Rath and Barry Conchie, the authors of *Strengths Based Leadership: Great People, Teams, and Why People Follow*, wrote, "Although individuals do not need to be well-rounded, teams should be." They see four distinct domains of leadership strength and argue that success comes from assembling teams that, among their members, can provide all four. I would say that your Extreme skills and knowledge can *get you onto* a great team, but what will make that team succeed is that the team becomes well rounded—as Extremers are not. That's why, to succeed in the long run, Extreme You needs some Extreme insight into your weaknesses and some Extreme support to balance them out.

I learned about that kind of support a few years later when I became friends with Francisco Nunez, at that time a rising star of the marketing world. Francisco and I could not possibly have been more different. Let's start with the fact that he legitimately did demonstrate incredible sporting talents his entire life—whereas I just wished I had. But Francisco quickly became a close friend. Today he runs all of global marketing for a major retailer—a huge and incredibly fun job. But if you had met Francisco in his youth, you'd hardly have pegged him for a role like that.

As a child he was extremely shy, preferring physical activities to talk. Mostly, he loved sports. As he explained, "I don't remember when I wasn't an athlete. I played basketball, ran track, and of course played on the Little League team, but my greatest love was always soccer." He went to college on an athletic scholarship, and, as he put it, "For me, training was 24/7. I got to everything else when I could." That included jobs and groceries. As a soccer player, he lived more like a starving artist.

Francisco was a soccer star, but he was plagued by injuries. He tried surgery and physical therapy, running up big medical bills, until slowly, reluctantly he realized he could not afford to go on. "Soccer had been the only thing that mattered to me," he told me. "It was my oxygen. Now I felt empty. I had lost the only thing that had mattered."

At one of his last tournaments, he started a conversation with a representative for the retailer where he bought most of his shoes. "I was so intrigued by the work he was doing. We exchanged info and this rep, Jesse, told me, 'Hey, there's a new store opening in the Los Angeles area.' Right then I made this split decision—this retailer was my favorite, and I wanted to work for the best. I'm going to go work for them!

"So I became a salesclerk, making seven dollars an hour and trying to figure out how to live on that in LA—from the standpoints of money and of pride. My family was like, 'You're doing *what*?' I wanted that job as a means to an end—to figure out what bigger things I could do for the company. But I had zero corporate experience. I was incredibly shy. Everyone who knew me would have bet against me being able to make it in a corporate environment. People in LA knew me as the soccer star, so I had to go from being that person everyone admired to the clerk in the shoe department, holding one of those Brannock Devices for measuring people's feet. It was the most humbling time."

I'm not sure I have ever known anyone who relied so exclusively on one Extreme strength. For his entire life, Francisco had been the Extreme Athlete, but now he had no choice but to recognize that that couldn't be the basis of his life. He had to get over himself and develop areas that he had never admitted he would need.

Although he had given up soccer completely, he had not given up the approach or the attitude that had made him a star. "Most people at the store didn't take the job too seriously," he said. "But I approached it the same way I approached my sport. I wanted to be the best at the job I was doing, and I wanted to go above and beyond to stand out." And that's exactly what he did, often staying after hours in the retail stores and impressing those around and above him. Eventually he moved from retail sales into product buying, which meant he was translating his hands-on knowledge of customer buying trends into decisions about the kinds of new footwear the company would sell in the future. Eventually he moved over to marketing, becoming a category manager by capitalizing on another side of his Extreme Self. "I was always exploring fashion, pop culture, whatever was important culturally—sneakers, style, street art. That was what I did on the weekends, how I played. I lived immersed in that part of pop culture that the company was trying to speak to." As a result, others in the company would seek him out to evaluate their marketing ideas, asking him, "Am I off base? Or are my ideas cool?"

But in time he discovered that there was a limit to the niche he had found. "I started to think to myself: You can't be in your mid-forties and be the coolest person in the room. One day that's going to run out." His bosses and mentors often told him that they felt he had more to contribute, that he could take more of a leadership role in the company if he could communicate more effectively. Jesse, the rep he had met at the soccer tournament when he first had the inspiration to join the company, was now running some of the meetings he attended, and in front of everyone he would push Francisco to overcome his lifelong shyness. Sometimes in a meeting, Jesse would say, "I think Francisco has something to add." Francisco found it infuriating. "At these big corporate meetings, everyone jockeys to contribute so they can be noticed, and that is just not my personality. It felt inauthentic. All through college, I never spoke. My philosophy was: I'll be the first one at practice every day, work the hardest, be the clutch player that always scores the goal, and be the last one to leave. My sport was a team sport, and my mentality was that if I do my part, the team will win. That was my style!"

He had developed himself as Extreme Athlete, Extreme Cool—and Extreme Introvert. But now his extremes were limiting his potential to move forward—to make his voice heard, to collaborate in meetings, to move beyond the model of the individual contributor focused solely on playing his own role, and to become a player-coach on a larger team.

But like me at Virgin Megastores, Francisco was ignoring the ways his familiar strengths hid unrecognized weaknesses. And he could have continued on at his professional level, maybe slowly losing his place as the coolest one in the room but remaining a category manager. Many people get stuck in traps like that. They cling to their pride and their past successes. Put simply, they can't get over themselves.

Pressed to change, Francisco turned angry and defensive. "I had a hot head, a bad temper." As a gay man and a Latino, both underrepresented groups at the company at that time, he felt like an outsider, as if no one actually knew him or believed in him, and that only intensified the feelings that kept him quiet. Finally Jesse told him, "You have a choice. You can do what you think is the right way, but that's not working. Or you can take the advice of the people you trust who are mentoring you."

Francisco knew that the part of him that was authentic, the part he could trust the most, was his inner athlete. He told me, "What I like about my personality is that I'm able to apply that athlete mentality to a lot of different situations. The athlete mentality asks, 'At the end of the day, am I going to win?' Everything is about winning, but for me now winning was not being the person to score the most goals. Winning was reaching the end goal, and for me now that end goal was moving up in an organization I'm really passionate about. Winning to me became figuring out how to thrive and flourish and grow. If I'm not doing that, I'm not winning.

"So while my first instinct when I was pushed to talk was to feel upset and angry, I began to try to flip the energy of that anger and use it to push myself." He still trusted to his athlete mentality, but he began to question the idea that his "style" had to be silence. Maybe, he decided, that was not style but fear. He was getting over his old idea of himself, acknowledging the liabilities that came with his Extreme strengths but doing it in a way that still felt true to his Extreme nature.

Once Francisco was able to find his own way of becoming a more communicative leader, the successes and promotions came quickly, even more than he had hoped for. He was made one of the top one hundred leaders in North America and entrusted with shaping the future of the entire company. As he told me, "I never in my life thought I would be in charge of something as big as this. As an athlete, yes, I had all these audacious goals, but from a career standpoint I never thought I'd make this amount of money or have this kind of life. And aside from the title or the money, there are the things that really make you feel good: you get invited to certain meetings because it's an important meeting and your point of view will be a critical part of where the company lands. Every day I wake up and feel, *Really? I get to do this?*"

Francisco had gotten over himself, which freed him to partner with people who could support his weak areas and help him develop new strengths. Boom ka-boom!

## NO GOLDEN TOUCH

Sometimes it's easier for Extremers to see the real potential of their unique strengths or the truth of their limitations by observing those same traits in role models and mentors. I thought of this when I had the chance to talk to Casey Wasserman, one of the biggest big shots in the sports world. He's the founder of the Wasserman Media

Group, which represents many of the biggest athletes, leagues, and brands—a dream business by anyone's standards. I got to know Casey in my days at Gatorade when we were working on negotiating an NFL deal together—the poor man has been stuck with me in his Rolodex of friends ever since because of his willingness to mentor me during one of the biggest deals of my sports career. For Extremers, no good deed goes unpunished!

Casey learned his approach to business one-on-one from his grandfather Lew Wasserman, who started out as an usher in a movie theater, became a talent agent, founded MCA, bought Universal Pictures, and for forty years was considered the most powerful person in Hollywood. Casey, though, knew from a very early age that he was never going to work in the entertainment business. "I wanted to make a name for myself and be judged for what I did and not my last name," he said. "When you're a kid of means, the greatest gift you get is the freedom to choose, but that doesn't protect you from making bad decisions." Casey wanted to choose a career he was passionate about, and through his own process of early discovery he started to realize that he had a passion for sports—not just playing sports but the business of sports. Yet at the same time, he wanted to make his career choice well and pursue it as effectively as possible. As he was developing his passion for his future career, he was quick to jump on the opportunity to accompany his grandfather as he conducted business and to be mentored by his many accomplished friends.

Casey assumed that he would discover the elder Wasserman's Extreme gift of making every deal turn to gold. "I always thought that everything he did worked, that he had a magic touch," Casey told me, "but it's exactly the opposite. The secret was how good he was at handling bad things. Today I understand that no one comes into my office to give me something for nothing. People come into my office to give me problems, and I have to be better at dealing with those problems than other people. That doesn't mean there aren't good days or that great things don't happen, but that's not how most people's success happens. Very rarely is it a line that goes straight to the top."

By observing his grandfather over many years, Casey was able to refine the Extreme style he needed to adopt when he faced similar challenges in his own business. "The best lessons I learned from my grandfather were about keeping an even keel. It's hard to be effective when you're riding an emotional roller coaster, because if you're riding it then your organization rides it with you." Casey came to realize that, just as in sports, both extreme ups and extreme downs can interfere with performance. "When I best understood tennis as a player, it was when I understood that keeping an even keel is fundamental. So many times a player celebrates a great shot only to have the next shot be a double fault. Once you have that perspective, you get a deeper understanding of how being consistent can be really valuable." By learning from his grandfather, Casey shed some of his early, naive ideas about business—that it was a game of dramatic emotional highs and lows, which you win by developing a magic golden touch—and reset his expectations: problems would keep coming in his door, and he would need the emotional balance to keep solving them well.

## EXTREME MOVES

A great CEO—and, I might add, a great doctor or parent or house cleaner—finds a way to deal with whatever challenges appear. Those challenges may require the Extreme knowledge and talents you have developed—or they may not. As Extremers, we must get over the expectation that we have been given some magic gift that will solve everything and instead develop our willingness to acknowledge and meet whatever challenges come along, including our own areas of weakness.

### 1. Identify Your Weak Bits—Before They Do You In

It's a risk for every Extremer. Exactly because you dig deep to develop your awesome combination of strengths, exactly because you have to believe in the combination of interests and skills that no one else has put together, exactly because you find the courage to Get Out of Line and show the world what you've got, it's easy to become blind to areas you have *not* developed. Working to make the most of your own unique awesomeness, you lose track of the things your awesomeness just can't do. Extremers need to be able to identify their weak bits just as clearly as their unique combination of skills. If you can't do that, you're seeing only half the picture. And if you're seeing only half the picture, you're going to realize only half of your potential, right?

So . . . how to do that? I like these suggestions collected by *Fast Company* contributor Gwen Moran, with input from David M. Dye, a leadership consultant, and Jim Haudan, the CEO of a human resources development firm:

- **NOTICE WHAT YOU'RE AVOIDING.** This is a good indication that it's an area you haven't yet mastered. That would have saved me a whole lot of humiliation at Virgin Megastores!
- **LOOK FOR PATTERNS IN FEEDBACK.** When there's smoke, there's often fire. I tend to come into organizations with a big,

bold new vision—and there are always people who don't get it, who value the old ways and don't want them to change. It's like I'm always the person at the retreat excited about the new T-shirt, while they're the ones still wearing the T-shirt from the first retreat, years back. But the people who don't get you are often onto something significant about you. It's worth listening to them—not because you should change from what you are to what they are but because they can help you identify your weak areas. For years, the criticism I received was that I "shot from the hip," made spontaneous intuitive decisions without proper research. I knew that perception was wrong—I did intense research and sought out lots of outside advice—but the people who didn't get me were right that my decisions came at them too fast. I hadn't worked hard enough to understand how they were receiving the information or given them a chance to express their input and really "buy in" to the vision. I learned that listening to the people who thought I had it all wrong helped me hone my ideas and perform even better.

- GET TO THE PUNCH LINE. If you're often the subject of jokes about being late, for example, consider the possibility that people are trying to correct your tardiness with humor.
- FIND SOMEONE WHO DOESN'T HOLD BACK. Embrace people who will tell you the truth, even when it's unpalatable. You don't have to wait around for someone to offer it, either. Think of someone you trust, then tell that person directly, "I feel like I could use more feedback in the area of X. What do you see as three of my strengths and three of my weaknesses?" (A special note for extroverts—I know it's hard. OMG, I know it's hard. But try to have a conversation with someone without filling in the silences. Just try. If you provide that person with space and fresh air, you'll love how much more you hear!)

### 2. Stand Proud, but Be Willing to Learn

Confidence? We Extremers *love* confidence—and we tend to have loads of it. It's superimportant that you live with a belief in your best version of yourself. Just be aware that there is a fine line between helpful confidence and the kind of overconfidence that can undermine your strengths. When I was flying high at Virgin Megastores, I felt cocky about my marketing ideas, and what was the truth? I had some great ideas. I had good reason to be proud of that strategic thinking, but I totally missed a chance to refine my skill set even further. The real challenge for Extremers—and this may sound a little strange—is to develop your Extreme gifts into understanding and skills you have every right to be cocky about, *while at the same time remembering you will always need help.*

### 3. Find Your Extreme Mates

Once you can acknowledge your weaknesses, the next step is to acknowledge that you're never going to be strong in every area. You need others to balance you and push you; you need a well-rounded dream team. Francisco's success came in partnering with colleagues as extroverted as he was introverted, and I know that because I was one of them. But I must have seemed pretty freaking annoying when he first met me. And for me, exactly because I specialize in a very extroverted form of leadership, I've discovered that my creative successes have all come when I've partnered with an introvert. I am a driver who always likes to be moving forward, so I do well when I partner with thinkers who can slow me down and make me reflect. I am stronger at innovative, disruptive thinking, so I've always sought out mentors to help keep me grounded in the fundamentals and historic truths of a business. I have a strong imagination, and I've learned that I need to partner with great analytical and engineering minds to help bring my ideas to life. I am extremely process-oriented, and I've learned to use that strength when I partner with great creative talent to focus them and unleash their abilities.

Who will your Extreme Mates be? Not people who look, act, sound, and think just like you. The people to partner with are the ones who have developed what you haven't, and chances are they will be unlike you in other ways, too. So a good moment to start scouting your dream team is when you're about to go out to lunch with the same crew you always go out with at work. Instead, think about someone you know from a totally different department who is unlike you, even the polar opposite. Ask that person out—go hang out—and get a sense of how he or she sees you, the team, and your company. And by the way, don't be put off if that person says no or if lunch is a little awkward. It takes time to build a relationship with someone very different. I think about how intensely awkward I have felt over the years when I've hung out with folks who don't immediately knee slap when I think I am being funny. And I'm like, "Oh, God, I'm *so* not interesting to this person." But give it time. Some of those people are my dearest friends now—they've let me in! Just because they process conversations differently doesn't mean they don't like you.

By now you've probably noticed that requirements for Extremers come in pairs. You need to wander along on your random walks—and then develop what you find with a ton of determination and drive. You've got to learn to Get Out of Line—yet, with all your skills and confidence, Get Over Yourself. So it shouldn't come as such a surprise that just as Extremers tend to have a whole lot of success, they also tend to be Extreme in their failures. That's where I left off in my story in this chapter—out of work and about to lose my dream. And that's where we'll pick up in the next chapter: discovering how Extremers turn their painful failures into awesome personal trainers.

# FIVE
# PAIN
# TRAINING

Long before I fully understood how Extreme Me had become a liability at Virgin Megastores, I had to deal with another problem: I'd gotten my ass fired. Now I had no job, and my application for US citizenship, which was being sponsored by my employer, was voided, which meant that if I couldn't find a new employer to sponsor me for a new work visa within three months, I would be boarding a flight back to New Zealand. This was a scenario I had never even imagined, the biggest failure of my young life—I was just ninety days away from losing my entire American dream.

How does an Extremer recover from a failure like that? At first I had no idea. In the days that followed my firing, I couldn't even pluck up the courage to tell my parents and siblings what had happened. I felt I had "let the side down," and I didn't want to admit it. I kept having conversations with them in my head, trying to come up with a credible story as to how this had happened and why it wasn't my fault, but there hadn't been a bunch of layoffs due to the headwinds in the music industry. Only one person had lost her job, me. So . . . I didn't tell them.

But there was no way to avoid telling Liam. He deserved to know right away, before he got on the plane to meet me in Los Angeles and maybe made the biggest mistake of his life. Yep, Liam needed to know that this high-flying businesswoman he was falling in love with was an imposter.

I gave him the news on the phone. Like the knight in shining armor that he is, he never missed a beat. Somehow, even half a world away, he projected calm and confidence, reassuring me that he would come to meet me just as we had planned. That helped me convince myself that things might be OK.

What I couldn't avoid feeling, though, was sheer and utter embarrassment. I kept remembering how I'd packed up my desk and walked out of the building feeling as if everyone were staring and whispering:

*"She just got fired."*

*"Holy shit, what did she do?"*

*"She so had that coming."*

*"She was a disaster anyway."*

How shocking to go in an instant from big girl on campus, rabble-rousing and feeling like your shit don't stink, to the loser everyone gossips about.

In shock and in tears, I spent most of that first day touching base with close friends. A couple of days later my team from Virgin called and offered to take me out to lunch, which was lovely of them. By the time we got together, I had reached the stage of feeling totally pissed off. My ego was hurting real bad, and I tried desperately to justify my actions to myself and to my former subordinates. We bitched and moaned about what a shit storm the company was, and I talked a big game, saying that I had a lawyer and I was going to go after their asses because there was no decent reason to fire me. (Yeah, it sounded good—but the truth was that a lawyer friend from my Air NZ days had taken pity on me and simply helped me to get two weeks of severance pay, and that was the end of it.)

## THE TRUTH HURTS

I continued to feel ashamed, angry, and unable to tell my family. But at least Liam had arrived. I know it sounds cheesy, but when I saw him walk through the arrivals gate at LAX, I felt that my soul mate had just walked into the picture. Soon we got into my little black Beemer—how much longer would it be mine?—and drove to a nothing condo in the mountains to spend a week.

The sheer excitement of having Liam in town helped me stop thinking about my failure for a while. We hung out, laughed a lot, and began to try to think about the future. After a few days, I found the courage to visit an Internet café with pay-as-you-go computer terminals, where I drafted an email to my brother, my sisters, and my parents. I remember it so clearly because it was so bloody hard to write. I reworded that email several times. In the first draft, the firing was all the company's fault—it was such a mess, the people there didn't understand the mistake they'd made, and so on. By the time I hit "Send," though, I had arrived at God's honest truth. Admitting to my siblings that I had fucked up so badly was really, really hard. Looking back, I know they would have wanted to help me and support me, but at the time I kept imagining how they'd feel about me now that the truth was out: little sis with the high-flying career had epically screwed up and revealed that she was a total loser. (That's the youngest-child syndrome for you.)

Emotionally, that email was my turning point. Once I had written to the family, I could pluck up the courage to tell my friends, who up to then had heard only my outrage and bravado. I did it—I told the truth—but wow, it was hard, hard, hard. At that age, my friends and I were all so competitive. Some were becoming partners in law firms. Others had gone on to complete MBAs. Plenty were making their way up the corporate ladder without the kind of setbacks I was facing. In the pecking order of careers, I'd felt I was not only keeping up but probably one of the best, but now I'd suddenly taken this huge nosedive that made me feel like a fraud and an embarrassment and left me imagining that everyone was laughing at me: "Huh—she had that coming!"

But what a difference it made to be able to admit to myself, let alone all my friends, what had really happened. To actually *feel* all that I had been trying to tough out and cover up with attitude. Once I had experienced that raft of really painful emotions, owning the failure and grieving it, the pain turned into anger and the anger into steely determination. *Fuck this! I am* not *a loser, and I am going to prove that to the people who fired me, to my family that I look up to, and to my mates who are probably laughing at me right now. I'm going to show them all!* My failure was turning into fuel. My drive, which seemed to have shut down, started firing again on all cylinders.

Of course, I'd been angry from the moment I was let go. I was full of resentment and ready to tell anyone who would listen what a stupid mistake my boss had made. But that kind of anger, which doesn't acknowledge the setback or feel the deep, miserable, loser-like disappointment, is really only fuel for arguments. I needed to feel the failure, to believe that I had failed, to let the hurt go deep enough that I began to question whether I was *ever* meant to succeed. Maybe the truth was that I was a failure. End of story. Did I have a champion in me, or had all my family and friends always known (as in my imagination) that I was just a high-flying fraud, bound to crash and burn? I had to feel all my big dreams slipping away, suffer the pain of it, and then dig down and say, *No goddamn way! What has happened sucks, but it's not a reason to give up on my Extreme dream—and I'm not going to stop until I prove it.* It's as though the pain of failure becomes a personal trainer, pushing you to do better, to prove what you're really capable of. I think of it as pain training.

Knowing for myself the power that comes from owning those feelings, it made total sense to me when I read what the researchers Christopher G. Myers, Bradley R. Staats, and Francesca Gino call the "ambiguity of responsibility." Most failures are ambiguous. Of course, I *knew* that getting fired was a failure, but was it my fault? Someone else's? Just bad luck? With each setback, we face a choice: place the responsibility elsewhere or take at least some of it on ourselves. And that choice, their research suggests, will determine whether or not we get the benefit of pain training.

Their experiment had two parts. In the first part, they asked their subjects to learn about and approve a car for participation in an upcoming race. But one critical piece of information was left out of materials they received: only by consulting an external research link would they discover that the race car had a 99.99 percent probability of a gasket failure. In the second part, the same group of subjects was given a similar test, but this time they were asked to identify a potential terrorist. Again, there was essential additional information missing, this time available only by email.

Now here's the really cool part. The participants who took responsibility for their failure to prevent the car crash in the first part—"I should have reviewed *all* the available information"—were more likely to identify the fictional terrorist in the second task. Those who attributed their failure to an external source—"Key data was missing"—were less successful. Taking responsibility for the failure turned the pain into a valuable trainer, and that brought out the best in the first group the second time.

## ARE YOU WORTH IT?

So many Extremers I look up to have lived their own version of this choice. I remember instantly wanting to becoming besties with Sage Steele, my favorite anchor on ESPN, when we met at a conference, and I sat in awe as she blew the doors off the room with charm and total charisma as the MC of the event. We got to chatting, and I discovered that she wasn't just a famous sports presenter, kicking butt and taking names in a male-dominated industry, but was one of the most determined Extremers I had ever encountered. (Her last name is Steele for a reason.)

Sage defied so many obstacles to get where she has gotten. As she puts it, "How did a shy, awkward, skinny tomboy, a big-haired girl with brown skin, become a confident woman paid to talk on TV about sports with a bunch of guys?" Sure, she identified the goal early—by the time she was twelve, she knew that she loved sports, that she wasn't good enough to make the Olympics, and that the answer for her was to talk about sports, even if that was a man's world. She had her father to talk sports with day and night, and at the end of high school, with her parents' support, she picked Indiana University, which had a sports communications major with a broadcast emphasis.

Even with all that going for her, she suffered some epic failures along the way. Generally a good student, she froze when it came to test taking in college. For three semesters in a row, her grade point average fell below 2.0. "Somehow, I had slipped through the cracks. I should have been kicked out of school after two consecutive semesters, but they didn't discover me until I had bombed three straight." Finally the college placed her on academic probation. The dean summoned her to his office. He called her "an embarrassment to the school" and said that if she didn't get her average up to a 3.0 in the following semester, she would be out.

"I was devastated and embarrassed," Sage told me. "I wanted to crawl under a table. That dean hurt me and he angered me—but maybe I needed that." She didn't fight with the dean, and she didn't deny the pain of what he'd said to her. She let the pain flow over her, accepted that her performance had been poor, but refused to accept that poor performance as a judgment on what she could do. "When he called me an embarrassment, I didn't view that as proof of what I could be or that the whole world was against me. I felt bad, I griped about it, but I was always taught: Don't dwell on setbacks. Go for what you want. So I asked myself: What can I do?"

Sage sought help with studying and test taking. She asked professors for extra-credit assignments. She worked as hard as she knew how. "And I scraped by. I barely earned my degree, but I have it—and it's the one piece of paper I'm so proud of."

Hearing Sage's story, I thought of a conversation I'd had with another friend recently about how she reacts to setbacks. She told me, "My father would always say, when something went wrong, 'You get twenty-four hours to feel sorry for yourself. Then it's time to ask: What are you doing about it?'" Admit your failures, feel the embarrassment and the loss, but then let the pain point you in a better direction and drive you forward.

With her degree in sports communications, Sage set out to get a foot in the door—any door—on her way to her dream job. She ended up taking entry-level positions writing and editing news—a far cry from her personal passion for sports but at least in an environment that enabled her to jump at the chance to volunteer for an on-air assignment when another reporter called in sick. Sage eventually landed her first on-air job, as a weekend anchor on a local sports program. "I was in heaven," she told me. "But I was also in over my head. I figured if I kept working hard I could only get better, but I found there were a few people trying to bring me down. A coworker of mine didn't like women covering sports, especially people with my skin color. And my boss seemed to have no interest in seeing me move forward. When I asked for my first raise, he said to my face, 'You're not worth it.'

"Now, I knew I was green, young, with a long way to go, but I didn't think I deserved to hear *that*. A boss was supposed to support the people who worked for him! At the time I was broke, actually in the red, so it was a hard decision to walk away from a job, but I couldn't accept what he said. I left to find somewhere that would support my potential." She didn't accept the setback and her boss's insulting criticism as proof that her Extreme dream was mistaken, that she didn't have what it took. She chose to see it, instead, as a chance to show her boss and her other doubters that they had gotten Extreme Sage wrong.

## ON A MISSION

Accepting failure, embarrassment, and criticism sucks, but it's like the joke about hitting your head against a wall—it feels soooo good when you stop! And the way to stop is to drive forward. For me, after a week in the mountains with Liam, I went from Sarah-sad-and-angry to Sarah-on-a-freakin'-mission. No way was I going to get thrown out of this country! So began "Operation Stay in America." Looking for a job became my full-time job. Every day, I would scour the boards on Monster.com in the morning. I made appointments for breakfast, lunch, and dinner with any and every business contact I knew. I put together a budget and figured out how much credit card room I had left to max out and how the hell Liam and I would survive. Not only did I have no legal right to work in the country, Liam didn't, either. Every penny mattered in our quest to stay financially afloat, so Liam even rolled up his sleeves and started washing cars in the garage of our apartment building to get enough cash to buy our daily coffees.

I have to laugh when I look back now and recall that of all the things to worry about, I was absolutely determined that we would not sell my little Beemer. That BMW felt like the one bit of material proof I had left to show the world I was a success. The thought of having to sell it and turn up to job interviews in some shitty old used vehicle was that much more fuel in my Extreme tank.

One of those lunches was with my dear friend Rob Remley from New Line Cinema, who had been my partner back on the Virgin "Shaglantic" marketing campaign. As we chatted about my situation and predicament, he suddenly said, "I think you should meet my friend Alyssa—she just took a new role working at a video game company, and I know she is looking for people."

Boom! A solid lead!

Alyssa Padia Walles has a vivacious, frenetic, larger-than-life personality, and when she walked into Starbucks to meet with me I was drawn to her contagious optimism and energy for her new company, a French video game publisher called Infogrames Entertainment. That seemed like a very dumb name, but I figured it was some exotic French word I didn't understand. I knew next to nothing about video games, but Alyssa assured me it didn't matter. She was looking for a big-brand thinker who could take the growing company to the next level.

I was certainly a big-brand thinker, and by that point it didn't really matter to me what the company did, as long as it could offer a job with a salary and sponsorship for my work visa. And in the glow of Alyssa's enthusiasm I actually did believe that this was a fantastic opportunity to participate in the fastest-growing segment of entertainment, the video game industry.

A week or so later, she called to offer me the role of vice president of marketing with a salary twice what I had been making at Virgin. Seriously! It was like one of the scenes from the movies when the character puts the caller on hold and busts out into a crazy big happy dance. Boom freakin' boom boom! Taking the phone off mute, I attempted to stop puffing and sound calm as I advised Alyssa that I would be delighted to take on the role. That night Liam and I celebrated with a sense of relief that I couldn't remember ever having experienced before.

## FROM BAD TO WORSE

Infogrames at that time was in the middle of a crazy acquisition run. The company ultimately bought three separate video game publishers: GT Interactive, WizardWorks Software, and Hasbro Interactive, which owned all of the rights to the Atari brand, letting us lose the dumb name and rebrand our entire company Atari. Every day, I worked my hardest to try to inspire our marketing team to step outside their comfort zone while trying to bring the new people who came with our acquisitions into alignment with the Infogrames people.

In my rush to get the job and stay in the country, I had overlooked something kind of important—as I soon discovered. I have zero interest in video games. I've never played them, don't understand them, and in fact, to be really honest, I'd always bought into the stereotype that video games were for fat loser boys with zits and bad body odor who didn't know how to have a normal social interaction, let alone get outside and be active. I had zero empathy or understanding for my core consumer and no specialist knowledge to draw on. *Whoop whoop whoop!* The sound you hear is the warning alarm going off . . .

The hard-core gamers on my staff noticed. They seemed to think I was some stupid, clueless woman from the bottom of the world. They ignored my direction and largely bypassed my directives. Even with Alyssa's relentless support, within a year it was clear that I was way out of my depth. I was "offered" a new role, working exclusively on the reinvention of the Atari brand, while a more seasoned and tenured executive whom we'd picked up in the Hasbro acquisition took over the chief marketing duties. Let's be honest—this was exile to the video game equivalent of Kazakhstan. Though I tried to feel fired up and energized by the opportunity of a project that was more in my wheelhouse, I knew I had been sidelined. My career was actually going from bad to worse.

Atari's overall business continued to falter. We'd gotten way ahead of ourselves with too many acquisitions, and needed to slim down if we were to grow in the future. I knew I would get the ax. In fact, going by my Virgin experience, I got my desk fully packed up, the photos taken down off my walls, and all the files exported from my computer six months before that ax fell.

These days, people talk a lot about failure. Every second day I see a blog post by some business leader with a failure story. Too often it sounds almost easy, as though it's some mildly enriching experience to cross off your bucket list, like visiting a Third World country and looking out at people's hard lives from soundproofed hotel windows and air-conditioned taxis. I worry that all this easy talk about failure gives the wrong message. When I talk about failure, I'm talking about Extreme failure. The kind that really fucking hurts.

And for me, it was starting to feel familiar: utter embarrassment and shame as I lost my job. Years on my résumé with really nothing to show for them. It was a very dark period, one that made me doubt my entire Extreme You approach. The questions in my head were pretty grim:

*Maybe I ought to be scaling back, looking for somewhere I could fit in and play it safe? At least then I could avoid another humiliation.*

*Can I ever get my career momentum back?*

*Maybe it's time to curl up in a ball and admit that I was never destined for great things.*

*Maybe I had it all wrong. All of it.*

I'd always believed I could be a champion, and I'd been well on the road to becoming one, but now it seemed as though I had lost the path, possibly forever.

It was terrifying.

## THE WORST THING IS NOT FAILURE, IT'S FEAR

Failure hurts like hell, but the worst thing is not the pain. It's the fear. Fear can wreck everything that builds Extreme You. It can shut down the engine of Magic Drive, breaking that essential rhythm: success, bigger ambition, bigger effort, and bigger success. It can shift your focus away from subjective goals you can control to objective ones that control you. *(Get me a job—any job!)* And the damage isn't only to Magic Drive. Fear can leave you too defensive and hesitant to Get Out of Line. It saps the confidence you need to Check Yourself Out and Get Over Yourself.

It's a freakin' nightmare.

After my firing from Virgin Megastores, I had overcome the fear enough to reach my short-term goals of a new job and a new work visa. But I hadn't realized the other ways that fear was screwing with Extreme Me. During the period I was interviewing at Atari, I badly needed to Check Myself Out, to see what kind of fit I had with video games—a terrible one, as it turned out, but I was too scared to look in the existential mirror and admit what I saw. Even if I was right to take the Atari offer just to have a job for the short run, I urgently needed to Get Over Myself, to look honestly at what unappreciated areas I needed to develop, so my new outcome wouldn't be Virgin Megastores all over again.

And now, fired for the second time, my self-confidence was shot. The real danger was that, in trying to avoid another failure, I would give in, edit myself down, accept a job in which I could never excel, and become too timid to take the risks that lead to success.

You might wonder why or how I found the resilience to come through and not give in to those fears. Turns out that the scars of failure from any moment in your life do a hell of a lot to toughen you up. In those hard months, I thought a lot about one of the most valuable, scarring failures of my childhood, the piano exam I'd taken when I was about sixteen. Did I just say it was a valuable failure? It sure was—my first great experience of pain training. Let me explain.

This was in those good old days when I imagined myself a future Mozart, encouraged by the fact that I had qualified to take the Royal Schools of Music Grade 7 Piano Examination. Definitely a big deal. The test helped separate the unremarkable kids taking piano lessons from the ones who might study music at university and make it their career. I had a vision of myself as a famous musician, and reality was tracking along rather well until six weeks from the exam date, when I participated in a school phys ed activity that involved a military camp training course. I fell off a twelve-foot-high wall and dislocated and broke my shoulder—and it wasn't just a small break; it was a "you need surgery" kind of break.

After four days in hospital, with two steel pins surgically inserted into my upper arm, I returned home still in incredible pain and discomfort. I couldn't lie down comfortably, so I couldn't sleep. I couldn't sit up comfortably, so I couldn't watch TV. I was all-around miserable. But I didn't withdraw my application for my piano exam. I felt certain that this would be my Niki Lauda moment. Lauda had survived a fiery crash in his Ferrari in the German Grand Prix, coming back to race six weeks later in the Italian Grand Prix; I was going to push through my pain to overcome adversity and continue practicing for that exam.

Let me tell you: playing four-octave scales is not easy when your shoulder is broken. But each day I would lift my left arm out of its sling and onto the piano and push and push and push myself to keep practicing and perfecting. When the day of the exam came around, my expectations were so damn high. It seemed impossible that I would not pass the exam after working so hard. I walked into the giant concert hall to find the grand piano awaiting me and the examiner waiting to grade my performance. My fingers were shaking with nerves, and I was more than a little sweaty under the armpits. But I played my heart out, and even though I knew I had screwed up a couple of the scales and the sight-reading test, in general I thought I had done enough to pass. For three months, I waited for the results to come in the mail. The necessary score to pass was 100. When the envelope finally came, it turned out I had failed—by two points.

I wanted to jump off a building.

Throughout the afternoon that I received my results, I managed to keep anyone from knowing how upset I was, but inside my heart was on fire. The exam was supposed to have been my proof that I really, finally was talented at something, and my failure felt like the end of my teenage life. How could this possibly be when I had worked harder than anyone else ever in the history of piano exams? I had pushed through pain and injury, for shit's sakes!

I held the feelings in until I was walking through the kitchen in bare feet toward the toasted sandwich maker with a container of grated cheese in my hand. The whole scene runs in slow motion in my head. I remember stubbing my toe on the edge of the refrigerator and then loading up my inner fire and just letting it rip. Cheese flying across the room and hitting the wall. Expletives spewing from my mouth—words my parents had never heard me say before. It was actually pretty impressive! I sprinted up the stairs to my bedroom, threw myself dramatically on my bed, and sobbed and sobbed into my pillow. I don't care who you are—or how big or small the goal you have set your sights on may be—when you miss it and you fail, it hurts. It really hurts.

But in time, when I could Get Over Myself, I realized that I hadn't failed for lack of effort. When I looked at the scores, I saw I hadn't fallen short because of the injury. I just wasn't a good enough sight reader. I wasn't an extraordinary musician, but I had made an extraordinary effort, and I had survived an extraordinary disappointment. I had survived. And that's how failure first became my personal trainer. Failure put me through some hard workouts, fear that made me feel I couldn't finish, couldn't survive, but it showed me that if I was willing to listen, failure had something to say to me. It said, *You know what? This felt impossible. This disappointment, this embarrassment, this heartbreak felt like it would kill you. But you're still here. You were terrified, and you still got through it. Remember that about yourself.*

When I talked to Sage Steele about overcoming the many set-backs on the way to reaching her dream career, I asked her, "Do you feel now that you've 'made it'? Do you know you're a success?" And she told me, "No. Many times I've doubted myself. Many times, even recently, I've wondered if I can succeed. Even having 'made it,' that doesn't go away. But I know now I'm a survivor. I know I'm going to be OK no matter what happens. And when I feel that doubt, I tell myself: Just put doubt out of your mind and keep driving. Keep learning and absorbing. Take the next step, and be better."

So: back to my impending fate at Atari—holy shit, I felt the fear, just as I'd felt the pain before. It was miserable—but it didn't kill me. And I still had Liam, now my fantastic and supportive husband. We were still living in America. And most important, despite the darkness in the depths of my canyon of career despair, I still had the recollection in my mind of better days. I had succeeded before. There was a time when Extreme Me had totally fuckin' hit it out of the park. I knew deep down that I still had all the capabilities I'd had in my high-flying days. And now I had something else, something new: the benefits of all my most recent failures, all the pain and fear that hadn't stopped me. I had resilience.

## EXTREME MOVES

The way you beat failure is to live through it enough—pushing yourself harder but also drawing on the supportive people around you—to realize it won't kill you, which means you can risk failing again. And the more comfortable we are with the possibility of failure, explains Professor Martin A. Schwartz of the University of Virginia, "the deeper we will wade into the unknown and the more likely we are to make big discoveries." But there's no course in business school that provides this kind of pain training. You have to experience it, feel it, and survive it. Failure has not only given me the fuel to overcome my setbacks, it has built up a deep reservoir of resilience in me—like an inoculation, a vaccine, against my future fears, so I can take the risks that will keep me true to my Extreme Self. My back-to-back firings turned out to be the greatest personal trainer of my life. I've learned that in frightening times I can look around at everyone else and think: *You all don't know you're going to be fine. But I do.*

Here are some techniques to get you through.

### 1. Tell the Truth and Feel the Pain
Okay, so you've had a setback. Well, a significant loss. No, um, actually, a great big stinking failure. You're probably not going to feel much like telling people about it. Or you're going to tell a lot of people, and yourself, a lot of stories—about how it was someone else's

fault or it couldn't be helped or it's not such a big deal, really. But if you want to turn your failure into fuel, you have to tell the truth about it, to yourself and to others you can trust. If nobody knows about your giant fuckup, it will be all too easy to sweep it under the rug—and things under the rug won't fuel you to overcome anything. You need to admit you failed. You do actually need to feel, for a wee while, that you *are* a failure. The pain and the humiliation give you something to prove, and that "prove it" feeling is what you rally against. *Oh yeah? I'll show you!*

Is it hard to get started on experiencing all that truth and pain and humiliation? Do you find you're haunted by a disappointment but not doing much about it? One of my favorite tricks is to sit down and write out the experience. Journal the whole story, what really happened, until you start to feel it, the real emotion underneath.

Does it really make a difference to write it out? Wouldn't you get the same benefit from thinking about it or maybe just jotting down some lessons for the future? Nope. University of California psychology professor Sonja Lyubomirsky, the author of *The How of Happiness: A New Approach to Getting the Life You Want* and *The Myths of Happiness: What Should Make You Happy, but Doesn't, What Shouldn't Make You Happy, but Does*, has been studying the difference that journaling makes. When she and her colleagues asked people to either write, talk, or think privately for fifteen minutes, three days in a row, about the worst thing that had ever happened to them, the writers reported better psychological and—get this!— physical health, and a month later that still held true. The ones who saw the biggest benefit were those who replayed the story in their writing rather than just analyzing it.

In the end, it's not about the failure; it's about how you react. So go ahead, write it out, imagine yourself as a big loser, can you possibly tolerate what it would feel like to be that person? Try on the feeling of giving up the dream. See how angry that makes you. Will you close the curtains and turn off the light, curling up in the fetal position and giving up? Or will you get so fucking angry that you turn your failure into fresh determination and desire?

## 2. Learn How to Crash

Most skiers, like most people in general, try hard not to crash. Extremers realize that there are times you need to crash *more*. The person who helped me to understand that secret is Bode Miller, the great American skier we met back in chapter 2. From his point of view, repeatedly crashing and failing on the slopes was what saved him from being just pretty good and trained him to become an Olympic and world champion.

When Bode started out, he told me, skiers were training by taking small, safe steps, improving incrementally and trying not to make mistakes. "They would work on technique and then, once in a while, go one hundred percent and see what happened. Then go back and work on incremental parts again." But for Bode, that approach had two problems.

First, he could already see that someone with his natural gifts would never get to the top by developing the same skills as other skiers and then practicing to minimize his mistakes. As an athlete, he said, "I'm not particularly gifted. I can't run very fast or jump very high. There are people my size who can tomahawk dunk a basketball. I could dunk a tennis ball. Maybe." He concluded that, even doing the maximum possible training as prescribed by sports science, he wouldn't stand out. "If I could make no errors, I would come in thirty-fifth every time. There was no reason to do that."

Bode couldn't become a champion by doing what others did; he needed to develop Extreme Bode.

Second, he recognized that working on small bits of technique, one at a time, was not in his nature. "The best outcomes for me came when I performed at my maximum, got comfortable there, and made my skill set catch up." Instead of practicing individual aspects of technique, he practiced racing to win: skiing as fast as he possibly could as much as he could. That turned out to give him an advantage in a race. "Other guys trained at seventy percent of their maximum speed. In serious competitions, they would go a hundred percent, and they wouldn't know how to do the simple things they should have learned years ago because they hadn't crashed enough to figure it out. Then they would blow out their knees."

Bode realized that he needed to crash *more*. He needed to fail more so he could learn what failure could teach him, and he was the right student for that teacher. "I was a durable little kid, big-boned, small muscles, flexible, stretchy, and comfortable on a trampoline. I could do flips and twists. And because I played every sport, I had a general athleticism." He learned how skiers get injured and how to avoid injuries even when he crashed. "So crashing was not my main concern. I mean, crashing into trees was bad—obviously you've got to pay attention to your spill zone—but I learned that if you are in a certain position in a certain point in a turn, there are things you can do that help. And because I had more crashes than anyone else, because I was constantly putting myself in these extreme situations in training, I developed a skill set to manage those crashes." Failure was teaching Bode how to ski Extreme with minimal consequences. Instead of letting painful crashes scare him into skiing slower, he let it train him to do just the opposite: to grow more confident and capable of skiing faster, not less but more willing to take the big risks. To make the most of your Extreme gifts, you must fail, and fail well, and then, by failing, fail less.

So I know what you're thinking: How do I show up to the office and tell my boss that I am planning to fail tomorrow? And fail at what? Well, you don't have to start by putting the entire prospects of your company on the line. Why not start with something in your personal life? Maybe you're into mountain biking but you always choose to take the easy route instead of the hard one. Go ahead—go hard for one day, and see what happens. Maybe you'll fall, maybe it will even hurt—but in the process you'll be pushing your skills, strength, and confidence to a whole new level. Or maybe you're preparing for the pitch presentation of your life and you're scared shitless because public speaking isn't your thing. Instead of playing it safe and planning to use a teleprompter, why not invite some friends over and go big—pitch to them as though your life depended on it, with no notes or visual aids, and see what happens when you crash and screw up embarrassingly in front of them. You'll live, you'll learn, and by the time of the big day, you'll be ready to deliver your presentation with more belief and confidence than anyone else in the room.

### 3. Drive On

Of course, a crash is still a crash. Failure hurts like hell. When I am in pain, I get relief by *doing something*. I need to get to work and feel a forward momentum toward a goal. If I can throw my energy into doing something positive, it at least helps to numb some of the pain.

In my last, unhappy months at Atari, I finally got the call I'd been trying to get since I stepped onto American soil. It was an internal recruiter at Nike who had received my name from a colleague at Virgin Megastores. (Who fuckin' knew? Despite my total train-wreck performance there, some people I had connected with were still looking out for me.) This time the potential role was regional marketing director for Nike, based in Los Angeles. That was a smaller role with a smaller title, but Nike was the brand I had been jonesing to work for ever since I was in college. Everything it stood for was in tune with my values, my passions, and my dreams. I immediately jumped at the chance, feeling in my heart that this was the career marriage I had been searching for all these years, with the potential to be my big break.

It was actually the second time I'd had a shot at Nike—back when I had been working for Air NZ in Los Angeles, I had met an Aussie guy who was running the Nike Australia office. He had been looking for a new marketing manager. I'd gone balls to the wall applying for that position, even though it would have meant walking away from my American dream to move back to Australia. This was Nike! The hiring manager and I had really hit it off, but the company had felt it was too risky to pay to relocate me when I had no significant sports experience.

Bugger.

So now came my second shot at my dream company—but the interviewing process was taking month after excruciating month. Lots of phone calls, an interview trip to Portland—but also lots of silence and indecision on their part. By the time I got laid off from Atari, I was about six months into that Nike conversation and I felt things were going well, but they were moving oh, so slowly. Having no job again meant my urgency switched into high gear.

Magic Drive, check: I researched every single Nike employee I would interview with so I'd be ready to have an amazing conversation with each of them.

Get Out of Line, check: I studied everything Nike and its competitors were doing in LA and put together a photo journal of my research and my observations and insights that I could send to the hiring manager to show my ideas for the future. There was no way anyone in the world was going to outsmart me for this job.

Check Yourself Out, check: Nike was the brand I revered. When I was fourteen, my dad had gone to America and brought me back my first pair of Nike Air Stabs. Running in them felt like bouncing on my own private little trampolines, and none of the other kids had ever seen anything like them. Since then, I had been fueling a big, obsessive, slightly stalker-ish dream of working for Nike. And when I had been studying marketing at university in the late 1980s, Nike had been redefining what it meant to be a brand. Its tag line, "Just do it," was a generational calling. It wasn't religious, but for me it bordered on that, a rallying cry for the ambitious and driven Generation Xers to get off our asses and make shit happen! At my wedding, my dear friend Sam, who gave the main speech, talked about the Nike posters on the wall of my dorm room:

THERE IS NO FINISH LINE.
NO PAIN, NO GAIN.
YOU DON'T WIN SILVER, YOU LOSE GOLD!

Here was an organization where I could fit in and where I would be willing to put everything I had into Getting Over Myself and developing whatever areas it needed from me. I had worked out with failure, my toughest personal trainer, long enough. I had crashed and crashed again. I was ready to play the game right.

When I finally got the offer, I can't describe the euphoria that I felt. Smaller title, pay cut, and the biggest celebration ever! I did not give a shit about the step down. It was freakin' *Nike*! Honestly, the company could have made me mail room girl and I would have been happy. Failure had become my fuel, and it had powered me all the way to a new opportunity where Extreme Me would be welcome.

So when you experience a failure, remember that the most important thing is to maintain your forward momentum. Remember what my friend's dad said to her? "You've got twenty-four hours for a pity party, and then it's time to move on." Give yourself the gift of your next goal. Yes, you are going to be processing your failure for weeks and months to come, but you can still start marching forward toward your next success. Maybe you lost the big tennis match or you didn't get the PR you were training for in the marathon. Commit to your next sporting challenge and face forward to achieve it. Or maybe you just missed out on a huge promotion. Scan the landscape around you, and set your sights on the next great mountain to climb. As Dan and Chip Heath, the authors of *Made to Stick*, wrote in *Fast Company*, "Retrenchment is the wrong response to adversity. Adversity calls for change, and change doesn't arrive via a miracle: It arrives via a kick start." So give that motor a kick!

What will happen next? Fear.

*What if I fail again?*

When that feeling comes, as it will, don't hide from it. Picture exactly what you fear might happen—and what you could do about it. Even in the simplest situations, such as preparing to give a speech, I imagine all the worst-case scenarios before I get there. What if my computer breaks down and I can't show my slides? It's OK—I've got the flow in a Word document, so if I have to, I can speak without my slides. What if the airline loses my bags and I don't have my business attire to wear? I'll show up in my running gear and make it into a great opening story. What if my skirt rips up the back when I'm walking up to the stage? (Oh, yes—that has happened before!) I'll just make sure as hell I don't turn around and face my ass to the audience!

Like Bode crashing on the ski slope and then figuring out what he could do the next time he lost balance that way, game-plan around the failure you fear. In your mind, welcome the fears, get to know them. Once you play them out in your mind and get comfortable with how you would handle even worst-case scenarios, you'll find you have not just more tactical ideas but waaaaay more confidence.

Time and again, I find myself at a fork in the road where I must choose the safe and familiar path or the more risky but potentially more rewarding one. It never stops being terrifying. But when I'm most afraid, to clear my head, I play out the possibility of failure in a dialog with myself:

*What is the worst that could possibly happen?*

I'll get fired. Again. Totally humiliating. All the recruiters in America will be stamping "LOSER" next to my name. I'll have to relocate my family to a downsized house on my own dime and then go looking for a new job all over again.

*Will that kill me?*

Honestly, if all that happens—I'll survive. I'll be okay.

*But how do I know?*

Because—it's happened before. And I lived through it.

*Now imagine getting fired again. Try it on. Remember how bad it felt. Are we scared of that?*

No.

*So drive on!*

When you can own your failures and use the pain to train yourself to set bigger goals and plan better to achieve them, then you are truly an Extremer. At this point, we've covered all five basic qualities of Extreme You. Now you're probably wondering: How can I put all this into action? How can I turn Extreme Me into Extreme success? And that brings us to the second half of this book.

# SIX
# STAY STUBBORNLY HUMBLE

**A** few weeks after I joined Nike, I learned that the company was organizing its first-ever leadership conference for women within the company. How cool was that? And then I received an online questionnaire that all of the attendees were asked to complete. That's when the fear and self-doubt started creeping up. The questions included:

*Did you play sports in high school?*
  Well, yes, of course!

*Have you ever run a marathon?*
  Yep, I sure have, and I sure as hell know that marathons aren't for everyone.

*Do you hold a world record?*

Cold sweat. Were Nike's women leaders all world champions? How average my childhood sports efforts would seem by comparison . . .

*What is your shoe size?*

I looked down at my Shrek-sized feet, realizing that working for a shoe company meant publicly announcing your shoe size on a regular basis. The voices of doubt in my head were growing louder. Sure, I was an Extremer, but could I really make it here? How could I turn my Extreme skills and knowledge into real and lasting success?

The first half of this book was about understanding and developing your uniquely Extreme potential. Now we turn to getting results by mastering what I call the Extremer Cycle, an approach you can use for your entire life. It starts when you find yourself in a new situation, possibly feeling as lost as I felt at Nike.

For so long, I'd imagined being part of this passionate, creative, amazingly successful organization, but now that I'd arrived, I often felt like a clueless, irrelevant outsider. In meetings, half of the discussion went over my head. Here I was trying to learn about an entirely new industry—shoes, apparel, sports equipment—while my new colleagues tossed around acronyms and shorthand terms as if they spoke a secret language: product engines, quick strikes, SMUs, MVPs . . . Feeling lost, I sat silent in those early meetings, aching to understand, let alone contribute something original to the conversation.

Nor did I yet understand the subtle signs by which Nike people indicated their status in the company's hierarchy. Only later would I come to understand that if you sported super-rare Air Force Ones (limited-edition shoes not yet released to the market), you were one of the coolest kids in the company, the "shoe dogs," or at the very least connected to them. By contrast, if you wore a pair of the freebie sneakers given out to all attendees at a management offsite meeting, you were probably in Human Resources or Finance. Then there was the term "hook up." It took me months before I understood that wearing shoes that weren't color-coordinated with the rest of my clothing (i.e., "hooked up") revealed that I hadn't made enough of an effort to use my wardrobe to show off my shoes. Hooking up was how you showed your deep commitment to Nike culture.

There were so many things to get wrong. How was I going to make my mark when I didn't even know which sneakers to wear? I was only too aware that I'd lost my previous two jobs, and now I felt out of place and worried that I might lose this job, too. To pump myself back up, I would remind myself of the Extreme You approach that had gotten me to Nike. I was still a ballsy, take-charge, super-prepared, and extroverted gal, full of ideas to share and willing to challenge the status quo.

But those private pep talks went only so far. I was discovering, painfully, what Wharton professor Adam Grant described in his book *Originals: How Nonconformists Move the World* as the difference between power and status. Power involves exercising control or authority over others; status is being respected and admired. The key difference is that power can be taken by force: if Jane gets promoted to be Joe's boss, Jane has a degree of power over Joe. Status, though, has to be earned. Back at Virgin Megastores, I hadn't earned enough status to make the changes I had wanted to make, and it had cost me my job. So now I knew I needed to build my status with this group if I expected to be taken seriously. I decided to give myself another sort of questionnaire:

*So. Was I going to lose three jobs in a row?*

No. I would become the person who could live up to my own ambition.

*What would I do differently this time?*

Whatever it took to make it freakin' work! After two failures, I felt such raw ambition that I knew I was not giving up for *anything*. I was going to strip away the memories of my high-flying past that might lead me to believe I deserved to be heard; I would earn my credibility and successes all over again. I felt desperate to prove myself to my new colleagues, yet I hardly knew where to begin.

One of the HR managers responsible for my hiring and "onboarding" kept reminding me to be patient. He told me, "Spend your first six months with your mouth closed and your eyes and ears wide open—just be a sponge." But let me tell you, that's not easy when you are in the middle of a fiercely competitive, team-based culture loaded with Type A personalities. It was impossible not to feel every day as if everyone was looking at me, wondering "Why the hell did they let *her* in the door?"

Still, I took his advice to heart. My entire career, I'd succeeded because I was the person coming in with all the big ideas. Now, suddenly, I had to figure out how to succeed by earning the right to share my thoughts.

Soon I attended a big sales meeting in Florida. I remember feeling like the new kid in the lunchroom who doesn't know where to sit: so *awkward*. Over dinner with the US marketing team, my new peers, everyone was laughing over great Nike stories from years gone by, but of course I'd never met most of the people in those stories, so I had little to contribute. After the meal, I happened to be passing through the hotel lobby as a group of Nike employees gathered to go see a movie together. I had not been invited. I remember in that moment desperately wanting to go back up to my hotel room, shut the door, order in some Ben & Jerry's, and watch *Survivor* on TV—with Liam back home on speed dial. But I knew I needed to pluck up the courage to ask if I could join the group. It was as nerve-wracking as high school, but to my huge relief, they said yes.

When we got back from the movie, again I wanted to go straight to bed. Even for an extrovert like me, it's exhausting to make conversation when you are the newbie. But everyone was heading to the bar, and I knew that joining them was the right thing to do to. The next day, I was able to get in on the conversation. That was my first real moment of belonging at the new company.

From then on, I worked so damn hard to build relationships and learn. Every time I went to the Portland campus, I made lunch appointments with my peers and my seniors. It became my full-time mission to be lunching, breakfasting, and dinnering with anyone who would give me his or her time. I was networking inside the company as intensely as I'd done outside it when I was unemployed. Even with the team that reported to me, I kept reminding myself to listen and learn from them before asserting my own ideas.

More than anything, I came to realize, I needed humility. Even an Extremer has to ask for help. I had to be open to what people said, to listen to their needs and their perspectives. I had to be patient, and I had to be willing to reveal my own vulnerability—to get over my own fear of not knowing *everything* so that I could learn *something* from every new person I met.

Finally, at the end of my first two years, I won a company award for my team's results in the Los Angeles market. Holy shitballs! I remember that moment so clearly—right in the middle of our big annual leadership meeting dinner, my name was announced. I felt happy and relieved. No one could have realized what a tough journey those past three years before Nike had been for me. To most of the people in the room, the award was probably just a run-of-the-mill company awards ceremony, but I'd been working at Nike as hard as I knew how. My success now was due to my willingness—born of pain and desperation, I'll admit—to strip away my old assumptions and habits, all the way down to bare ambition: *I want to succeed here, and so I'm going to have to go in humble.*

Being humble—earning your place by listening before you talk and showing that you care about what matters to those who were there ahead of you—isn't just good office politics. It's not just the price of admission; it's a lifetime commitment that Extremers need to keep renewing throughout their careers. You might think that when you are accomplished enough, you don't need humility anymore, but for Extremers like Angela Ahrendts, whom we met in chapter 1, leaving her role as CEO of Burberry to take one of the highest-ranking positions at Apple, the lesson was the exact opposite.

She told me, "Humans, the higher up they go, they more they feel they're *supposed* to know, so of course they then *act* like they know. You see it constantly in big business, in politics, in celebrity culture. But I've found that the higher up I go, the more I *don't* know, because I am removed even further from thousands of decisions that are made every day without me. So I need to listen *more* and I need to connect with many more people so I can feel the business and take in as much as I possibly can. It is physically, humanly impossible to micromanage thousands of people and even more the daily decisions they are empowered to make. You can call it humility or just call it being really smart in knowing what you know and what you don't know, every day. Humility is not a box I tick, it's a value that's embedded deeply in my DNA."

Humility is not just a style of leadership, it actually predicts success. Professors at the University of Washington Foster School of Business conducted a series of studies evaluating the effects of humility on professional performance. They defined humility as having an accurate view of yourself and a desire for honest feedback, being teachable, and being willing to showcase other people's strengths. Another study, by Professor Brad Owens at the Marriott School of Management and colleagues, reported in *Organization Science*, assessed the humility of students and employees, then tracked their performance on both individual and team efforts. *Humility was the strongest predictor of high performance*, even more than intelligence and conscientiousness.

How much does that rock? Seriously—for all of you out there, like me, who weren't born with crazy obvious natural talents, this is *huge* news. Just by having humility and a willingness to listen and learn, you might end up speeding past and outperforming everyone around you.

## PRIDE GOES BEFORE A FALL

The more experience and success you get, the harder it can be to stay humble—and the more you have to be on the lookout for the dangers that come with success, no matter how well earned it is. In fact, as hard as this is to admit, the award I won at Nike and the success my team and I had been able to achieve in Los Angeles almost led me to self-destruct once again.

After two years of leading a team in Los Angeles, I was relocated to Nike's global headquarters in Portland, Oregon, and promoted to USA brand director. I was now leading the team responsible for all national marketing for the women's fitness category, including public relations, advertising, retail windows, the Nike.com website, and live events. It was a great opportunity to step up and lead in a bigger, more complex part of the Nike environment. It was also a significant time to be taking on the role, because we were making a shift toward what we called "integrated marketing," where all of the elements of the marketing mix were meant to work together around one key idea. It didn't take long, though, before one of my regular team meetings turned very, very awkward. The first time I gathered all of the team members together to review our progress, a young woman from advertising spoke up, offering a completely different idea for the campaign. I calmly but firmly explained to her that although her advertising idea sounded great, it wasn't in line with what the rest of the team was doing. She was respectful and agreed to update her boss, Nancy Monsarrat, the head of advertising, on our discussion. But at the next meeting of our integrated team, she was back, explaining that Nancy wanted to stay the original course. My plan, she explained in front of everyone else on the team, wasn't going to work for the advertising team. What's more, she continued, they had a better idea, which they had been working on since before I arrived in my new role. I told her no again and sent her back to Nancy with my decision, but the next week it was the same thing: advertising would prefer to continue with its original plan— and since she reported to Nancy, not to me, I didn't have the power to overrule her.

How humiliating. With every dreaded meeting I was losing face in front of my team—and even with myself. *How can they just ignore me?* I would wonder. *Could it be . . . that I don't know what I'm talking about?* I would try to shore myself up by mentally recounting all of the reasons I knew I was right and telling myself to press on. Then would come the next meeting, and still nothing would have been resolved.

Here's what we disagreed about. In those days, Nike was still predominantly a sports performance company, leaning heavily toward sports associated with men. Products for women made up a smaller percentage of the business, because the women's market had not really been the primary focus. Many of the products for women had tended to be feminized versions of products for men, an approach sometimes known among the female employees as "shrink it and pink it." But the company's new global strategic plan recognized an opportunity for huge growth if we could create a deeper connection to women consumers, offering products, experiences, and marketing designed specifically for them. The plan called for us to reinvigorate our efforts to become a women's brand by creating a new athletic category for women, which we called "fitness dance." Essentially, we would focus on women who worked out in gyms, and given that dance was a booming trend in group fitness classes around the world, we decided that not only would we create new footwear and apparel for female gym goers, we'd also collaborate with leaders in the fitness industry to create a new fitness class called the Rockstar Workout.

The advertising team, however, didn't feel confident that women would connect emotionally with fitness dance. They didn't see the idea as a broad enough "umbrella" for the entire women's business. Given that so many of the young women we were targeting had grown up playing sports and on teams due to the positive outcomes of the Title IX legislation, they felt that sports would be a far stronger point of connection. What's more, they wanted the Nike brand to connect emotionally with women, and they felt that the way to do it was by using magazine ads to start a conversation about athletics and body image. In the past, the assumption had been that women didn't want to look like athletes because muscles didn't look "skinny." But the advertising agency had done compelling new research showing that young female customers felt a strong body was a badge of honor. Personally, I couldn't have agreed more with that insight, but I didn't see how it would help us promote the fitness dance concept. Even more important, in my time at Virgin and Atari, I had seen the shift away from the traditional model of advertising, in which people's feelings about a brand grew in response to big TV or print ads, to a far more interactive approach in which people connect digitally with a brand, communicating back and forth with a company in ways that traditional ads can't offer. In my view, the advertising team was chasing the wrong goal in the wrong way.

But that was just one voice in my head, call it the voice of my Extreme knowledge. There was another voice—call it the voice of humility—that also called up that disaster at Virgin, when I'd had the long-term vision and the technological know-how but not enough status and "buy in" from the team around me. What I had learned was that in the end, when there are dissenting points of view, the team ends up losing out due to that lack of alignment. I knew I needed to get aligned with Nancy.

But I was scared. Really scared. I didn't want to worsen a conflict that could turn my Nike peers against me. I couldn't bring myself to talk to Nancy, a major player with a shitload more experience than me and a ton of influence in the company. If I admitted what I didn't know, would I look unqualified? Weak? I didn't realize it at the time, but studies of leadership, including a survey by the Forum Corporation in 2013, have found that the most common reason leaders won't admit to mistakes is that they're afraid for their reputations—they think it will make them look incompetent. And so, in their fear of looking bad, they persist in their mistakes. *Tell me about it.*

I skirted a direct confrontation and instead complained to my boss. Maybe he might talk to the advertising team and get them on my page? Oh hell, no! He wasn't going to let me off the hook that easily. He said exactly what he ought to have said: that I should sit down with Nancy and talk it through. When I finally met with her, we had a respectful and open-minded conversation—a major improvement from my days at Virgin. But by then the advertising campaign had already been produced and it was too late to resolve the differences in our two approaches. My team was selling the new fitness dance products. The advertising team was starting a conversation about women and body image. There was no overlap.

As soon as the advertising team's new body-image ads hit the magazines, consumer reaction was swift and powerful. Friends and colleagues congratulated me on the brilliant, brilliant Nike ad campaign. Yeah, that was awkward, given that I had basically opposed it all the way. Despite the fact that we had put no public relations plan in place around the campaign, lots of media outlets picked up on it, too, leading to positive coverage on major television programs such as the *Today* show about women and body image and why it matters when brands such as Dove and Nike help to lead the conversation. The campaign blew up in the best way. My counterparts in advertising had been right all along.

To be fair—my team's marketing effort for the Rockstar Workout, and our execution around fitness dance at retail, also did OK. But what I had totally missed, because I had never worked on a brand like Nike, was how a brand that consumers believe in can lead a national conversation and how that conversation will inspire people to associate themselves with the brand even more. And so I missed the chance to align the body-image message with the fitness dance campaign, which would have had a far bigger impact for my team and for the business.

It took a couple of pretty intense morning runs before I admitted to myself that I owed Nancy a giant apology. In my fear of looking as though I couldn't do my job, I had made the typical mistake of the newer executive trying to be disruptive, discounting the value of experience. But now I could see that if I found the humility to learn how she did what she did, it would make me a gazillion times better as a marketer in any medium.

So I plucked up the courage and apologized, knowing it might be too late. She had every reason to write me off as a smart-ass upstart. But this woman is a freakin' legend, a mentor to the stars! She accepted my apology and even went on to support my future work in the company. And thank God I realized my mistake when I did. Within a year, we would both change jobs and become peers managing different categories but needing to work very closely together for the good of the overall brand. We became a powerful work duo, close confidantes, and great friends. She helped me evaluate ideas I was developing and advised and encouraged me about juggling motherhood with my career for the first time.

The underlying challenge wasn't just that I needed the humility to build relationships and understand the needs of others. I needed a deeper humility as well, enough to admit that even though I was the Extremer with the vision, I didn't see all of what needed to be done or all of how to do it. And no one can, not even the heads of our most successful companies. As Deborah Ancona and the co-authors of "In Praise of the Incomplete Leader" argue in *Harvard Business Review*, it is impossible for a leader to possess all the expertise, creativity, and charisma necessary to steer a company single-handedly. Instead, she must acknowledge that she is incomplete and either develop certain capabilities or find others who can compensate for her own lacks.

I had misunderstood the conflict. It wasn't about who was right and who was wrong; it was about building the greatest possible success by bringing all the Extremers on the team together to collaborate. That takes humility, the kind I hope I never grow out of.

## BOTH STUBBORN AND HUMBLE

The lifetime commitment to go in humble—and keep going in humble—requires an Extremer to maintain a balance between two opposite impulses. On the one hand, as Angela Duckworth has documented, it takes a heroic stubbornness to do whatever it takes to succeed. That I had in spades. On the other hand, even as you remain stubborn about succeeding, you need to be humble and flexible, always willing to learn new ways to achieve that success. And it's not only Extreme individuals who have to manage that balance but wildly successful Extreme companies and brands, too. So often their ongoing success comes down to stubbornly returning to humility and listening—again and again.

A great example is Zumba dance fitness. It was created by Alberto "Beto" Pérez, a Colombian dancer and choreographer, who, back in the mid-1990s, forgot to bring the recorded music he usually played at the fitness classes he taught. Not wanting to cancel class, he grabbed some Latin and hip-hop tapes he had in his car and improvised a new class on the spot. That was the start of Zumba, the dance fitness program that now boasts fifteen million students in one hundred eighty countries around the world. (Did you hear that?

Fifteen million means more than three times the entire population of New Zealand, all doing Zumba fitness classes every week. Zumba is a freakin' game changer of a business!) The story, as you would expect, involves stubborn commitment and relentless hard work, but when I spoke with Beto and his cofounder, Alberto Perlman, so much of what they told me was about what they *hadn't* known, the surprises and adaptations they'd made along the way, humbly.

For the first few years, they told me, they had thought of Zumba as a fitness program competing with lots of other fitness programs for that one hour a day when their customers worked out. Around 2007–8, they were expanding, and Alberto's younger brother, Jeffrey Perlman, joined the company as head of marketing. Jeffrey asked them, "Why do your marketing pictures show the students' whole body? Why don't you do close-ups that show people smiling through the class?"

His question pointed out an important confusion in the way the partners understood their business. Officially, you could say, it was a fitness business, and they were promising what fitness businesses promise: weight loss, stronger muscles, six-pack abs, and so on. That was the world they knew. But what they heard from their most devoted instructors and students was something far more emotional: "Zumba changed my life." People brought them a broad range of stories about surviving illness, getting through divorce, or in other ways putting their lives back together because of Zumba classes and the emotional support they offered.

As Alberto told me, "Beto knew this was how people viewed Zumba, because he had been watching the transformations of students and teachers in the program. But for us on the marketing side, it was frightening. This was a direction no one had gone in the fitness space before. We had to come around to accepting that the brand was telling us something. Fitness brands are all about exercise, but Jeffrey was pushing us to talk about music, about joy, about transformation."

This is the kind of moment that fascinates me. Here was a successful marketing team—that is, a group of people who were good at their jobs. They had been using one approach successfully for years. Then a new idea came to them unexpectedly, something that was going to force them away from their established strengths and into areas that were unfamiliar and frightening. Were they willing to be like humble newcomers again, to do whatever it took to learn a new approach?

In their new promotional materials, they began showing the faces of people loving the class, rather than hard bodies. They launched a campaign for Zumba apparel that emphasized real women appreciating their real body shapes. Alberto explained, "We changed the sizing of our apparel—instead of medium, we called it marvelous, instead of large we had lovely and extra lovely. We saw how that resonated with people." On the company website, they began collecting inspiring "Zumba stories" of personal transformation, and although they still had a category for tales of weight loss, their top illustrations of what Zumba means for its students were categorized by themes such as Adversity, Love, and Unsung Heroes. Humility had taken them a long way from the conventional pictures of six-pack abs.

Alberto came to realize that there was a whole lot to Extreme success that he hadn't learned when he'd studied business. "Everything you learn is just a foundation," he told me. "When you get into the world, you get punched in the face every single day. You have to listen—to the brand, to your customers. You can't be hardheaded and stubborn. If we hadn't heard what world was telling us, we couldn't

have built what we built. You have to be part of the evolution."
Zumba had already been successful, but it grew more successful, far
more than anyone had imagined a dance fitness class could ever be,
because its people kept listening, collaborating, and changing their
established approach. They stayed humble.

## EXTREME MOVES

Extremers have no shortage of ambition, drive, and confidence, but
that takes them only so far. Without humility, stars tend to flame
out quickly. To be a true Extremer, you need to keep your pride in
check and remain eager to listen and learn. Humility is a scarce and
valuable resource, and it's hard to keep enough of it on hand. Here
are a few key moves Extremers should practice throughout their
careers to be sure they remain in touch with their humility.

### 1. Admit What You Don't Know

Pulling off the protective layers of overconfidence and mistaken
certainty to find the humility to admit what you don't know—to
others and sometimes to yourself—can be awkward and even painful. It's bad enough privately suspecting that you may have weaknesses and areas of mild to severe cluelessness, but revealing it to
others truly sucks. It's easy to think that keeping your blind spots
and insecurities secret is necessary if you want to be perceived as
a winner, but research by Erika Andersen of Proteus International
suggests that even CEOs benefit from admitting that they have
areas they still need to develop. "If a leader starts by demonstrating
that he or she is excellent in many of the core skills and capabilities
needed to lead," she wrote in *Harvard Business Review*, "the people

surrounding that person will have confidence that he or she will be able to learn the rest of what's needed, and will see that person's openness to learning as a positive thing."

Stanford Professor Zakary Tormala has suggested that experts become *more* influential when they admit to some uncertainty, even though it makes them seem inconsistent. "Inconsistency is surprising," he wrote. "It draws people in. And as long as the arguments in a message are reasonably strong, being drawn in leads to more persuasion."

I have often been surprised that as soon as I asked for help, others didn't see me as weak—in fact, they seemed to gain respect because I took the time to develop a missing skill. In the Forum Corporation study I mentioned earlier, employees were more trusting of leaders who admitted their mistakes and encouraged others to admit them and learn from them. Trust, in turn, was highly correlated with employee engagement. In other words, humility brings others closer to you and gets them more engaged with the work itself.

That's especially important if you're hoping to have multiple successes in your life. Every success creates the potential for new opportunities—and every new opportunity puts you into a situation to confront what you don't know. The more you live Extreme and seek to step from success to success, the more prepared you need to be to park your assumptions at the door, tolerate approaches that may seem, at first, to have no point, and respect the fact that others can help make you better if you will let them. We may imagine, as children, that when we grow up we'll know it all, but in fact the Extreme Grown-ups are the ones who never stop not knowing—and admitting it.

No matter where you land on the humility scale, you can always do better. So today, pick someone you are close to whom you really respect and admire. Ask that person to lunch and tell him or her you are wondering if you are humble enough to really succeed. How does he or she perceive you? Push that person to be brutally honest—threaten him or her with a guacamole food fight if he or she tries to give you "nice talk"! At minimum, ask for three tips on how you might become even more humble than you are today.

## 2. Learn from Everyone Around You

The fact is, you can learn from anyone and everyone around you. Don't assume that only those above you in the hierarchy can teach you new things. I have never felt as though I should be hanging out with people of a certain level in order to climb the ladder or be seen a certain way. Actually, when I think about many of the people I now consider to be mentors, some were my bosses but many were junior to me when we worked together. When I had my first role as a general manager in Nike's Western Region, in 2006, which meant having responsibility for more than just the marketing function I knew so well, I chose to sit in on merchandising sessions, the meetings we held for our salespeople, so I could learn what they did. I felt like a giant goofball sitting in the back of the room—the GM who needed "remedial sales training." At moments it felt super awkward (who wants the boss sitting at the back of the room?), but I just kept telling myself, "I will never get this if I don't make the effort to try and learn."

I try to admit what I don't know not just down the hierarchy but also up. When I was first offered that general manager position, with sales and finance people reporting to me, I was freakin' intimidated because I had no experience in those areas. But I had befriended the top finance guy in Nike's apparel division. On my trips to Portland, I always asked to meet with him so I could pepper him with questions about finance. I did the same with one of the top sales executives, asking him to explain some of the lingo and chatter I'd heard that I hadn't understood.

Being vulnerable like that was surprisingly easy at Nike. For one thing, I felt so fucking humble coming in off the back of two firings that I was more than ready to admit I didn't know it all and to ask for help. Second, once I started asking, I got such positive responses that it was easy to continue. And third, Nike is a competitive culture, but it's not knives-in-the-back. I never really felt unsafe admitting what I didn't know.

But that's not true everywhere. In a later job, I remember a veteran warning me, "You have to stop openly saying that finance isn't your strength. This company is run by the finance people, and if they think it's a weakness, they will eat you alive!" He went on to explain to me that he felt I was often too hard on myself, projecting weakness instead of a sincere desire to continue to learn and grow. Instead, he would take the time to explain things to me privately as I needed it. So make this Extreme Move with care. Look for situations where you can safely admit what you don't know in a way that reflects your humility.

But by all means do it. In fact, right now, repeat after me, "I don't know. Explain it to me." The more you use this phrase, the more you'll learn and the more allies you'll develop.

### 3. Go Ahead—Get Awkward

As the leadership expert Erika Anderson, whom I quoted earlier, puts it, "Every time we need to learn something new, we'll be bad at it when we begin." If we're pursuing new learning and experiences with humility, looking awkward doesn't have to feel so bad—and it doesn't have to count against you with others, either. Indeed, when you open yourself up to others, they are more likely to show you compassion and generosity. And later on, when given the opportunity, we can return the favor, sharing advice and insights with others who find themselves in the middle of one of those inevitable awkward career moments. At the same time, it's prudent to test the waters before you spill your guts to a colleague. Sadly, not everyone will have your back, so pick your moments carefully, expressing your inner thoughts and self-doubts selectively and strategically.

Now try this: Get out there and suck at something. Commit, today, to exploring a new experience that you know absolutely nothing about. Feel again what it is to be humbled by your lack of skill and experience. Write about those feelings so you can refer back to them any time in your life and career when you kinda sorta suspect you might be getting ahead of your skis. If you're not experiencing those feelings with some frequency, chances are you're not stubborn enough in your humility. (Learning a musical instrument is an easy place to start. Just wait until you face the mortifying moment when you have to play in front of your instructor and you know you kind of suck!)

#### 4. Treasure Your Setbacks

For hardworking Extremers, it can be difficult to accept that not all skills can be learned through sheer willpower, that sometimes it takes time and patience to master a new skill. Later in my career, I had the chance to interview the basketball legend Michael Jordan at a sales meeting. He told us, as he has told many audiences, that he had never made the varsity basketball team in high school. He credited that intense disappointment with spurring his success in the rest of his career, that disappointment haunted him and kept him humble and willing to work hard. I remember thinking that his disappointing experience was almost like a treasure he carried with him, and I've tried to do the same with the memory of my Virgin flameout.

A fail doesn't have to be epic to have value. Think about a team experience when things went horribly wrong and your teammates just didn't love "passing the ball" to you—it's OK, we have all had them. Write a blog post (even if only to yourself) about the role you played in that experience and what you might have done differently.

Maybe the best reason to stay stubborn *and* humble is that it's an Extremer secret weapon; by admitting what you can't do, you increase what you can. In the next chapter, we will meet Alli Webb, an Extremer and stay-at-home mom who rode her humility and her willingness to seek help from those around her all the way to founding a hugely successful business.

# SEVEN
# PLAY YOUR SPECIALIST GAME

**W**hen you hear the story of how Alli Webb started a game-changing, blockbuster business, you're going to agree: it sounds like a business miracle. I mean, who could have seen Drybar coming?

A former hair stylist turned stay-at-home mom, Alli eventually began to feel that she needed to get out and a do a little outside work. Six years later, her Drybar salons had spread nationwide, with three thousand stylists and $70 million in annual revenue. Amaze-balls! How did she know she could do that? She didn't. Who told her how to put the pieces together, to turn a skill and some ambition into a business phenomenon? No one. So how did she turn a pretty quirky list of Extreme interests and skills into a major success story? I just had to find out.

For sure, she developed herself as an Extremer. Her Magic Drive got kicked into high gear by a force I think anyone who has ever been responsible for small children can understand: "I'd been a stay-at-home mom for almost five years, and I *really* needed to get away from my kids for a couple of hours a day," she told me. "It wasn't about money. Now, don't get me wrong, I like money as much as the next person—I've got a shopping problem and all that—but it was much more about getting out of the house and *doing something*."

She began to brainstorm about where that drive to get out and do could take her. Checking Herself Out, she recognized certain Extreme qualities that had been there from the start—though not necessarily recognized by anyone else as skills or areas of expertise. "I had naturally curly hair," she told me, "and from the time I was a little girl, I was obsessed with getting my hair straight. If my hair looked good, I felt better." Working as a hairstylist before she'd had kids, she'd realized, "Most women don't have the patience or the time to make their hair look the way a professional can. There is something magical when someone else blows your hair dry. Technically, they can stand above you and get a better angle. I spent thousands and thousands of hours on my own hair and learning on other types of hair as well. "

Back when she was struggling with her own hair, Alli had often wished for someone to come to her house and help her. Now she had the idea to go to women's homes and blow out their hair for them—no salon, no haircut, just the part she loved best. But in the salon world she had known, blow-outs were considered undesirable work. There was more money to be made cutting and coloring. Even so, it was something she'd always wished for herself—and it was part-time work she could fit around her children's school schedules. She started making house calls with her blow dryer, calling the service Straight at Home.

Part of her approach was a sensibility she took with her into her clients' homes—a second Extreme skill that went back to her childhood. Her parents had run what she described as "mom-and-pop sportswear clothing shops." The challenge they had faced in selling sportswear to women was that the husbands who came shopping would lose patience while waiting while their wives tried on clothes. So Alli's parents developed an approach to customer service that would take care of the whole couple: "In their little stores, they would have a row of chairs for these older women and their husbands. Mom would take care of the ladies—the customers—and my dad would bring in orange juice and bagels for the husbands. They made people feel really at home, really comfortable. We knew all their names. My brother and I grew up in that environment, and that approach was embedded in us: that's how you treat people."

Okay, now: time for an Extremer quiz. When you look at that list of Alli's interests, skills, and experiences, is it obvious to you how she went from stay-at-home mom to the founder of a $70 million fashion juggernaut? Here's that list again:

She was driven to get out of the house and work.

She cared a lot about her hair and had put a lot of time into learning to do her own hair.

She'd worked in a salon.

She had previous experience in a highly customer-focused retail business.

She combined those elements to invent a part-time gig, blowing out women's hair in their homes a couple of hours a day

So is the basis of her success crystal clear now? I'm going to guess: no. Not obvious at all. Even when you learn that she had the humility to learn from others about building a business, it only adds up to an Extremer with experience and skills around hair care and customer-focused retail. It doesn't add up to megasuccess.

This is an example of a challenge any Extremer will recognize: it's one thing to develop your drive, interests, and skills, to Get Out of Line while staying humble, but it's very different to turn your Extreme qualities into a breakthrough success. The secret to that kind of success, I've found, is specializing—in two different ways. On the one hand, to develop out of the broad range of your extreme skills and interests one narrow, specialized method or product or area of expertise, something that's all yours. On the other hand, to find an equally narrow, specialized audience that absolutely needs and loves what you've got to offer. When you take the specialized offering to the right specialized audience, stand back! You are now playing your Specialist Game—and amazing things are going to happen.

Alli knew that she had a rare knowledge and expertise when it came to blow-outs, but she also knew that no one had ever made blow-outs the basis of a business. So she paid very close attention to her potential audience and what they might want and need. When she priced her at-home service, she explained, "I didn't want to be greedy. I thought at forty dollars a pop, women would do this—it was two twenties. That was easy, women would pay that. And I learned that at this price, going into women's homes, I was soon saying 'no' more than 'yes' because I didn't have the time: I had to pick up my kids!"

When she found herself turning down more clients than she accepted, she began to see the benefit of playing a Specialist Game.

Those women were like her—they shared her longtime wish for someone to help blow their hair dry. They wanted what she was offering. "When I saw how busy I was getting, it hit me: Why doesn't this exist? I've got to do this!"

Now here comes the part of the story where I put myself into Alli's shoes and get a little sweaty under the armpits. Alli had never launched a business, and she knew very little about the financial and legal aspects, among other important functions in running a business. She wasn't even sure how to evaluate the viability of her business idea. That has to have been as scary as all get-out. But her husband was in advertising, and she tried the idea out on him. "He's so skeptical and cynical and used to rejection," she told me. "But he said, 'Wow, this is a great idea. We should do this.' That gave me courage."

The couple decided to put up their life savings—"which wasn't a lot"—to launch the first store. SWEAT. BULLETS. ON. FOREHEAD. I mean, think about it—they have kids at home, and they are putting their entire life savings on the line. Holy shit! And even that wasn't enough. So she asked her brother to help. "My brother was always the overachiever of the family, with a good business mind. But he was bald, so he didn't know a thing about hair. And his wife had beautiful, stick-straight, dry, perfect hair—like maybe one percent of the population. What I desperately wanted as a kid. So my brother didn't understand why blowouts could be such a big deal."

Alli explained to him that in her experience, the vast majority of women have hair they can't manage. "We all want what we don't have. If I have straight hair, then I probably want curls and volume." She explained to him that when women come out of a salon, they don't just *look* good, they *feel* very good. "It's like you're getting red-carpet ready, like someone has made you look kind of the best version of yourself." And she explained the response she was getting from the specialized audience she had found—women with hair concerns like hers. In response, he lent her the rest of the money to open her first Drybar salon. On behalf of women with unruly hair all across the world I just want to say, "Hooray for Alli's brother!"

That said, getting your completely unproven idea funded is one thing; turning it into a successful, profitable business is another thing entirely. The pressure to succeed was intense. "I can remember like yesterday lying in bed at night, thinking: if we can just do five blowouts an hour for twelve hours a day, this can work. . . . In my gut I had a feeling that there would be enough women like me out there." Alli's gut was telling her that she had found the specialized audience for her specialized offering—"women like me." And that's the heart of playing what I call a Specialist Game: you don't create a general approach or a method or product that everyone will like. Out of the broad diversity of Extreme skills and knowledge you have developed, you create a narrow specialty that a narrow group of people will absolutely love.

But *why* will they absolutely love it? Harvard Business School professor Clayton Christensen has observed that there are 30,000 new consumer products launched each year, and 95 percent of them fail. The ones that succeed, he argues, make it because they do a job for the consumer that the consumer needs done. That's what Alli Webb was realizing—not just that she had a unique service to offer (there are all sorts of unique and uniquely unnecessary services) but that among the things she had to offer, this one did a job that *women like her wanted done.* Christensen says, "Crawl into the skin of your customer and go with her as she goes about her day, always asking the question as she does something: Why did she do it that way?" When you know why others want the things they want, you can tell if what you've got is something that will matter.

## MY ISLAND OF MISFIT TOYS

When I've tried to discover how the diverse, jumbled experiences and interests inside me could come together into a new specialty for a narrow audience, it has almost felt as if, inside me, I were managing several different people. It's like getting a team to work together. So managing an actual team is great practice for learning to develop a Specialist Game. I learned that when I was given my first team to manage at Nike. Although we were all talented, hardworking, and well meaning, with a broad range of skills and interests, the truth was that at first we got nowhere. Of course, we knew in a general way that we were supposed to serve the Nike customer, who was an athlete. But we didn't share any obvious passions or clear skill set that gave us a unique approach or advantage. Before I arrived, though the others were called a team, they hadn't really been asked to work as a team, and they were certainly not a well-rounded team in that very necessary sense I described in chapter 4.

Here was the deal. This small collection of individuals I would be managing worked out of a small rinky-dink office in a strip mall in Marina Del Rey. It was horrifically messy—like a teenage boy's bedroom. But officially we were a whole new department—like a little start-up within this huge company, Nike. Our nasty office was the only one available near the Nike Entertainment Marketing Office, a gorgeous space where the company gave away free shoes to famous people, cultivating the celebrity relationships so essential to marketing in Los Angeles. Before I arrived there had been little collaboration expected between the Entertainment Marketing Office and the "start-up" in the teenager's bedroom.

My new teammates were all Nike veterans, placed in their current roles months before I arrived. Drew was a former college football player, impeccably dressed and movie-star handsome. Jason was a former state champion swimmer, obsessed with surf culture and basketball, and had started his career when he was handpicked by Nike founder Phil Knight to join the company. The team was fleshed out by a few more part-time consultants with equally deep backgrounds in sports, street culture, and event production, people whom Jason and Drew had recruited to help with their efforts. I'd been told by my hiring manager up in Portland that the team needed support and direction; they sat in the same office each day but didn't have the forum to engage in one another's ideas or activities. In their six months together before I arrived, their most memorable "output" had been turning a car into a Nike shoe-mobile that drove all around the city and was described to me by my impeccably tasteful boss as something "that sucked"!

Nevertheless, I'd heard that Jason and Drew were widely known and respected throughout the organization, which meant they could make or break my success because they were so well connected internally. And let's not forget the frame of mind I was in having just waded through the shit storm of the last four years of my career—nearly deported, two unceremonious firings from two different jobs. On day one, it's fair to say I turned up feeling super freakin' intimidated.

Our first meetings were cordial, but the message I took away was clear: "Who are you, crazy-lady-with-an-accent? And why are you here? You've got no sports credentials whatsoever."

And yeah, let's be honest, from their point of view they were right. Not only had I not worked in the sports industry, but my sports knowledge grew from my childhood in New Zealand. I could talk cricket, rugby, and field hockey until the sheep came home but much less about sports in America. When Drew and Jason started trading basketball and football statistics, they were like a foreign language to me.

My goal was for all of us to come together and create a success that would break us out of the teenager's bedroom. Before I could do that, though, I had to prove I belonged. How could I earn their respect?

Each morning, I went to work determined not to let the intimidation factor get to me. Each night, I came home exhausted. I wanted so badly to prove my credentials and win the team over. But even if I could have spent the next year at home watching *SportsCenter* and studying sports stats, I would never have come close to their level of American sports knowledge. And nothing I'd done could compare to the kinds of brand-related events that those guys had been involved with before. I mean, Jason frequently talked about one of his greatest memories being the "guerrilla tennis" events that he had put on in New York back in the heyday of the Agassi-versus-Sampras rivalry. My God, that stuff was legendary for anyone in the marketing industry. Honestly, I didn't know what to do with this team.

## NARROW YOUR FOCUS, BUT DIVERSIFY YOUR TEAM

Then I began to think of the team like an Extremer who needed to play a Specialist Game. For a single Extremer, like me, the formula was: bring all your diverse interests, idiosyncrasies, and skills, then narrow your focus to specialize for a narrow audience. Could I take that same approach with my team?

One day we were all asked to join a national conference call for the launch of the Shox NZ, a major new running shoe. The national office in Portland asked my team to put on a local marketing campaign in Los Angeles. A campaign like that fell outside anyone's usual areas of responsibility, because even though the category of focus would be running, the expectation was that the entire city of LA would hear about it. And so, as if I weren't already feeling enough pressure, I realized that the initiative was going to be high on the corporate radar. It was a make-or-break moment for me in my fledgling career at Nike.

I had to do something to focus my new team, so I decided to bring this group of strong, smart, but independent personalities together for an afternoon of brainstorming. I prepared a very detailed plan to facilitate our creative work and showed up with my extremely me style of collaborative and creative leadership: a highly structured set of activities with a lot of room for fun and improvisation within that structure. Instead of just putting everyone in a room and saying "Okay, guys—let's brainstorm!" I decided we would start by imagining the consumers we hoped to reach, mentally bringing them to life as if they were people we knew, with names, jobs, friends, and tastes. What was their day like? What kind of opportunities did their everyday activities give us to connect with them?

My team and our colleagues from the beautiful Entertainment Marketing Office arrived looking slightly perplexed—pissed off?— that I was wasting their time. But I said, "Guys, let's just try and have fun with this and see where we land." Do not underestimate the extreme anxiety I was feeling treading into what was such unfamiliar territory, but to my massive relief, that awkward beginning led to a playful afternoon throwing around all manner of crazy possibilities. Finally we came to a big insight: runners in LA weren't just any old runners; this was the land of entertainment, so lots of runners in LA were hugely into music. Hugely. And when we thought of creating a marketing platform that was highly focused on appealing specifically to musically oriented runners, suddenly the narrow focus led to a big idea: stage a 10K running event where we would get "one-hit wonder" bands from the eighties to play their most famous songs at each mile of the race, motivating the runners with an unforgettable, once-in-a-lifetime, live sound track.

As we brainstormed together, we laughed our asses off about how funny this could be. Did the guy from A Flock of Seagulls still have that spectacular fountain of hair? Would MC Hammer still wear parachute pants? How would the entertainment marketing team pitch an aging rock star on the idea of playing the same song over and over and over again for the full hour of the race? For the first time, we felt like a team. And we came up with the most epically perfect name for the event: Run Hit Wonder.

What was so special was that we landed on the idea together. The shared experience of surviving the decade called the eighties did loads to break down the barriers between us. (Who knew that shoulder pads, mullets, and leg warmers were such a shared global experience?) But, more important, because we all felt ownership, we freely contributed our diverse gifts and resources. Drawing on their sports knowledge and Nike relationships and history, plus my strategic and marketing skills, plus the company's entertainment marketing ideas and connections, we focused our whole diverse range—an unruly mess that had seemed as though it would never go together—on the narrow goal of creating an unforgettably fun running event for a very specific kind of runner, and in a way that would draw attention from all over the city. For the first time, this unlikely group of edgy Extremers was functioning as a well-rounded team, combining very different strengths to make a unified whole.

In the end, Run Hit Wonder was off-the-charts awesome. The Nike national team came down from Portland to run in it, and on the day of the race we went from being the Los Angeles Island of Misfit Toys to a high-energy, innovative, and cohesive group that had put on one of the most successful and memorable events in Nike history. Soon the company launched a national tour, bringing Run Hit Wonder to other areas where runners were passionate about music. Nike teams started coming to us for off-sites to discover how we worked. Our team had learned to play a Specialist Game.

## GO DEEP

One reason we succeeded is what I've emphasized so far; we focused our Extreme skills and knowledge on one very narrow way of serving an audience. Another is that each of us had already developed our unique skills and knowledge. We had depth. Jason had created and executed a number of world-class events, Drew had a brilliant knowledge of Nike products and how to articulate their benefits, and Ferrell and her entertainment marketing team were the best in the business when it came to ideating and executing around music and talent.

They were all Extremers, and Extremers take the time and find the patience to get deep into their areas of interest and skill. Think back to Sam Kass, the chef introduced in chapter 1. When he traveled to Vienna, he came to realize he was drawn to work in a restaurant kitchen. As I said, he didn't half-ass it—he showed up day after day that semester abroad, taking on all the work they could throw at him until he was forced to leave because he didn't have a visa. That was Sam Checking Himself Out, and when he left Vienna he had identified a new interest and area of skill. After he graduated, he went deep. He kept on cooking and learning about food all over the world. In those years, he went from Checking Himself Out to developing his newfound interests and talents as a versatile, original professional chef. By the time he came back to America, he was one of a kind. That's depth. That's how to play the Specialist Game.

Or think of Alli Webb, whose obsession with straight hair led her to practice on herself and others from the time she was a girl. That wasn't a hobby. She got licensed to do hair care, she worked in salons, and by her own account she spent thousands of hours styling her own and others' hair. If she had had the realization that there were lots of women like herself who would pay to have their hair blown out but had never developed the depth of knowledge and skill in hair care and customer service, her inspiration to open a shop wouldn't have taken her far.

Once you know what you love, your competitive advantage derives from setting yourself apart at your "thing," whatever it is. It's as true of businesses that reach their potential as it is of individuals who do. Nike's specialty is its understanding of athletes. My specialty is business innovation and transformation—having the unique ability to imagine a bigger future for the products, brands, and businesses I get involved with—and I've stuck with it across many different industries, developing an approach that is all my own. Back when the headhunters didn't get me and told me I needed to stay where I was because I was an "airline person," I had to develop depth in product development and marketing on my own; I chose to get extra experience in direct marketing with my business diploma and sought out experiences in digital technology that would help me understand how to be innovative. (How geeky is this: I was seen lying on a beach in Fiji reading the book *HTML for Dummies* in my twenties.) Then, as I moved from the airline industry to the music industry and next to the athletic shoe industry and then the beverage industry, I kept enriching my knowledge base until I had a unique depth of understanding I could bring to whatever came next.

One of the all-time greatest examples of depth I know is the artist and designer who calls himself Mister Cartoon. He has mastered an amazing array of art forms, going deep with illustration, sign painting, decorating low-rider cars, graffiti, apparel, shoe design, and even filmmaking. He has found specialized commercial audiences that no one, not even Cartoon himself, would have expected. I feel so lucky that my career crossed his during my time at Nike in Los Angeles. Little did I know that I would learn as much from the guy about life as I have about art.

Cartoon first got noticed as a graffiti artist when he was growing up in a Latino neighborhood in East Los Angeles. He told me the story. "One day someone pulled up to my school and asked all the girls in the front, 'Hey, who's the best graffiti artist in the school?' So some girls came and grabbed me out of class. They said, 'Some white man wants to talk to you!'

"So I come out front and I see a blond-haired man who said, 'I'm a photographer for *Car and Driver* magazine, and I want you to paint some graffiti. I'm going to put a vintage car in front of it and a girl is going to wax the car—kind of a bikini issue.' I did a couple of covers. Then I was walking in the supermarket with my mom, and I saw I had a cover of *Car and Driver* magazine! I was sixteen."

With that early experience of getting connected with a specialized commercial audience for his talents, and with the encouragement of his father, who played him inspirational recordings about how to succeed in business, Cartoon began trying to picture his ambitions in his mind's eye. "I'd been drawing since I was a little boy, but I started stepping back and saying: What's my dream situation? If I won the lottery, what would I do, what kind of company would I do? And I wrote it down: I'd be a tattooer, I'd have a big lot with cars in it, and I'd design my own shoes."

In time, Cartoon realized that the art form he wanted most to master was tattooing. He was already accomplished with pen and ink, but he discovered that tattooing was much harder. "I knew illustration, commercial work, and I could do it standing on my head. But skin on skin is hard to get used to. It's a curving, living, bleeding canvas, so I really had to focus. I spent ten solid years on tattooing to feel I could master part of it. Living in a tattoo shop, submersing myself in it, living and breathing tattoo. I spent a lot of time watching other tattooers, and some would drop some jewels on me, technical shit. But there's no shortcut. You just have to do it till your hands cramp and tattooing is coming out your ears."

At the time he was going deep with tattooing, it was no one's idea of a mainstream art form. He remembers, "Back in the day it was only for the hard core: gangsters, strippers, bikers—all the -ers. Eventually, fortunately, a bunch of pro athletes and Tupac and other entertainers started to get tattoos. So my timing was right." His best friend was a tour manager for a major hip-hop act, and at music festivals such as Lollapalooza, his friend would spread the word about Cartoon's talents. "He'd pull the guys from Outkast, Eminem, and tell them, 'Hey, you need to get tattooed by my homeboy Cartoon.'" When Eminem appeared on the cover of *Time* magazine, Cartoon's work was right there in the picture. The long, hard work of going deep was paying off, and his new specialty was reaching a new specialized audience: music lovers.

## A BILLION DOLLARS

Alli Webb and my team for the Run Hit Wonder are examples of inventing and launching new ideas, but playing a Specialist Game is just as important when a person or company is already established but needs to keep growing. For that reason, I loved hearing the perspective of Angela Ahrendts, whom we met in chapter 1, on Magic Drive. Starting with her work at Liz Claiborne, she has made an astonishing career out of helping businesses of all sizes understand what differentiates them and gives them the chance to succeed with their audience. She calls this their core.

"At Liz Claiborne Group, we acquired three, four companies a year. Out in California, for example, we bought Lucky Brand, the denim experts, and Juicy Couture, the T-shirt pros who also created the incredible modern-day sexy tracksuits. I oversaw twenty-two different businesses, all apparel, but with very different founders, products, and price points, and each targeting different audiences. So what was my role? What was my job?" Angela had the power to be a "dictator," making decisions for those companies, but she realized that the most valuable thing she could do for them was to keep them focused on playing their Specialist Game. "A company can get to a million in sales, ten million, but to get to a hundred million or a billion, you have to be laser-focused and cut through the competitive clutter. You've got to have a compelling core that people desire. What made Lucky Brand was that well over half of the business was done on their core product, which was a couple of pairs of perfect jeans. What made Juicy Couture become a global sensation was T-shirts and tracksuits that drove nearly 80 percent of the business. Both Juicy and Lucky Brand had found a core that was seasonless, ageless, timeless—something that everyone [in their specialized audience] needed, wanted, and could afford."

As Angela freely admits, she couldn't give the founders of Lucky Brand advice about how to create the greatest denim, because she wasn't part of their specialized—young, trend-seeking—audience. But she could guide them to trust their own Specialist Game. She did the same thing in her massive success with Burberry. She partnered with another brilliant creative person and they started from Burberry's historical core, the trench coat. "The outerwear category was always going to be the anchor but the trench coat was always intended to be first and foremost in everything." Whether it's Alli Webb looking for a little part-time work or Angela Ahrendts leading a global fashion phenomenon, the key to success is committing to play a Specialist Game.

## WHERE DO I START?

I know exactly what you are thinking right now: "But wait, *what* is my specialty—and how do I know if I'm focused on the right one?" Finding the precise specialties you can offer and matching them with a specialized audience is one of the more challenging, nonlinear parts of living Extreme You. So it's good to know you can start developing your Specialist Game by working on any aspect of it. You might build up extreme skills and knowledge, as Mister Cartoon did with tattooing, and trust that you'll find your audience along the way. Or follow a personal obsession, as Sam Kass did with the politics of food. Or get to know an audience you want (or need!) to serve. What matters most is that at some point you knuckle down and get focused.

It's the same for individuals and for businesses: experiment until you land on a core specialty, and then focus like hell. A great example is Strava, the fitness mobile app and social network that made its first big splash with cyclists. (Full disclosure—I love this company so much that I went ahead and joined its board of directors!) When I first learned about it, I assumed that the founders, Michael Horvath and Mark Gainey, would be hugely obsessive cyclists—you know, the type of dudes who are more than happy striding around a coffee shop in uncomfortably tight spandex after a big long ride. But no. They didn't come from cycling families at all.

Sure, they had worked together before, creating—are you ready for this?—customer email management software for businesses. Not exactly the background you'd expect for the guys who founded the hottest social network for athletes. As Mark told me, "People think Michael and I were avid cyclists, but that's far from the truth. I typically end up in hospital when I ride too frequently! I enjoy being out on the dirt, enjoy riding with people, but our intent was to pick a customer base we could go deep with."

Like a lot of Extremers, Mark and Michael wanted to be champions at something, but what? They didn't know. So for two years they talked about what sort of new company would be motivating to them. And actually, what I love the most about Mark and Michael is that they've basically been besties for more than twenty years. They rowed crew together in college and have had an amazing lifetime of shared experiences and passion as competitive athletes. So they were uniquely positioned as a duo in their pursuit of that unique customer base that they could understand and focus on.

They finally settled on "something touching the world of the athlete—someone who had decided that health and fitness were important. We wanted to complement how they were already living, not change them." They still hadn't decided who exactly that health and fitness audience would be or what kind of specialty they could offer. They even picked their name for the business before they knew for sure who it would serve. "Strava means 'to strive'—anyone striving. It's not built just for elite athletes, for those who have to be the fastest—you might be striving to run an eight-minute mile or complete your biggest hike. We know what it's like to have the challenges: finding time to work out or being injured and feeling it isn't fun to exercise anymore. This was the audience we wanted to build for, the kind of person who we thought would be our customers. We conceived and pursued different ideas in parallel and finally settled on starting with cyclists, a group who seemed like they were not being served, yet who were quick to adopt new technologies such as GPS mapping of the length of their rides or power meters for their bicycles." It was only after they identified an audience they could serve that they set about getting to know them and how they could be served. In that, their approach was the exact opposite of Mister Cartoon, who knew he wanted to offer the world his distinctive vision of tattoo but didn't know that his first specialized audience would be hip-hop fans.

## EXTREME MOVES

To play a Specialist Game, you need to bring together an Extreme You approach or product with a specialized audience who has reason to love it. And the secret to making that work is in what you *don't* do. To win with your specialized audience, you have to learn to say four different kinds of "no" to everybody else.

### 1. Be Spectacular for a Few, Not Average for Many

Your specialist game won't please everyone—and that's actually awesome. You have to please only the people who truly need what you're offering. The Strava guys recall that they got a fantastic validation that they had found their specialized audience when they met with a consultant a couple of years after they'd started the business. The meeting was at Starbucks, and the consultant asked them a key question for companies seeking to play a specialist game: Who is your customer? "When she asked me, I said, 'See those guys in the corner with spandex and cycling shoes? That's our customer.' And her eyes lit up! She told us that too many times at meetings like these, the person she's talking to looks around and says, 'Anyone here would be a great customer!' But when you know who exactly you're speaking to, you can have this amazing rapport."

Ultimately, the Specialist Game is about building relationships—with a million customers or one team at work—that last because the fit is so good. You find that unique fit by developing a wide range of diverse possibilities and then narrowing the offering to suit your audience in a way they've never known before. It's impossible to predict what that combination will be before you find it, but you can be sure that it will combine elements that didn't originally seem to go together. Diversity matched with unrelenting focus makes you relevant. Just make sure you have both.

When we start businesses or develop our careers, it's human nature to develop FOMO (fear of missing out). We want to do everything, so we don't miss out on any opportunity. But I just love this blindingly simple insight that Mark shared with me. "It's better to be number one in a market that looks small, because if you're number one, people will listen to you. If you're number four in a big market, that's noisy. So you have to be prepared to say the market might look small now, but we can go on to have a rich, long-lasting relationship with them." I know now I'd rather be number one at being the cheerleading, hypercompetitive, big-thinking business innovation leader Sarah Robb O'Hagan than I'd want to be number four in a large collection of people who can be described the same way as me!

### 2. Become Good at Saying No

So now you've identified a specialized audience that needs what only you can give it. Now comes the hard part: refusing to be distracted. Saying no. It's not hard as a concept—as the Strava guys told me, "Everyone says, 'Focus.' Everyone says, 'Choose what not to do.' But then comes the noise of opportunity. You have a small success in one area, and that makes people say, 'You should go after this other thing . . .' Pretty soon you're doing too much. You've lost focus by trying to appeal to everyone, and you've lost your way. "

What do you do after you learn to say no? Say it a lot more. As Warren Buffett, the superstar investor, put it, "The difference between successful people and very successful people is that very successful people say 'no' to almost everything." Alli Webb was trying to offer the best possible blow-out in the most customer-friendly shop while everyone else, from her clients to her investors, was pushing her to widen her focus. "Women sit in the chair and say, 'It would be so great if you could do my makeup, too!' They feel, 'I'm sitting here anyway—could I get a manicure?' And, as the business grew, our investors would say, 'You have this audience of millions of women. Why don't we sell them more stuff?'" Alli had to defend her specialist game by saying no—a lot. "In my humble opinion it would take away the intense focus we have on blow-outs and customer service—stylists blowing hair out the way they're supposed to and also being nice to people." Hmm . . . saying no again and again and again—maybe her years caring for small children were the perfect preparation for playing an entrepreneur's specialist game.

But seriously, in the moment, it can be hard to say no. So I wanted to summarize Adam Grant's "8 Ways to Say No Without Hurting Your Image," from LinkedIn Pulse. The Wharton professor and author of *Originals* is a great friend of mine and one of my favorite thought leaders in the world today. He's also the most epic example of a person who gets an enormous amount done because of his exceptional focus on the stuff that matters. I have often asked him if he has a few clones of himself because he's so freakin' productive, but no. He's just very good at prioritizing without offending people. He suggests that instead of looking someone in the eyes and telling them flat-out no, you could try:

1. **THE DEFERRAL:** Offer to help at a later date, which will filter out the people who are too lazy or disinterested to follow up.
2. **THE REFERRAL:** When you can't (or don't feel qualified) to do something, share resources that may help instead.
3. **THE INTRODUCTION:** Offer to put people in touch with someone who can help them better than you can.
4. **THE BRIDGE:** Facilitate connections between people who can help each other.
5. **THE TRIAGE:** Employ someone else to act as an initial filter.
6. **THE BATCH:** Find ways to efficiently combine requests in a way that makes it possible to help several people at one time.

7. **THE RELATIONAL ACCOUNT:** Reference your commitment
   to other people when rejecting someone's request, e.g.,
   "With more than two dozen speaking invitations rolling
   in per week, my wife and I have set a limit for speaking
   engagements, and at this point I'm maxed out."
8. **THE LEARNING OPPORTUNITY:** Just be honest: "I'm sorry
   to disappoint. One of my goals for this year is to improve
   my ability to say no—you are a tough audience. I suppose it's
   good practice."

### 3. Play the Long Game

Saying no is challenging not just because of potentially awkward
social moments but because each time you say no you are giving
something up. You might be saying no to money right now for the
sake of a specialized relationship that is going to take time to build.
You might be saying no to an opportunity that seems easy, when
your specialist game is feeling hard. For Mister Cartoon, early on in
his career it got hard to say no when a friend got him the chance to
be part of an event at Nike. At that time, no one at Nike thought of
him as a designer. They knew only his tattoos, so that was what the
company asked for. "When Nike came to me," he explained, "they
just wanted me to tattoo in a booth at the event. I was like, 'I'm not
really down with that—better that I'm there as a tastemaker.'

"My buddy who got me that job was upset, like, 'Hey, man,
what's wrong? That's really good money!' But I thought, if I take
that money for doing that tattooing, I'll never be accepted as anything more. If I'm the taco man in the tent in the back, they're never
going to look at me any other way. So I had to show myself like the
other designers who would be there.

"I gambled on it, I told them how I felt, and I got to go to the party as a designer, where I had a conversation with Mark Parker," who was not only the CEO of Nike but a legend in the world of design. He continued, "It was worth it (a) to know he knew who I was and (b) just to rap to him." With that conversation, he introduced himself as a designer to the top person at Nike. In time, he was asked to collaborate on the design of a Nike Air Force 1, the most coveted shoe to design and insanely hard to get hold of. It's called a "quick strike," which means it's a limited-edition production run, superhard to buy, and destined to become a collector's item.

Everyone who has successfully played the Specialist Game has had to turn down opportunities. They could have had more gigs, more certainty about their cash flow, and more satisfied customers—in the short run. What they would have given up was the long-term positioning as a specialist and the relationship with the people who would value their Extreme talents and products the most. They might have felt more comfortable for a while, but they would have lost at the Specialist Game when it really counted.

### 4. Streamline Your Commitments

Cartoon's success, as much as anything, is a story of cutting out distraction and streamlining his life in every aspect. "I stopped drinking and smoking weed for thirteen years," he explained. "I was like, 'OK, I want to get all this work done. The last thing I need is drinking beer. What am I celebrating? I'm not even close to where I want to be.'"

And the closer he got to where he wanted to be, the more he had to be careful of the people around him. "The more good shit that happens, the more people want to hang out and start acting weird. My studio was set up like a barbershop or a clubhouse—tattoo shops are known for guys coming by and bullshitting. There's nothing more distracting than that shit. You have to be precious with your time and get a lot done. You have to have creative people around you to build off. Do you want to do a restaurant? You have to find a badass chef; you have to find a badass designer. *Those* are the people you want to hang around with. Other than that, you're got to constantly shrink your circle.

"Especially when you have kids—then fuck everybody. These days, I'm not trying to make everyone happy and be at all the parties and art shows and events. I'm trying to lock it down and create content. You lock yourself down and make stuff, and then you bust out again."

Never were truer words spoken.

There's a reason it's said that there's no such thing as overnight success, because to truly develop your potential, it takes time to learn where you shine the best and discipline to become the best in the world at it. That might seem like a lot of hard work—and it is. But every great Extremer will tell you that when they're playing their Specialist Game, all that hard work feels amazingly satisfying. And when you do find your specialty, it's still not the end of the journey. Hold on tight, because it's just the beginning. In the next chapter I'll explain how developing a narrow specialty can lead to game-changing innovation and success.

# EIGHT
# CHANGE THE
# GAME

Extremers dream of going big. We want to find the things we're best at. We want to use *all* of our potential. So let me be clear: the Specialist Game I described in the previous chapter does *not* mean you have to settle for small ambitions. Just the opposite—it's a technique for breaking into the big leagues. Once you're there, you have a chance to succeed on the biggest scale you can imagine—by getting so good that you change the entire game around you.

That was true of Strava, whose founders dreamed of being the top social network for athletes. They started narrowly, with cyclists, but they always believed the potential audience for their product would be much larger than that. And just like that, they indeed changed the game. In a landscape where "social network" meant one thing and "fitness tracking app" meant another, Strava combined the best of both that tapped an unmet need among athletes who strive to be better.

## WHAT IT CAN BE, NOT WHAT IT IS TODAY

If you want to go crazy big, you need to build your skills and the opportunity over time—*and* you need to stay open to the possibility that you might ultimately discover your full potential in unexpected ways. I had assumed I'd have my biggest successes at Nike. After all, Nike had been my dream company. The entire time I was there, the fact that it had hired me at all felt like a miracle. I was just so chuffed to have made it in the door at all, and I thought that as long as I managed not to get fired, I'd absolutely stay forever. I made so many amazing friends, and gosh, my first two kids, Sam and Joe, had been born during my time there, so the company had so much personal relevance for me. For years, I didn't take a single head-hunter phone call because I had zero interest in being anywhere else until the fateful day when I was starting to feel antsy for more of a challenge and just happened to pick up the phone.

It was a recruiting firm telling me that PepsiCo was looking for an innovative leader to revive Gatorade, the iconic sports drink brand. Daaaaaaaamn! Impossible not to be intrigued! Not by Pepsi-Co's corporate culture, where it seemed that left-brain quantitative presentations led the decision making and suits were still required four days out of five. And definitely not by the PepsiCo campus, which featured one of the finest sculpture gardens in America but lacked any kind of sports vibe. (I had been spoiled by the Nike campus: soccer fields, running tracks, and gyms everywhere and nobody dressed in anything they couldn't pair with sneakers.) So why was I possibly considering walking away from the coolest company on the planet?

PepsiCo offered a chance to express my Extreme Self and play my now well developed Specialist Game in a far more audacious way: the job promised to give me the chance to take full responsibility for reinventing a brand. And not just any brand. Gatorade was then the second largest sports brand in the United States, with as deep a heritage and as much credibility in the sports drink space as Nike had in athletic footwear and apparel. Some badass was going to lead that transformation, and it wasn't lost on me that if I didn't get the job, it would likely go to one of my Nike teammates.

At my interview, I hit it off with Massimo D'Amore, CEO of PepsiCo Americas Beverages. Just as those PepsiCo cultural signals were making me think I'd be a bad fit, here I was having one of the most daring and energizing career conversations of my life. Massimo was a classic Italian with all the brilliant hand waving and body language that you'd expect. But more important, he was a bold and hugely ballsy change agent with a reputation for being one of the most successful leaders in the industry. PepsiCo had just brought him in to transform the North and South American beverage business.

Soft drinks and beverages in general, like so many large businesses in the mid-2000s, were facing a rapidly evolving competitive landscape full of many new start-up competitors enabled by new technologies. Consumer preferences were shifting away from unhealthy sugary ingredients, and that was changing the entire beverage business. Massimo looked me dead in the eyes and said he was on a mission to find the best sports marketer on the planet to run Gatorade. And as I sat there trying to make the case that it surely had to be me, he paused and said with utter confidence that if I thought I had worked in competitive industries before, nothing would compare to the world of beverages.

BOOOOOOM! Boy, did he know how to turn the fire in my belly into a raging furnace! The kind of bold individual leadership he was seeking, I realized, was impossible at my level at Nike, a team-oriented company where it felt as though every meeting had stadium seating. And because Nike was so very successful, there was almost nothing—not even failures of new products or missteps in new categories—that slowed it down much. I absolutely loved the camaraderie of the great team successes we had at Nike, but I certainly never felt that my actions could make or break us.

This conversation came at a time when I'd been wondering something about myself: what was the truth about Extreme SRO? Was I really capable of leading great business success, or was I just another loyal deckhand on the good ship Nike? The crisis at Gatorade represented a challenge I could rise to, a service I could perform, and an opportunity to see what I was really made of. I would never get to meet that challenge if I played it safe within the enormously successful Nike machine.

A big part of the allure was that Gatorade was no ordinary soft drink. Developed by scientists at the University of Florida, the home of the Gators football team, it had been meant to be an "aid" to Gators playing under the ferociously hot Florida sun. But in the years since PepsiCo had acquired it, the parent company had massively ramped up its growth by leveraging its powerful distribution system and selling it like its other beverages, bundling it with corn chips as part of PepsiCo's ongoing competition with the number one soft drink brand, Coke. "Stack it high and let it fly" had been the mantra as PepsiCo pushed Gatorade far and wide through the huge network of retailers that it served. But that approach had now reached its limit. Sales had stalled, and what the company needed, I believed, was someone who could get back to Gatorade's Specialist Game by aiding real athletes to improve their performance. That, I felt, was the only way to reinvigorate the brand and take it to new heights.

For Extreme Me, the choice to leave or stay was surprisingly clear. At Nike, I was and would always be a solid player on a championship team. At Gatorade I would have the chance to be the captain of a Specialist Team that was struggling but still had championship potential. Here was a chance not just to fit my Extreme skills and knowledge to a specialized audience but to make a big bet on myself and my capability to lead an entire brand in a new direction. There would be no middle ground—I would be either a smashing success, taking Gatorade to the next level, or a crushing failure. And I would be putting a lot on the line. I had the sense that Nike wasn't the kind of place to welcome back those who left.

Then fate intervened. Returning from my trip to the PepsiCo campus for my first round of interviews, as I boarded the plane and finally settled into my seat for the six-hour journey home, I slowly became aware of a really gnarly feeling of nausea that was all too familiar. Holy shit—I was pregnant with number three! I told Massimo my news, thinking this meant good-bye to my Gatorade hopes, but to my surprise he answered, "My deeeear, that's woooon-derful news. We looove babies!"

And so I left my dream job—incredibly excited about the possibilities ahead but equally sad and homesick about the door closing behind me. Nike had allowed me to regain my confidence and hop back onto my career trajectory. It was the place where I had made some of the best friendships of my life. Would I survive without the strength of that "family" behind me?

## DRINKING FROM THE GATORADE FIRE HOSE

When I arrived in Chicago in July 2008, three months pregnant, Massimo summed up the situation: sales had stalled because the brand was dated. The only innovation in the past few years had been new flavors. Our goal, Massimo said, was to turn sales around by reenergizing the brand and reconnecting it with its core audience. Quite naively, I thought all we really needed to do was jazz up the logo, packaging, and marketing and we'd be laughing again. Massimo had already made some big moves by hiring a new advertising agency for the brand: TBWA\Chiat\Day, which was known for its iconic work with such brands as Apple and Adidas. And I had quickly felt a real connection with my key new team members. Opokua, our wonderfully bold leader from Research and Development with a long history of creating great food and beverages; Carla and Morgan on the marketing team, who were fantastic marketers with a personal passion for all things Gatorade; Scott and Mary in sports marketing who'd worked intimately with Gatorade users from high school coaches all the way through to the world's most elite athletes; Pistol Pete, firing up the publicity machine; and Heather, who'd led consumer insights for the brand for many years and was a walking encyclopedia of athletic consumer knowledge. I mean, with this awesome team and this awesome brand, how hard could it be?

Turns out . . . really hard.

Marketing for general beverages at PepsiCo was very different from that at companies like Virgin and Nike, where I had earned my chops. PepsiCo was about mass-market reach with highly sophisticated research techniques to create flavors and marketing campaigns that appealed to the greatest number of people. Instead of targeting a specialized audience, it needed to appeal to "humans with throats" in order to achieve growth on a mass scale. And its method was to find ways to "steal share" from competitor brands in the Coke portfolio. Now I was starting to understand what Massimo had meant by this intensely competitive industry. In the "soda wars," the language of battle was everywhere, and as members of the blue army, we were expected to do anything and everything to stop the red army.

Then, in September 2008, just three months after I arrived, came the worst economic downturn since the Great Depression. Gatorade sales went from flat into decline. This was unheard of for this brand, which had been the "workhorse" of the PepsiCo portfolio for so many years. Our market research revealed exactly what was happening: under pressure from the recession, consumers who were not athletes, and therefore had no real reason to drink Gatorade, were giving it up, often switching to tap water because it was free. Boy, we had work to do.

Our biggest problem, I came to realize, was that the teen athletes who should have been our specialized audience weren't feeling the brand anymore because it came across like an Oldsmobile among sports cars. I wanted to give it a new, fresh look and feel so that Gatorade would feel more modern and innovative—right at home next to Nike, Under Armour, ESPN, and the other brands teen athletes valued. Those brands were all digitally savvy, but Gatorade still spent 90 percent of its marketing and communications budget on television ads, with barely any resources devoted to digital promotion. If we could give Gatorade a younger, cooler, more athletic feel, I thought, and present it in the ways young athletes liked to communicate, that would be half the battle. (Or half the bottle, as it were.)

Before I was hired, the team had already been working to re-design the outdated Gatorade logo and packaging, and they were about to make their final recommendation to Massimo. I remember looking at the new approach and feeling it was "cleaner" and certainly more modern than the current packaging, but boy, oh boy, it still looked safe. I was reluctant to overwhelm the meeting with strong opinions when I was so new, but I also remembered Massimo saying that we were in a crisis and needed to change our trajectory massively. My gut just screamed at me: playing it safe was not going to be the answer.

I asked Shawna, our packaging manager, if there had been any other options presented by the agency. Her eyes lit up, and she told me there had been one that everyone thought was really cool, but they'd decided not to present it because it felt too risky. So of course I had to see it, and the minute I set my eyes on it I just knew that we *had* to do it. Literally within thirty seconds of seeing this concept, my brain was bursting with the many ways it could be embraced by young digitally savvy teens. So I thought, fuck it. If we keep on playing the game the way every other beverage team plays it, we're going to fail anyway, and we're probably all going to get fired.

So with the support of my courageous new team, I pushed for that radical approach, including a big fat mysterious teaser campaign to rename the brand "G." We were taking inspiration from Apple's "Think Different" campaign, which had intrigued customers with the idea that a big change was coming but held off revealing what it was. In that way, we'd buy time to figure out what exactly the change should be. So even as we delved into the options for creating a new beverage behemoth, we also began planning a teaser campaign that would ask, "What's G?"

We would have less than three months to do a shitload of work.

First we'd have to complete new designs for every single packaging SKU and then get them processed and into production in order to hit our planned launch date of January 1. Next we'd have to align, shoot, and edit all new advertising materials and arrange to change the logo of Gatorade everywhere across millions of point-of-sale displays across the country. Talk about epic teamwork! At the same time, we had to present our plan to our retailers and sales teams. Little did I know that those folks were not so good with change. In meeting after meeting with retailers, I would share our new vision for the brand, only to be met with looks of confusion, fear, and worry; after the fact, those same people would take their complaints directly to Massimo: too risky, they'd say. To his credit, every time he heard those phrases, he would tell them the new campaign was happening no matter what.

On December 14, I presented the entire launch plan at our "all hands" employee meeting. We were rolling the first "G label" bottles off the manufacturing lines that week, and our final ads had been tweaked and were ready to show, including a TV spot to kick off the teaser campaign. It featured every famous Gatorade-sponsored athlete of all time—think Michael Jordan, Peyton Manning, Usain Bolt, Serena Williams, Derek Jeter, and Mia Hamm—asking the question "What's G?" That TV spot would be followed three weeks later with another TV ad that would reveal the answer to that question. (Gatorade, of course.)

I felt so confident—against all odds we were pulling it together! But as I presented the work, there was a split reaction in the room: excitement from the younger crowd and fear and confusion from the older crowd. I tuned out the negative responses and continued to tell myself to be strong because we had a blockbuster on our hands.

The next day my obstetrician told me that my fluids were running dangerously low and I needed to have the baby immediately. I said, "OK—cool. Let me just hop back to the office and wrap a couple of things up and go home and get my overnight bag." To which the doctor replied, "No, I mean now. We need to get this baby out *now*. You're being admitted!" Yikes! I found myself checking into the hospital to have a baby with nothing except my laptop. (I'm not exactly sure how I thought my laptop would be useful in the delivery . . . )

Thankfully, it was only a couple of hours before Liam arrived with my overnight bag, and later that evening we welcomed our precious wee girl to the world. It took us a day or two to land on her name, Gabriella, or "Gabby." When Massimo called to congratulate me, he said, "Well, you've given birth to two G's this week—the big G and your baby G." So for a little while Gabby was known as Baby G.

For two weeks, I enjoyed maternity leave, getting through a very cold and snowy Chicago Christmas and adjusting to the sleepless nights. I'd sit up feeding Gabs and indulging in my favorite guilty pleasure, midnight *Gilmore Girls* marathons. (More Gs again.) Then New Year's Day arrived and with it the debut of our "What's G?" campaign. I sat on the couch at home with Gabby and watched it roll out from afar. Within five days of launch, we were getting an enormously positive online response to our TV advertising. We broke a record for the most-googled search term with "What's G?" Things could not have gone better, right?

But alas—the economy was still sputtering, and it was the coldest winter in years. Gatorade sales nose-dived at retail. Within two weeks of the relaunch, revenue was down up to 20 percent *each month*. (Off a $5 billion revenue business: you do the math!) In many stores the shelves were a total mess, with new G and old Gatorade labels mixed together. The retailers were up in arms, complaining that shoppers didn't know what "G" was and the whole rebranding was a giant disaster.

Back at PepsiCo headquarters, not surprisingly, fear and confusion over the sudden and dramatic downturn of the Gatorade business reigned. Therefore a recommendation was made that we immediately change all of our "teaser" TV spots and billboards to "reveal" immediately to try to turn things around. Massimo called me to ask what I thought we should do. I pleaded with him, saying it was too soon and we had to hold our own. We managed to keep the teaser campaign in place for two more weeks. In between breast-feeding sessions and diaper changes, I was on the phone and email at all hours and working essentially full-time on crises associated with Gatorade's perceived implosion. Maternity leave? Yeah, not so much.

We were counting on our Super Bowl ad to change things. The team had prepared a hilarious spoof on *Monty Python and the Holy Grail*, featuring a number of our famous athletes as Knights of the Round Table. But in the confusion and concern at PepsiCo HQ, the spot seemed very risky. I was desperately trying to get in on the discussion on conference calls from my basement office at home, but I was still too new to the company, probably considered too naive, or perhaps just too far away to convince them. So we had to rerun one of the spots we had been running all month. I was devastated. I felt I was failing my team and my vision for the future of the brand.

It was no surprise, then, that our Super Bowl spot landed almost at the bottom of the Ad Meter. In February and March, sales got worse. From our retailers to Wall Street analysts, everyone seemed to think the problem was that my team and I were idiots who had blown the redesign of the labels and bottles. Could anyone blame them when the business was in total free fall? There was tremendous internal pressure to go back to the strategy that had caused the brand to stall in the first place—even to change the G labels back to the old, dated Gatorade ones—and return to waging an all-out war with the competition the way Pepsi had traditionally done with Coke.

I found myself trying desperately to be all things to all people—an attentive mother to my baby and two fast-growing little boys, a supportive wife to my husband, Liam, who was trying to settle our family into an entirely new life, and a focused and courageous leader to my newly formed Gatorade team going through a fight that was tougher, in an economy that was far worse, than anyone had expected. The *Wall Street Journal* ran an article with the headline "Pepsi Sweats over Gatorade." I imagined my former Nike colleagues gasping with horror at the hot mess I had made of my career.

After nine months of this, I was physically and emotionally exhausted. Liam put his foot down and forced me to get on a plane home to New Zealand for a month of real maternity leave, family time, pampering, and perspective taking. He was right: a bottle of good Kiwi sauvignon blanc with your mates will solve all manner of problems. Once I remembered how to laugh again, though, I had a decision to make. So many people at PepsiCo were pushing for us to take a less extreme approach and return to the familiar Pepsi marketing playbook. And with hindsight I have to say that I don't blame them—as they weren't on the inside of our specialist team, it was damn near impossible for them to see that we might actually be onto something. I just knew that this amazing brand, with its deep specialist point of view and the hard-earned trust of its core audience of athletes, was never going to win if it continued to reenact the traditional battle of Coke versus Pepsi. Years of fighting that battle was what had driven Gatorade into this mess in the first place. Even before the so-called disastrous brand change, the business had already been stalling, so in my mind going back to our old approach wasn't an option.

The research we'd done around our brand launch showed that we actually *had* succeeded in reinvigorating our relationship with our specialized audience of young athletes. For the first time in years, we were in the thick of the social media buzz among the athletic kids we cared about most. But with the economy in free fall, that wasn't a big enough success to compensate for our lost sales. We needed to build on our specialized success to fulfill a much bigger ambition—to take our new approach the whole way, beyond a splashy advertising campaign to a full business reinvention. It wasn't going to be enough to play the old beverage game better. We would have to change how the game was played.

Before returning from my trip home to New Zealand, I wrote what I called my "Jerry Maguire" manifesto, explaining how things were going to be from there on out. No longer would we allow our fears to be fanned by the opinions of those without specialist knowledge of our athlete consumers, our market research, and our new strategy. No longer would we focus on chasing our competitors the way Pepsi chases Coke. The only way I was willing to continue to climb this incredibly steep mountain was if we made every decision by listening to the voice of our athlete consumers. I wrote the document and emailed it to Massimo, making clear that I was putting my job on the line. To fail by doing what I believed to be right would be acceptable to me, but if the higher-ups really felt the only way was their traditional beverage strategy, I was the wrong leader for the company.

The week I returned to the office, Massimo took me out for breakfast. It was clear: he got it. He told me that he was willing to accept that our sales numbers for the rest of 2009 would be terrible. He was betting that if he protected me and gave the team air cover, we'd figure out how to turn this bad boy around and start growing sustainably in 2010. That breakfast was the moment our relationship went from boss and employee to partners in an incredibly tough fight. Now we knew each would have the other's back, no matter what.

We'd had meetings before to discuss broad innovations for the brand, but now the innovation meetings changed. Before, the team had mainly been responding to internal pressure urging us to find some magic ingredient to put in Gatorade to "make it advantaged" compared to Coke's Powerade—that is, do something new to make our product seem better than its direct competitor. For a while, Massimo had us exploring a new ingredient, which, in high doses, helped athletes get more oxygen to their system, improving endurance. There were only three small problems. First, it was fluoro freakin' yellow, so it made Gatorade look radioactive. Second, it was sourced from only one forest in Brazil. Third, you needed to drink about a keg of it to get any performance effect. (As the Gatorade research and development team kept reminding me: *If there was a magic ingredient, don't you think we'd have found it by now?*) The point was that we had lost focus. We were spending too much time trying to reassure corporate executives instead of addressing our athletes' needs.

## SEEING THE GAME DIFFERENTLY

To refocus our efforts, I bolstered our team, hiring a few more athletically savvy people from different business backgrounds: Andrea from Nike, who had a whole depth of experience around retail that we needed; Stanley, whose agency could help us reimagine our packaging through the lens of athletes' needs; Jonah, whose agency was great at developing new innovation concepts; Phil, who was a brilliant and seasoned project manager; and of course the incomparable Gordon Thompson, whom you met back in chapter 1, who brought a deeply needed design and strategic capability to all of our efforts. At the same time I made sure to elevate the voices of those from the original Gatorade team, who deeply understood our athletic consumers, our history, and our unique opportunities. Playing by the rules of the old game, we had seen our product as a beverage and fought to get more people to drink ours over our competitors'. In the new game, we would be serving athletes, and our product was whatever athletes needed to fuel their bodies to perform. The breakthrough came when we realized that athletes playing their best need more than a drink. By listening more intently to many of the original Gatorade team members, who by this stage had lasted through years of difficult change in the business, we were able to tap into oodles of research stored away on computers that nobody had ever really leveraged. The research showed that athletes need a full range of specialized nutrition—before, during, and after an event.

I still remember the meeting when we wrote "Before," "During," and "After" at the tops of columns on a piece of paper and came up with distinct product ideas for each of those columns. We eventually called it "sports fuel," and soon we discovered that even world-class athletes didn't know where to find it. (Even Usain Bolt, perhaps the greatest sprinter of all time, was still eating Skittles before Olympic races—for real!—because he couldn't find anything better designed for his needs.)

We realized that Gatorade innovation could touch everything from the cooler on the NFL sideline (we redesigned it for better dunkability and called it "the cooler cooler"!) to squeeze bottles that helped measure hydration doses to gummy chews that gave energy before an event (thanks for the inspiration, Usain!) to post-workout recovery shakes. We could innovate ingredients, packaging, food forms . . . And it didn't stop there. We also realized that no other company in the world had as much scientific knowledge and research about sports nutrition as we did, thanks to our Gatorade Sports Science Institute—and that there was nothing stopping us from totally reframing our marketing approach and sharing our knowledge with our young, digitally savvy consumers in a fresh way. We decided to call the new relaunched product line "The G Series": Gatorade Prime for energy before the game, Gatorade Perform for hydration during the game, and Gatorade Recover to rebound afterward.

We began 2010 with the same horrible headwinds facing us, and our first-quarter results showed even more declines. We had not yet launched any of our new products, and we were running out of room to fail. The media and market analysts were crushing us. Three weeks later, I made a presentation at a huge PepsiCo financial analyst meeting. This was a companywide event with top executives from all brands presenting the future of our businesses to the leaders of Wall Street. It was up to us to give them reasons to continue to invest in PepsiCo. I got up that morning and ran down the East River from my hotel, blasting Eminem's "Lose Yourself" and thinking this was *it*—the moment this entire freakin' eighteen-month nightmare would end. I was on fucking fire! I felt wind at my back as I presented the Gatorade vision with more passion and conviction than at any time in my life. And boom! The presentation went great, I managed to answer every probing question with confidence and clarity, and the reports coming out of the presentation were, to everyone's pleasant surprise, cautiously optimistic. Now at least the skeptics could see we had a real plan. And by the way, that plan was badass—nothing like anything they had seen in this category before. Now there was nothing to do but wait four more weeks for our launch.

In late March 2010, our first G Series ads hit the air: "If you want a revolution, then the only solution is to *evolve* . . . introducing the G Series." Unlike at our launch the previous year, we had developed a far deeper approach to connecting with our core audience. Yes, we had inspiring, amazing TV spots, but now we also had a digital army of young, passionate athletes talking about our brand in social media, amplified by our social media command center, called Mission Control, to ensure that our inspirational and educational messages would spread among our specialist audience. The pre-workout energy pouches and the post-workout recovery drinks started to hit the shelves while we anxiously looked at sales reports every single day.

And then, holy shit, it *happened*! Suddenly sales turned around. Did you hear what I just said? *Sales turned around.* That's right. In the month of March, we hit our sales targets for the first time since I had joined the company. By June, we were significantly surpassing our monthly sales targets and well on the way to exceeding our goals for the year. In consumers' minds, our innovations had not only given them new Gatorade products to try but had made the original product, the sports drink, seem more innovative, too—because now the beverage was part of the new category we had created called sports fuel.

In the end, our dedicated and passionate team turned Gatorade from a flagging sports drink to one of the fastest-growing brands in the PepsiCo beverage portfolio. Through all those twists and turns, we had discovered that the potential market for athletic nutrition was far bigger than the market for sports beverages. Suddenly we had far more room to grow the business. In "sports drinks," we already had a huge majority share of the market, but "sports fuel" was a new playing field that was far bigger and untapped by a brand on our scale—so, not surprisingly, we held only a tiny share of athletic consumption. And the piece of data I love the all-time most—the proof that a Specialist Team playing its own game is unstoppable—is that well after my time on the team, Gatorade went on growing. From 2009 to 2015, sales per year increased by more than a billion dollars.

By changing the game, we had found a new playing field where we could have far more success on our own terms, rather than fighting for existing turf. It's similar to what W. Chan Kim and Renée Mauborgne have called "blue ocean strategy." They wrote, "In blue oceans, demand is created rather than fought over. There is ample opportunity for growth that is profitable and rapid." By contrast, in red oceans, "increasing competition turns the water bloody." And in their research, they have observed what we proved at Gatorade: "A blue ocean strategic move can create brand equity that lasts."

So why would Extremers stay and fight when we can find bluer oceans and succeed? It seems so obvious when you hear about a successful ending like the one Gatorade had, but the truth is, blue oceans always look scary and uncertain for an existing business when you first identify them. It was one thing for our specialist team to pursue a new path that made so much sense to us, another thing entirely for the chairman and CEO of PepsiCo to support us with all manner of external stakeholders as we broke the mold with such a large and strategically important business. I've often looked back and thought to myself that we were damn lucky to have a CEO in Indra Nooyi, who was a former strategist—for whom our seemingly crazy dream for Gatorade must have made all the strategic sense in the world! Indra showed me the importance of enabling a team like ours to bring out our Extreme—a skill that has served me well ever since.

## GOING BIG

Many of the biggest, game-changing successes build on the opportunities you create by learning to play a Specialist Game. They can come in two ways. For some people, it's the act of continuous development and improvement in an area of passion that leads to a new way of doing things. For others, it's the willingness to ask a game-changing question about your audience, whether it's your team at work, your boss, or the demographic for a product or service you offer. Ask yourself: *I have already proved I can do X for them better than anyone, so what else do they need that I am uniquely qualified to deliver?*

I like to think of needs as if they were on a map. Mentally I put my finger down on a need I can satisfy. Then I look around: What needs are next to the one I already know? Can I keep drawing on the same Extreme skills, knowledge, and passions to help the audience do more of what they want? Do my skills open up the chance to find my audience's undiscovered needs? Some examples:

You're an athlete who needs my sports beverage to boost your performance? Okay—what other products do you need to boost your performance that we know how to make for you?

You make one pair of jeans that all the hip young women of a certain demographic feel they must have. Now, if you extend my skills and learn to make other accessories in that same style, might they want those, too?

You're a young college graduate, and the only way to secure your first job is by participating in a standardized process of personality and experience testing that won't show your strengths. Looking through the lenses of your specialized skills and passions, what distinct insights, experiences, and skills can offer your potential employer?

Will you be able to successfully bring your skills to another area? You will if you put in lots of hard work and don't lose sight of the specialist knowledge that grounds you. Will your audience trust you to move from the narrow specialty you've proven into new territory on their needs map? They will if you're already number one for them in some area. Will you know them well enough to expand? You will if you never stop learning about your audience and how your Extreme approach might benefit them. You can see how far this method can go by looking, as I have done, at the brands you love. Nike started in footwear and extended its reach into apparel and equipment, all while maintaining its original focus on athletes. Apple started in computers and then developed a complete digital ecosystem, all while maintaining its focus on the customer's experience. David Bowie changed the definition of what it is to be a musician, constantly evolving his musical style and his personal brand, all while keeping his original fans and finding new fans through the decades. Serena Williams became a female icon well beyond the tennis courts through her athletic power, intensity, and fashion sensibility.

Who inspires you?

## WHEN THE GAME IS PERSONAL

It's easy to see a game being played in a new way when a brand does it by identifying the new needs of an audience. You can track the product's evolution, you can analyze marketing campaigns, and you can chart growth in market share over the course of those efforts. But the Extremer's approach to Changing the Game works just as well when it comes to personal reinvention. The principles are the same: first, become a specialist; then use your unique talents and insights to create a whole new way of winning.

One of the most inspiring examples of this approach is my husband Liam's sister, Mary. Mary is a powerful force of nature but, more important, she is proof that even for Extremers who find themselves in a position of massive disadvantage, there is hope and the possibility to bust out and succeed. Now, hang on tight, because this is a completely different kind of story, a world away from marketing. But it's an awe-inspiring example of an Extremer developing her own "specialty" and then using that approach to help change how the game is played—not just for herself but for many people around the world.

In her late teens and early twenties, living in New Zealand, Mary O'Hagan began to experience disruptive mood swings and feelings of utter hopelessness. For many people, being in your twenties is a time of wonderful freedom and self-discovery, but Mary would "get into very dark places where I couldn't even put a sentence together." She spent five years in and out of psychiatric hospitals. On top of these dark periods, she faced serious external obstacles. As she explained it to me, in those days "the game" for the treatment of mental distress made her situation even worse. Everywhere she turned, she was faced with what she calls "benevolent pessimism." The doctors told her, essentially, "You've got a serious mental illness we can't cure, and you just have to wait for the pills to work. We'll look after you while you're sick." There was no expectation that she would ever recover. "I was told, 'You'll never be able to achieve what you would have been able to achieve. You won't be able to work full-time, you'll have a very interrupted life.'

"The other thing they told me was that I should think very carefully about having children because they believed I had a genetic condition—which was a lot of bullshit. So, you think about a smart young woman of twenty. The two things she wants are: the choice to have children and the choice to have a career. They said I could have neither, and they were totally wrong. I have taken enormous pleasure out of proving them wrong!"

Mary endured for many years at several different hospitals because she wasn't given the opportunity to participate in the decisions regarding her own treatment. Her doctors' notes, which she saw many years later, made clear that they didn't understand what was wrong with her. They said things like "She gives an impression of overdramatization but with underlying gross psychological turmoil. She dresses unconventionally." They didn't know what to make of her, and they didn't know what to do for her. What Mary needed was not just to find another conventional psychiatrist—all the doctors she found in New Zealand saw her the same way—but to find an entirely new approach to her mental health, one that would create the possibility for her to make an independent and satisfying life. She needed someone who would recognize that she had the ability to understand her own condition and work to improve it—that she was a human being in a desperate struggle to improve her own life.

Then, during a very bad episode, she told me, "This kind of parable came out of the blackness to me, telling me that I had to take responsibility for my own life, find my own power." She described it this way in her memoir, *Madness Made Me*:

> *One of the last times I went mad I lay on my hospital bed with my eyes shut and my thoughts started sliding off into nonsense. This terrified me so I tried to make some sense of things by taking bits out of nonsense and putting them into a sequence: An old woman and her grand-daughter lived by a great ocean. Every day the old woman went fishing. She yelled in awe to the ocean, "Let me take the life out of you with my net." She always returned with fish and cooked them for herself and her grand-daughter. One day she gave some of the fish to her grand-daughter and said, "Cook these for yourself." The girl wailed, "I can't." The old woman replied, "You must find your own power." But the girl didn't understand and went to bed hungry. . . . That night the girl woke from her dreams to a booming voice from the sky: "You have the power of the old woman and the great ocean flowing into the core of you. Now, take meaning from the rawness of life and cook it for yourself without fear." At first I just repeated the words over and over to myself to ward off the chaos. Later I realized the words had arranged themselves into a story, a story that was telling me I didn't have to go mad anymore.*

Her "parable" became the inspiration for her to make "a transition from being a passive patient to being an active agent in my own future. It enabled me to think: I can't just let these experiences sink me. I've got to manage them."

Mary attributes to several factors her ability to start seeing her mental distress and her life in a different way, as part of a different and more hopeful story. First, she had been a "rebellious teenager, always saving the whales and going on marches and that kind of thing." Her noncompliant nature had often gotten her into trouble at school, but now that rebelliousness helped her to question the conventional narrative that she would have problems for the rest of her life. Second, she had people in her life who believed in her and gave her "messages of hope," even when she didn't get them from her caregivers. I loved the way she described this for me: "I think there is a well of hope in all of us, that even when things get really tough, you are able to reach into a place of hope because there is always a future to look forward to." And third, she came from a family that had education and a progressive approach to the world in which young women were expected to speak out and to achieve for themselves. And although no one on her medical team saw it that way, her rebelliousness, her hopefulness, and her family's expectation that she would speak up and accomplish things were all Extreme skills she could develop in herself. They gave her the chance to play a Specialist Game, becoming the best possible guide out of madness for an audience of one: herself. She learned to use the "mad" thoughts in her head to show her a way out. "My own pictures of madness came in the form of words and metaphors. At their most powerful my words floated in from the blackness and passed through me on to paper. I made meaning not in spite of my madness, but because of it."

The change did not come thanks to a single vision. She went through a long period of learning "how to pick myself up multiple times when I'd been knocked down." Even after she was out of the psychiatric hospitals, she struggled to make a life for herself. And the life she found came from going beyond her narrow Specialist Game—finding a way out for Mary—to question the entire "game" of understanding and helping people with mental distress. Mary helped found what came to be known in New Zealand as the "mad movement," which was created in the 1970s by and for people who had been forcibly treated and institutionalized. It was a protest movement, something like the women's movement, which valued peer support over traditional psychiatry and insisted that madness is a "profoundly disruptive but full human experience." In this view, survivors of psychological distress are uniquely positioned to help others deal with their own bouts with madness.

Mary became the first chairperson of the World Network of Users and Survivors of Psychiatry, an adviser to the United Nations and the World Health Organization, and a full-time mental health commissioner in New Zealand between 2000 and 2007. She is now an international consultant in mental health and a developer of PeerZone—peer-led mental health programs and consultancy. And get this—in 2015, Mary won the incredible honor of being appointed by the queen of England (yes—*that* queen!) to be a Member of the New Zealand Order of Merit, an incredibly impressive accolade. Her career trajectory and satisfying life would have been unthinkable had she not set out to question and help to change how the "game" was played. Her brilliant summary of her story is that she's glad she *didn't* expect to achieve so much in her life, because if she'd told one of her old psychiatrists that she was hoping to do these things, he would have upped her antipsychotic medications on the spot.

My examples of a psychiatric patient and a beverage brand are radically different, I know. But their stories have two things in common: systems that were broken and people stuck within those systems, at serious risk of failure. Desperate for a new approach, they triumphed because they were able to Change the Game.

## LOVE HOW IT FEELS

The impulse to Change the Game and the material and commitment to make it possible don't have to come from negative emotions, such as the fear my team felt at Gatorade as our sales nose-dived or the profound despair Mary felt. It can also come from inspiration and love. Often it takes both time and patience to make the connection between your growing Extreme set of skills and an audience that is ready to receive them. But if you're starting from a place of sheer joyful love, chances are you will stick it out and make your "match" in the end.

Bozoma Saint John, known as Boz, describes the entire arc of her career, from freelance writing that didn't pan out to financial success that felt empty to an amazing marketing career that finally landed her at Apple, as following a path of love. Boz is one of the biggest personalities you could ever meet in your life—starting with her insanely beautiful bouquet of hair that you can see popping up above even the most crowded of rooms. So it's kind of shocking and amazing to me all at once that we both worked at PepsiCo at the exact same time, yet we never met. Yet when we were introduced years later, we instantly hit it off. I have followed her brilliant light ever since, so I was determined to ask her to chat with me about her Extreme journey.

When I meet super successful businesswomen, I always make the assumption that for them to get where they have gotten, they must be massively ambitious. But when I heard Boz's take on it, I felt, Wow! That's so damn refreshing! "For me," Boz told me, "it's not ambition, it's about the feeling. Doesn't matter about title or salary. It's not ambition for the role or even the power. It's about falling in love! Those other things come with finding the job or project that you love. People say 'Do what you love,' but for me it's 'How do I feel when I'm in the job, doing the job, how do I feel when I'm in conversation about the job?' If I feel good, if I want to brag about it, talk about it. Often I've left not because I hated the job I was in but because the new thing spoke to me in a way that made me want to run to it."

Boz was an English major, and after she finished college, she quit her job to see if she could make a career out of writing poetry and short stories. Within three months, she knew writing was not for her—too lonely! What she did love, she told me, was "running around the streets of New York City with my artist friends and my pop culture friends. There is a certain magic in culture that is not tangible—you can't predict it, you just have to watch for it. You keep your finger in the air and feel the winds change."

To support herself, she joined a company that was more like a recruiting company. It paid her bills and let her dig deeper into New York's art and pop culture scene. Soon she found she was good at it. "Funnily enough, even though I didn't have my heart in it, I was making what seemed like a ton of money. I had my own apartment, and the company felt that at twenty-five I was ready for a vice president title, ready to start running things. I didn't love it, but I didn't hate it. I could have kept going along, but I got a call from Spike Lee's company, Spike DDB. They wanted to tap into my art and pop culture stuff to help shape ideas for their clients such as Pepsi."

This new job would also mean "going back to the nothing money I was making before and the long crazy hours. There were people who told me, 'Don't do that! You have the promise of good money and promotions!' But I wanted to prove you could use the love of pop culture to drive business. At the time, my choice looked like the stupidest thing on the planet."

Boz worked on projects for Spike DDB before she was poached to work for PepsiCo full-time, participating in the traditional process of brand building for brands such as Pepsi and Mountain Dew. She didn't have an MBA degree, and she hadn't come into the organization with a class of peers, all hired at the same time and trained in the same ways. Her projects were successful, but she ran into trouble during performance reviews. "Managers would say I was 'not analytical enough' or that I 'didn't understand the business enough' to be promoted. I knew what I was doing was good and made sense, but I was not accepted for the whole me. I felt my contribution was not appreciated." When she received an offer from a fashion company, she took it.

Boz told me that today she sees that part of the reason she left was "narcissism." She didn't feel that she was liked and appreciated enough at PepsiCo, and it hurt her feelings. But she also sensed, to put it in Extreme terms, that her managers weren't letting her play her Specialist Game. She'd been hired to use her Extreme understanding of street culture to market PepsiCo products in new ways but had then been prevented from using the very skills that made her contributions so special. And so she had to leave.

Once again, she was warned she was making a mistake. "People said, 'Aw, man, you got in! You got into Pepsi in a way most people can't. People go to grad school to work for a company like that! They apply for internships, they get turned down. Why would you give all that up?' But I was like, why in the hell would I stay? I'm doing good work here, and if there's not the opportunity to do it to the full hundred percent capability, then I've got to go."

Boz had always loved fashion, and her new position was exactly what she'd wanted—on paper. She was now the head of marketing for the company, managing a big team. But loving fashion and having a feel for fashion as a business are two different things, and she found that her specialized knowledge of art and pop culture didn't give her the depth of understanding she needed to lead fashion marketing. Meanwhile, she heard from friends still at PepsiCo that management was becoming more open to new and more specialized approaches to marketing and consumer engagement. She thought, "Wait a minute! That's what I was trying to do!" And after many conversations with PepsiCo, she went back, now with her own team of music and entertainment specialists focusing on pop culture initiatives across the entire beverage portfolio.

Here's an example of the kind of success Boz was able to have when her team worked on the Mountain Dew brand. The consumer target for that brand had long been described in the company brief with words such as "aggressive," "male," and "exciting." That led to campaigns featuring images such as "testosterone-filled white men jumping off roofs." But at that time, what was happening in the culture to bring young men together was more likely to be coming from young men of color, for example hip-hop music, which had crossed over and become the most popular music form among young white men, too. Boz set out to express the identity of Mountain Dew—the "brand idea"—by targeting young men of color. "That came across in street ball, which is basketball with an edgy component to it, more aggressive, harder hitting, more exciting." Street ball was having a cultural moment—soon ESPN would create a reality show around it. This was the kind of cultural shift that Extreme Boz could feel on the wind. "You could see it coming eighteen months before. So we used that to drive the business, and by the way, it worked! We started communication with the young men in this way, diversifying the message, and that gave us an edge we didn't have before." Boz continued to rock it out at PepsiCo for a few years, and not surprisingly her efforts got noticed industry-wide. She's a trailblazer who's in it for the love of *her* game—which led her to run to the amazing opportunity of leading marketing for Beats Music when it launched its new music service. So now she's crushing it at Apple, playing her own multicultural marketing game in the way only Boz knows.

## EXTREME MOVES

An amazing range of accomplishments is possible when you Change the Game—like building a career around the interest you love most, restoring a faded brand to its former glory (and then some!), or re-building a life that doctors had essentially given up as lost. Why isn't everyone doing it? Too many potential Extremers get distracted by how others play their game or how they decide which risks are worth taking. Here are three ways to keep your focus.

### 1. Cultivate Extreme Independence

If you want to Change the Game, it won't be enough just to think outside the box and work incredibly hard. As important as creative thinking and hard work are, you will also need what psychologists call "field independence"—a willingness to do what you intuit is possible, what you love in your heart and feel in your gut—and to ignore the doubts and overcome the obstacles of those who don't feel it. When I think about my team at Gatorade, about Boz Saint John, and about Mary O'Hagan, what we all had in common was being told repeatedly by experts and people with power over us that we were wrong. Dead wrong. Wasting our time. Making a terrible mistake. And we had to insist that we were going to play our game, our way, anyway.

Do you have your own sense of Extreme independence, or do you need to develop it? Think about some of the most pivotal decisions in your life—a risky job offer that you desperately wanted or a school that you wanted to attend. Did you follow your own Extreme intuition despite advice that told you not to? By looking back on your own significant decisions, you'll start to see if this is a trait you need to develop to start changing the game around you.

### 2. Forget the Competition

It's not just that doubters and haters can stop you. Even other people's successes can steer you wrong. We all have moments of doubting ourselves and envying whomever seems to be in the lead. You may have found yourself thinking, *Why didn't I do that? Couldn't I be more like her? Couldn't our organization be more like theirs?*

But that question is wrong. Other people are always going to be better at being themselves than you are at imitating them. Other companies are always going to be better at what they do best than the companies around them. The extreme wins come not when you try to do what others do best but when you look for broader inspiration, then take your own specialties and use those to change how the game is played.

So stop worrying so much what your competition is doing. I don't mean to forget *being* competitive. Extremers are super competitive. Put Extremers on a treadmill, and they will inevitably steal a look at their neighbor's stats. (Admit it—you've done that!) But Extremers also know that the competition that matters most is the competition with themselves. They want to improve their own personal best. And the ultimate version of improving one's personal best is to insist on playing the entire game your way. As a leader, I love to take people's minds *off* the competition.

For that reason, I loved Michelle Greenwald's list in *Forbes* of examples where one industry has looked not to the competition but either to nature or to totally unrelated industries for inspiration in innovation. Japan's Shinkansen "bullet train" design didn't grow from competition with other train systems but from the aerodynamics of the hummingbirds' long, pointed beak. Velcro was inspired by thistle burrs. The design firm IDEO helped think how to make hospitals' nursing stations more efficient and effective by studying Formula One race car pit crews. And the founder of Pinterest reportedly came up with the idea for the digital platform based on the mounted insect collection he had as a kid. I will never look at Pinterest in the same way again!

In my personal life, too, I have tons of people whom I admire and turn to for new ideas and insights. But there is no competitor I want to be and no personal nemesis I'm trying to bring down. I've learned that if you try to keep up with the Joneses, you'll just wind up an imitation Jones. I'm not trying to be anyone except Extreme Me. So take a moment alone to ask yourself a candid question: When you rate your own performance based on how well you are doing at work, at school, or in life, are you competing with yourself or with others? There's only one way to go if you want to be Extreme!

### 3. Don't Wait for Proof

When you're out to reframe the game, by definition you're trying to do something that hasn't been done before. A whole new ball game. That means that it's uncertain, it can make you crazy, and there will be many days when you wish someone could come along and give you proof that it will work. The trouble is, though it may be possible to prove that a certain approach *won't* work—the numbers don't add up, the theory is faulty, the product is too expensive to make— there's really no way to prove it will work except by *making it work*. So don't wait around for proof. You have to trust your gut and make a decision. When I think about how I unleashed my own strength to stay the course all those months at Gatorade with no certainty of success, I credit my amazing career coach, Dr. Anthony Salemi, who gave me a great line when I was in my most scared and fearful place. He said, "Stop worrying about whether you've made the right decision with this transformation, Sarah—just make that damn decision *right*!" Lots of people told Boz Saint John not to leave a secure job to work for PepsiCo. Then lots of people told her not to leave PepsiCo. She had to make her decisions without any proof that she was right. Alli Webb got lots of advice about business, advice that may have saved her from making some fatal mistakes, but in the end she trusted her gut and her experience that there was an audience for what he had to sell. Will Dean of Tough Mudder was told that no one would pay to run a race that wasn't timed, but he went for it anyway.

Changing the Game is a voyage of exploration—the only proof you'll get is when you arrive at success. So go ahead, think about something going on in your life where you're struggling to make a decision. It might be a job you want to take, a girlfriend you really need to leave, or a house you want to buy, but you're scared of the commitment. Whatever it is, just get on and make a decision—and commit to yourself that you're going to make your decision right!

Every Extremer I spoke with for this book had to make a personal decision to go with their Extreme plan, and they did it without guarantees. But they did have a secret weapon I need to tell you more about, the skills of imagination leadership—and imagination followership! In the next chapter, "Calling All Extremers," I'll show you how to use those skills to bring out the extreme in others.

# NINE
# CALLING
# ALL
# EXTREMERS

I would never have met Liz Miersch if she hadn't been facing a career crisis within a bigger crisis. Not just her job but also her entire industry—in fact, the intersection of two industries—were being disrupted by powerful forces of change, and the game was too big for any one Extremer to change on her own.

Liz was a fitness editor for *Self* magazine. Her career combined her passions for writing, health, and fitness, so much so that she'd even become a certified personal trainer. But as she honed her writing and editing craft in the world of big magazine publishing, she realized that both journalism and the fitness industry were being profoundly disrupted by the emergence of digital media platforms and new fitness start-ups. She'd built her career as a bridge between two mountaintops; now it turned out that they were both active volcanoes. Ambitious Extremer that she is, she didn't see the down-sizing of magazines as a reason to question her career choices—just the opposite. She saw a big opportunity to take her well-honed journalistic knowledge and skills and become a change agent in the front lines of these burgeoning new fields.

Liz was quick to Get Out of Line when a chance meeting at an industry party led to her joining the luxury fitness company Equi-nox. Equinox operates gyms, a far cry from magazine publishing, but its CEO was thinking ahead of the game—he could see the landscape shifting, and therefore he wanted to develop editorial content to support the brand. Liz arrived with a very clear vision of what could be achieved.

In the world of fitness editorial content at that time, you found lots of pictures of shiny, muscled men and overly airbrushed women selling their five best tips for six-pack abs. Nothing inspiring, noth-ing thoughtful—just hard-core cheesiness. Liz recognized an un-tapped opportunity to create something new that would combine the company's scientific knowledge with her chic and inspiring style, thus allowing Equinox to become the trusted authority in the space. Just nine months after arriving, she launched "Q by Equi-nox," a blog featuring polished articles and engaging videos that ed-ucated and inspired readers to reach a higher level of performance.

What was particularly cool about her approach was the way she managed to enlist so many of her workmates to support her in this new endeavor. It would have been easy for her to sit alone in the cor-porate office, telling herself that her colleagues didn't understand publishing. But somehow she knew that taking the time to bring others along with her would pay off in the long term. She reached out to dozens of Equinox trainers and instructors and asked them to spread the word that she was looking for amazing stories for her blog. It was like a talent call to enlist them in her videos. Talk about firing them up—on every level, people were in clubs videoing themselves doing crazy moves in the hope they would get picked for the blog; they realized that the exposure from her video channel would bring them more clients and perhaps even some Internet fame. It wasn't long before the whole company was raving about her efforts.

Every story her team wrote and every video it released helped build a reputation for Q as an authority in the fitness/lifestyle space. (All those years you'd been told not to eat the egg yolk because it was bad for your cholesterol? The Q team researched the facts and blew that misunderstanding and so many more like it out of the water with provocative and entertaining articles that were grounded in science.) Her team had its first major breakthrough with a yoga video that was like nothing the industry had ever seen. Instead of the typical yoga participants in a studio, this was a highly sensual peek into the private hotel room of a top Equinox yoga instructor performing awe-inspiring yoga moves while her partner lay asleep in their bed. The video, called "The Contortionist," raced up the YouTube charts with millions of views, thanks to its provocative, sexy, and aspirational content. With this one video, Liz and her team had changed the expectations of what fitness content could look like. Its viral success proved they had tapped into something potentially huge—not to mention inspiring some hilarious spoof videos, including one showing an overweight man in uncomfortably tight spandex pants attempting to pull off some of those yoga moves himself.

But even with the success of the Q blog, Liz was still only one Extremer in a company that knew almost nothing about magazines and publishing. Her team was playing a strong specialist game within the company, but there was so much potential yet to be unlocked.

Liz had begun to see an even more audacious vision: that Q could become a stand-alone digital magazine, a true pioneer of this new form of journalism, supported by a superpassionate audience and highly curated brand partners as its advertisers. Yet every time she thought about it, she reminded herself that there was so much she didn't know about how to bring this badass vision to life. And that was where I entered the story, as the new president of Equinox, thinking about how I could possibly assist in making that happen, to help Liz bring out the Extreme in herself and in her team.

Now, wait up—hang on—hold it! I know what you're thinking. Wasn't I just leading the charge at Gatorade? How did we get here, at the cutting edge of luxury gyms and fitness? There is a short answer and a longer answer, the latter of which only became clear to me with time (and which I'll discuss in the next chapter), but they both come down to the thing I love best: bringing out the Extreme in the people around me. Let's start with the short version. In my years of career dreaming and planning, I can't say I'd thought about the fitness industry as a place where I might land. But when the opportunity presented itself to lead Equinox, the world's leading luxury fitness provider (and the place where, back in my twenties, I had spent many hours enjoying free Kiehl's shower products and indulging in free air-conditioning), it suddenly made perfect sense. In case you haven't noticed, I am a fitness junkie. Any twenty-something who skips nights out partying in New York City in order to be able to afford a fitness club membership clearly has a passion for fitness. But more important, as I got to know more about the company and its huge ambitions to grow, what I saw in front of me was an incredible manifestation of my Specialist Game—and one hell of an opportunity to learn to inspire not just a small team but a massive, high-energy workforce of more than ten thousand potential Extremers.

When I started at Equinox, I consciously said to myself that I wanted to elevate my leadership approach. At Gatorade, in the heat of the fire, I had always been needed, in person, to handle a lot of the tough stuff because the vision for change had very visibly started with me providing the bold "north star" for the rest of my teammates. But Equinox was already a successful business. This wasn't a turnaround situation like the one I had faced at Gatorade—it was quite the opposite. Here was my chance to go Extreme in a company that was already extremely successful and already loaded with an impressive group of individual Extremers. It presented me with an exciting challenge: to build a bigger vision out of the promising ideas the team already had.

Liz's hunch about a new kind of publication was just one example. Another example came from David Harris, a twenty-five-year company veteran who was the vice president of personal training. David was exploring the idea that fitness isn't just exercise; it's far more holistic than that. He knew, through his own exploration and meetings with many of the leading scientists in the space, that to achieve high-performance fitness, we require not just movement and exercise but a focus on nutrition and what he called regeneration (sleep and recovery). I just loved that approach. To think that getting better at sleeping is just as important to my overall fitness as doing an extra hour of exercise—who's not up for that?

It didn't take me long to realize that David's ideas, when mashed together with what Liz had started with the blog, might represent the beginning of a super game-changing vision of a gym—not just as a place to go for your hour-long workout, not even as just a source of information about health in all its aspects, but as a digital lifestyle partner, "always on," available to inform, accompany, and celebrate you in a highly personalized way as you pursue your health and fitness goals, any time of day or night. Extremers such as Liz, David, and others had brought their own visions to the company, and their visions inspired my imagination, so that I could see a much bigger, bolder, more powerful whole. In this new leadership role, my job would be to figure out how to leverage all of those Extremers' Specialist Games into a broader vision that would allow us to change the playing field. In other words, my leadership challenge would be to imagine how to make all of these great ideas even bigger, bolder, and more badass.

Instead of trying to copy what others were doing with new technologies such as Fitbits, Jawbones, nutrition-tracking apps, and fitness trackers such as Strava, we could leverage our Specialist Game, drawing on all of our great knowledge and experiences, to create an entirely new game. Sure, in order to realize that vision we'd need to invest in new capabilities such as a world-class technology platform to personalize holistic fitness recommendations for our members, but the major pieces of the puzzle already existed inside our company, thanks to the wonderfully bold individual visions of our leaders.

So when it came to Liz and the many chats we would have in my office about her team, her successes, and her giant dreams for Q's future, I realized that it was a huge opportunity to help her go as big as or even bigger than she was thinking. Why did Q have to just be a brand content blog that was forever playing number two to its parent brand, Equinox? What if Q could be evolved into a stand-alone editorial business with its own name—significantly increasing the size of the team and the breadth and depth of the content and bringing in real paying advertisers to make it a self-funding, revenue-generating powerhouse of its own?

Liz looked me square in the eyes and told me it could be done.

She believed with as much conviction as anyone I have ever seen that that "white space" was ripe for the taking. But she also told me about her questions and her fears. Up until then, she had been an Extreme editorial talent, not so much a holistic business leader. She didn't know how to write a business plan, let alone pull a financial model together. How on earth could she turn this little blog into a business when she'd never performed half the roles that were required to make it happen?

Booooom! That's exactly what I was there for: to support her, guide her, and help her find the ultimate team of Extremers to complement her brilliant skills and go on the adventure together. I still get wee chills when I think about the day Furthermore launched and the excitement we all felt as the vision become reality. Within its first six months in business, the team beat its revenue targets. For me, it was particularly rewarding to see how that Extreme form of leadership could empower others and help take the company's game to a new level. That is what I call imagination leadership.

So far I have focused mainly on what it takes for individuals to develop their Extreme Selves. But take another look at the stories I've shared with you. Extreme Me could never have done it alone. Every step along the way, I have benefited from others' having the imagination to recognize my potential and the wisdom and experience to help me reach it. Even though I was rough around the edges—and dropping a few too many F-bombs—they stuck by me and gave me the chance to prove myself. They pushed me, they prodded me, and they supported my dreams, even when those dreams weren't perfectly clear or seemed too risky. That takes imagination. That takes leadership. Extremers put the two together.

Extremers can't succeed without leaders who recognize the value of their unique specialties and who tolerate, even encourage, them to Get Out of Line and sometimes fail. Without imagination leadership, ideas tend to get edited, drive tends to get dialed down, and potential gets zapped. It takes a symbiotic collaboration between leader and follower, each helping the other, to really go Extreme.

It comes down to this: Some people go to work to do what they're told. Some understand that the company has a vision that they're expected to share and to follow. But there's a third choice, the Extreme choice, which is to go to work and actively imagine how your company could achieve its vision and how you could personally contribute to it, beyond even what your supervisors or job description might say you should do. And if you're in the position of leading others, the challenge is to imagine how to unleash their talents to elevate the vision to a new level.

Whether you are a leader or a follower, the key ingredient is imagination. Too often, that's what's lacking. Start-up founders constantly ask for meetings with me, then turn out to have only copycat ideas: the Uber of group fitness; the Lululemon of kids' wear. That's not imagination leadership, that's just copying what's already there. If you really want to play the Extreme Game, you need to use your specialist knowledge to imagine solutions to people's unmet needs. You need to let your imagination take you as far as it can, and then you need to surround yourself with people who will push you to stretch a little bit farther still. That's how the rules of the game get rewritten, that's how big change happens, that's how Extremers do it.

## THE FOLLOWER BECOMES A LEADER

When I talk about using imagination leadership to bring out the Extreme in others, I don't mean something that's limited to people in formal leadership roles. Sometimes all it takes to exercise imagination leadership is a tweet. I was contacted on Twitter by some guy named David Burstein who said he'd read about my Gatorade experience in *Fast Company*. He was interested in the way I had included young people on my team. Now, plenty of people randomly tweet me, asking me for jobs, advice, mentoring, and favors with absolutely no relevance or reason. And I can assure you, in the stream of communications in a given day, the likelihood that I'll respond is basically zero. So what made David different? How did he manage to get past my Twitter bullshit meter?

First, he engaged me with an incredibly relevant and insightful answer to a question I had posed about the new workforce. Then, when I responded, he continued the conversation and made me laugh. The guy was smart, with a great sense of humor, and he wasn't just randomly asking me for something. Of course, I googled him and learned that he'd written a book about Millennials (a topic that was fast becoming a fascination for me). So when he asked if he could take me to lunch, I was totally interested to meet him.

At lunch, he listened to my story and told me his. Then he described his initiative called Run for America, designed to get next-generation leaders to run for political office, because right now many talented people are not choosing to serve their country. (They're trying to become Internet millionaires instead.) His idea was that they can do both, and he captured my imagination with his leadership; he was reminding me that our country was founded on a vision, and he had imagined his own way to contribute to it. Soon I realized that he was doing everything I have just described. He had a bold vision and a practical plan, and he'd contacted me as part of his effort to gather the sort of people who would be inspired by his vision to help him spread the word. He was very specific about the ways I could help him, such as providing introductions to some of the high-profile individuals in my network, giving him advice on his strategic plans, and introducing him to marketing agencies. So even though I didn't understand all the technical details (I am not a political expert, after all), I was able to build on his vision with ideas from my areas of expertise.

When I asked him to return the favor and help me with some strategic planning for the Women's Sports Foundation—not exactly his thing—he signed up immediately and was an awesome help. Not only did he come to our meeting with incredible insights about our Millennial consumers, but before he arrived he spent an entire evening watching documentaries on Billie Jean King, to get himself up to speed on the organization's founder and heritage. He showed up brimming with passion for our cause.

Eighteen months after we met, he already had some major momentum behind his initiative because he'd enlisted a very strong imagination army of bigwigs from politics and the private sector to join with him. It made no difference that I was the one with the formal leadership title global president of Gatorade and he was some stranger tweeting to ask a favor. He showed me he was an imagination leader who knew how to bring out the Extreme in me.

## THE MOST SUCCESS YOU COULD EVER ACHIEVE

It may sound as if I'm putting the focus on Extreme followers and what they need, but it is through selfless leadership that leaders get what they want most. All of us discover at some point that no matter how much power you acquire, and no matter how fully you realize Extreme You, in the end you're still only one Extremer. Your dreams will always be greater than what you can achieve on your own. The limit on your success is ultimately not something in you; it's how effectively you can bring out the Extreme in others.

That realization came to Beto Pérez and Alberto Perlman, two of the founders of the Zumba dance fitness program whom we met in chapter 6, when the company's growth started to take off. Beto, the Colombian dancer and choreographer who had created the Zumba classes, was responsible for training all of their instructors. He told me, "I was training people every weekend, traveling to thirty countries a year. I'd killed myself working very hard all my life. I was so tired. Then Alberto tells me one day, 'Beto, it's too much for you. We need other master teachers. We have to do it in order to break out and expand.'" But Beto couldn't imagine that any other master teacher would give as much as he gave. "I said, 'What? Are you crazy? You think it's so easy?' I thought that it was going to be hard to find people with the right mix of talent, heart, and humility."

Beto was afraid the new master teachers would not be loyal to the company. He worried that they would not respect him as a leader or uphold the values of Extreme Zumba. And he was partly right. Some of the new master teachers acted like divas and made demands on the company that Beto had never made. Some quit and became competitors, stealing his methods and trying to create imitation Zumbas.

Around the same time they were struggling to hire master teachers to teach their instructors, the company hit a similar difficulty finding senior executives who were the right fit. In four years, it hired eight senior executives and had to let four go. Those were highly qualified hires who were willing to work hard, yet the founders were not able to bring out Extreme Zumba in them. Meanwhile, there was an employee from the early days who had started at a very junior level and been promoted, then promoted again, to the point that she was now running marketing. She had succeeded where others in senior management with far more impressive résumés had failed.

As Alberto and Beto observed the master teachers and the executives who made a good fit with the company, they came to see a pattern. Beto explained, "Being a Zumba teacher or master teacher is not always easy—their lives are hard, they travel all over, they have to give their best all day long, performing all the time. The ones who are in it for the money never succeed. The ones who succeed are the ones who care about their students, who truly care about people." The early master teachers who had been disloyal, trying to steal the Zumba method and make a quick profit, had little success. It was those who put the students first who went on to have great success becoming important leaders in the instructor community. The company now has one hundred fifty amazing master trainers who have trained a huge army of instructors that reach fifteen million people a week.

Alberto, the CEO, told me that he had never believed in the idea of "corporate culture," but with those developments he had been forced to take a second look. "I didn't understand why culture is important," he said. "Some people in business talk about culture, culture, culture, but what does that mean? A Ping-Pong table in the office? Free ice cream for everyone? I thought it was just business-book BS. Now I realized that people can be talented, but if they don't fit the culture, they can never make it in your company. It made me realize that it didn't matter if we hired the most amazing CMO on paper with a ton of experience, because if that person didn't care about our instructors, our Zumba community, and our brand as much as we do, it wouldn't work."

The two founders shifted their approach to hiring, now looking to build a team of Extremers who would share the company's vision, in which "everything is seen through the lens of Zumba's purpose: Does it deliver joy and happiness? Does it make our instructors more successful?" To support their team, they set out to model the Zumba approach in their own everyday behavior. When a teacher traveled to visit the Zumba headquarters in Florida, Alberto made it a point to welcome him or her and give a tour of the office. He told me, "I stop what I'm doing and ask the teacher what we could do better to change more lives." Some of his employees at Zumba headquarters have objected—why is he interrupting a meeting?—but he wants to show that the company puts its teachers first, just as it wants its teachers to put their students first. "You have to act like you want *them* to act," he told me.

And the result? Beto is now fully satisfied that he can trust the master teachers and executives with the approach he's given his life to building. "I feel so happy," he says. He has found the success and happiness that come from bringing out the Extreme in others.

In the end, the important thing is not leaders making use of followers or followers making use of leaders. It's symbiosis, with both sides benefiting. The need to shift perspective was recognized as far back as the 1980s, when Peter F. Drucker argued, "The center of gravity in employment is moving fast from manual and clerical workers to knowledge workers who resist the command-and-control model that business took from the military 100 years ago. Economics also dictates change, especially the need for large businesses to innovate and to be entrepreneurs. But above all, information technology demands the shift." With innovation more urgent all the time and information flowing so freely, Extreme leaders depend on their Extreme followers to handle more information more independently and use their own imaginations to judge and make use of that information collaboratively as it comes in.

To me, being a leader of even a large global business is less like commanding an army than putting together a Tough Mudder team. A Tough Mudder course is not the kind of thing you can do alone. When I as leader decided to form my first team, I needed to smack talk, cajole, and basically steamroll friends and colleagues to come get covered in mud and get electrocuted with me. And in every instance the people I was pushing (sometimes against their will!) to be my followers entered the experience with variations of complete dread—and came out the other side signing up to be on the next team I put together because it was so much fun. But fun for whom? All of us! I simply couldn't have done it without that crazy band of misfits, and I'm guessing they'd never have signed up for such an experience without my pushing them. A leader who sets a vision needs followers who get the vision, an imagination army willing to step up and to "vote" for the leader's vision with their enthusiasm, energy, loyalty, creativity, persistence—to give their all, with the support and protection of the leader. One can't succeed without the other.

## EXTREME MUTUAL SUPPORT

It's not just leaders and followers who can bring out the Extreme in one another. Some of the most powerful imagination leadership is the kind that goes back and forth between equal partners who push, inspire, and hold each other accountable to achieve their greatest ambitions. In my own career, I think of my closest friends, many of whom I've known since high school, who provide a unique and important viewpoint when I am making big life decisions. My dear and cherished bestie, Randa Abbasi, has been pushing and inspiring me since we were nine years old. Our lives and careers could not be more different. Randa is the world's most Extreme occupational therapist, bringing her outrageously big and warm personality to inspire people to find strength and push through some of the toughest moments of their lives. She has been there for every big moment of my life and career—the highest of the highs and the crashing, embarrassing lows—she's traveled the world to be at my side whenever I have needed her. And because of that and her own extreme life experiences, she is able to bring a whole new kind of advice to me when I am thinking things through. And then there is my wonderful, inspiring "co-driver," as I used to call her: Sam Perkins. Sam was the most special, free-spirited hippie-ish bundle of love and care—completely different from hard-charging, driven Extreme Me. But it was our differences that drew us together, and I grew more from her friendship than I even realized was possible at the time. She taught me that it's much more fulfilling to be a human "being" than a human "doing." Her life was cut woefully short, but somehow she understood the universe in her thirty-three years much more clearly than most people twice her age. I can always find answers when I am chewing things over by asking "What would Sammy say?"

As well as my close friends, I've had many mentors. I seem to pick them up in every job and never let them go: from Norm and Tony, who took me under their wing all those years ago at Air New Zealand and still patiently give me the time on the phone when I am noodling over a big career or business decision, to Massimo from Gatorade and Scott and Larry from Equinox. They are the great wise ones who've faced the challenges I am taking on before, who can give me the courage to leap when I need it the most or tell me the honest truth when I am not playing at my best.

Going even deeper, I think of my siblings, who in my mind are like a fantastic team that I am constantly wanting to live up to. When I was a kid, so much of my drive came from a desire to make my family proud of me. My oldest sister, Anna, recalls that as kids we were all told, "Just you remember when you go out of this house you are representing the whole family, so don't let the side down!"

At about the age of twelve, I stole some change out of my mum's wallet and went to play Space Invaders at the video parlor with a girl that mum had warned me not to hang out with. When she found out, she told me I had let the side down and broken her trust and that it would take me a long time to rebuild it. Knife in the *heart*! Wow, she knew how to get into my conscience. After that I worked my ass off to help around the house and get my mother's trust back because I didn't want to ever feel that kind of guilt again. With Mum, "letting the side down" was more about doing the right thing and not getting into trouble, while with Dad it had more to do with working hard and applying yourself properly. At the end of each school term when we got our school report, we would be called into my dad's small home office, where he would review our grades and the effort we were putting in. If there were comments in your report that suggested you were slacking, he'd give you an earful about it, reminding you not to squander opportunities. I suppose every family has its own ways of talking about poor behavior and weak effort; putting it in terms of the family being a team created a sense of shared pride among us. We knew that we were part of a special family, the kind of family that was known for creating a lot of fun for those close to us, and that each of us was lucky to be part of "the side." That left me with a real sense of duty, of wanting to live up to the standards of that special side that I was a part of.

Even when I have made solo moves, even when I have been at my most badass, I've known that all those supporters were there listening, advising, and caring. And likewise, when I have returned the favor and helped them work through their challenges and problems, it has been incredibly eye-opening for me. At times they have helped bring out the Extreme in me; at times I've done my best to do the same for them.

When it comes to Extreme mutual support, the person who has been paramount for me is Liam. I've built my career on a willingness to make whatever Extreme Moves were necessary to succeed at work, and I was lucky enough to find a life partner who helps me do that. From our first days together, when I was in despair over my firing from Virgin Megastores, to my crisis after the birth of Gabby, when Gatorade seemed to be going down the tubes and it was too much to try to take care of my new baby, my team at work, and the rest of my family, Liam was there to support me emotionally, to believe in me, and to patiently put up with me for the hours, days, and months that it might take me to go round in circles figuring out how to tackle my greatest challenges. It's friggin' hard to be married to an Extremer like me—someone who is constantly drawn to the gnarliest challenges. But Liam's tireless strength has unquestionably been the secret ingredient that has enabled us to navigate it all as a family.

Before we were even married, Liam and I realized that I was the one best suited to taking the lead on career and he was best suited to be what we call lead parent, the first port of call for all things to do with the family. From organizing every detail of the kids' annual schedules, to volunteering and participating in the school community, to feeding, clothing, and watering the kids, to being the first responder whenever issues come up, Liam has taken the lead. By taking that role, he has brought out the Extreme in me, allowing me to focus on building an Extreme career, and I have made it possible for him to be involved as a father in a way our own fathers could never have dreamed. He has blogged about his experiences in the Huffington Post:

> *I'm forging a new path, one that is on the male extremes, but I never felt my choices were particularly radical. They were logical. Sarah was clearly more career-oriented than me. So it made sense personally and financially that we would end up in the roles we have. I would credit my parents for equipping me to slip into the role of lead parent without undergoing a crisis of masculinity. My mother was a feminist and my father supported her when she went into business after we children left home. He learned to clean and cook. But it wasn't until my mother's eightieth birthday that I realized she was probably equally proud to have had two sons who stayed at home while their wives pursued their careers as she was to have three daughters out in the world.*

I'm profoundly aware of the hard work and sacrifices that Liam has made for our family, so I wake up each day determined to reach the best of my potential so Liam and the kids can benefit. Each of us has been the imagination leader who brings out the Extreme in the other.

In recent years, Liam and I have gotten to know Anne-Marie Slaughter and her husband, Andrew Moravscik, who is the lead parent for their family. Anne-Marie has written a book, *Unfinished*

*Business: Women Men Work Family*, arguing that for couples and families to thrive, we must all value the work of caregiving as much as we do conventional work. She suggests it is time to "stop talking about work-life balance and start talking about discrimination against care and caregiving." Or, to put that in Extreme terms, if we are going to enable all family members to be their Extreme Selves, we must together provide the kind of support and care that we all need. That will require society to value caregiving a whole lot more.

## EXTREME MOVES

We have entered the greatest era of change and innovation that our world has ever known, and if we as individuals, companies, and even countries are to remain competitive, we must play to our highest potential. I believe it's our duty to learn to exercise imagination leadership to unleash Extremeness everywhere. Every Extremer will play both roles—leader and follower—many times in his or her career. I still have experiences every day where I play both roles and, no matter which, I take the same approach.

### 1. Imagine the Future

Extreme leadership starts with imagining something great or noble or fun or necessary that could be in the world—but isn't yet. It might be that you are the leader of a huge organization needing to see a new and bigger mountain to climb or are someone within a great team who has to imagine better ways of getting things done. Either way it's about having a vision, yes—but how exactly can you do that? By using your imagination. I remember as a kid that my older siblings enjoyed teasing me for the fact that I had an imaginary friend called Sally. The entire family knew who she was and even when her father was on business trips. When I saw the same behavior in my own children, I got so fired up that they were starting to cultivate their own imaginations—the magical tool that I now see has led me to so many wonderful places.

To imagine the future, you must start by getting super-deep into the knowledge of whatever you're working on or concerned about. Then look all around you for ideas, cultural shifts, new break-throughs or technologies that might spark your thinking. When you bring the two together, you'll be amazed how vividly you will start to imagine how you would wish things could be and how you might get there. Make sure you take the time to imagine a clear destination. Once you can see the vision in your own mind, talk about it clearly and with passion to enlist other people's imaginations to share the vision and join in the journey.

### 2. Step Up and Stand Out

No matter whether you are in the leader role or the follower role, be the one who pursues the vision. If you aren't the leader—and much of the time, you won't be—then there is always an opportunity to be what Derek Sivers has called a "first follower," the one who steps up for a visionary leader with the courage to take practical steps. If you're the leader, don't be afraid to start small—you don't need to get everyone on board right away, because if you have a big success with even a small group of Extremers, the whole culture will shift behind them as others seek to be part of their Extreme. Every great story of leadership starts with one follower and then blossoms into a small group and then a movement. Your early followers are easy to spot—grab them and support and champion them because their passion will be infectious.

If you're the follower, remember that the way to become a leader is by taking the initiative without being asked. Don't wait to be told what to do. You may get a flimsy medal (or a measly raise) just for showing up, but promotions, new opportunities, and breakthrough ideas don't come from running in place.

In contrast, Extremers are always looking to take the initiative. They might offer to write up the notes of a meeting, pitch in to help the field team with operations during a snowstorm, or put together meetings, plans, or networks that can benefit the team—or just go ahead and do what needs to be done faster than anyone else. And they do it because they share in the vision, they see where the group is trying to go, and they want the team to get one step ahead. Every day, they are looking to collaborate with their team, seeing that there is a better way or a potential opportunity. But let me be clear: these kinds of Extremers are not taking the initiative with the intent of getting noticed or promoted, and they certainly don't ask to be paid more in order to put more time or effort in. They're just doing it because it's the right thing to do for the team. I am the poster child for knowing that all the extra effort and initiative are rewarded in the end because of the depth of experience you get along the way.

### 3. Have No Fear

The opposite of Bringing Out the Extreme in others is making them afraid. All it takes is for someone to start implying that risk taking will be punished, that the boss is running out of patience, or that old procedures must be followed to the letter, and the collaboration between imagination leaders and followers starts to fall apart. This happens in corporations the world over, and the entire place seizes up with fear. The most effective leaders I've known combat that fear with curiosity, always looking to explore unknown territory and reward people for being innovative. Of course, by "leaders" I mean any Extremer with a vision he or she is pursuing, no matter what his or her official role might be.

### 4. Push Hard; Support Even Harder

When you become the leader and you're trying to bring out the Extreme in others, your most important role is as mentor and supporter. You've picked them for their extreme skills and expertise, now let them use it. Don't edit them down, drive them away, or try to tell them how to do their jobs. Once your team of Extremers gets to work and they're headed in a productive direction, let them play their own Specialist Game and follow where it takes them. It's truly the most rewarding feeling in the world to see other people take an idea and blow it out farther and better than you ever could.

But it's not about passively waiting for the team to deliver. Your role is to hold them to the highest standards of performance while supporting their ideas. You have to do two very different things for the people working with you at the same time: be clear about your vision and what you expect from them, but at the same time be just as clear that you will support their approach to getting it done—no matter how novel and unfamiliar to you it may be—and protect them long enough for them to succeed. It's not a choice between being tough versus being nurturing. Extremers need to do both.

When I was researching this book, I had the chance to discuss leadership with the psychologist Angela Lee Duckworth, whom we met in chapter 2. Angela has made a career studying the "grit" that enables people to succeed. I asked her about how she applies her ideas about fostering grit to her own team of scientific researchers. She told me, "For people who work for me, I am relentlessly demanding. They know that if they come to work for me, their work will never be good enough. There's no draft of a scientific paper they could write that would make me respond, 'Great—we're done!' They are going to get reams of feedback from me about how we could do better, so we are all continuously improving. But also, when you come to work for me, it's like now you're in my family. I will do anything for you. If you need me at two in the morning, call. If you need forty letters of recommendation, I'll send them. I'll introduce you to anyone I know. It's this combination of letting people know you are a demanding leader but you're a supportive leader."

### 5. Pick the Best Pit Crew You Can Find

Here is the most important piece of advice I give to people just starting out in their careers: be sure you find really strong partners and mentors who will handle the things you can't and who will push you and tell you both the good *and* the bad. You need to hear the honest truth about what you could be doing better and to feel that your mentors believe you can succeed—and will do anything to support you along the way. Whether it's friends, family, a life partner, or a mentor, Extremers need at least a few extra close relationships with folks who will say those things, bad and good, that others won't. That's an Extreme supporter.

So much has been written about what to do after failure, but what to do after you succeed? At first, of course, the answer's easy: Celebrate with your mates! Enjoy the big win! But after that . . . what next? In the final chapter, we'll explore what to do when your imagination leadership succeeds, victory is yours—and then the Extremer Cycle begins all over again.

# TEN
# BREAK YOURSELF TO MAKE YOURSELF

I t's taken me years to understand fully that great old Nike slogan from many moons ago: "There is no finish line." We tend to set our sights on goals and imagine that once we reach them, once we make it to the top of the mountain, we're going to be satisfied that we've "made it." But once an Extremer, always an Extremer. Reaching the summit only opens your eyes to the many wonderful new mountains that you can now see—and feel compelled to climb. That was what happened to me at Gatorade. We had that peak experience of Bringing Out the Extreme in one another and Changing the Game, and that success showed me other mountain ranges on the horizon with their own unique views. I could have stayed comfortably on the Gatorade summit forever, I suppose, but as I wanted more, I found that I'd need to start over.

I've been amazed at how many of the people I admire most, people with truly awesome success stories, have experiences like that in their pasts. One of the people I was most psyched to interview for this book was Condoleezza Rice, the former secretary of state. I had the extraordinary good fortune to meet her when we were both speakers at a conference on opportunities for women in sports. Condi was the keynote speaker kicking off the day, and to speak on a panel after her was humbling, to say the least. She stopped me in my tracks with her powerful words. The incredible stories she told of her own life experiences coupled with her challenging and empowering messages for young people made me realize that she was an ultimate Extremer and I'd just have to figure out a way to include her in this book.

Condi's path to her epic career in politics took a dramatic shift in college, and it required her to break herself in a profound and painful way. She hadn't gone to college with any intention of political service. In fact, she was and still is a highly accomplished classical pianist. She told me, "I was a piano major until my junior year of college, when I realized I was never going to be talented enough to play Carnegie Hall—and thus I decided I needed to find a new major. Luckily enough, I wandered into a class on Soviet affairs taught by Josef Korbel [the father of Madeleine Albright, the first woman to serve as secretary of state], and I was hooked. My passion for the USSR and international policy only grew from there as I learned more and more about the world outside of the United States. I always tell people: if you want to know the road to being secretary of state, it's that you start out as a failed piano major."

That last line just blew me away, because of course today she's known around the globe. But imagine how she felt during that semester in school, the one when she came to feel that she wasn't good enough—would never be good enough—to achieve the dreams that had led her to major in piano. Accomplished as she was, she considered herself a failure in terms of her own aspirations. She could never play Carnegie Hall.

Now try to imagine being that discouraged young ex–piano major with no plan, hanging out with her music major friends who were still working toward their dreams. I'm sure that later, working hard to catch up with the other students of her new love, international policy, she reached the point that all that studying "hurt so good." But to begin, I have to think, she just hurt. She'd given up one dream and was going to start over as—what? She didn't know. She was just a "failed piano major," as she put it, choosing to acknowledge the brutal facts, wandering into different classrooms with no clear way forward.

That's the moment of breaking yourself. The moment when you are already successful in one realm—after all, Condi was an incredibly accomplished musician by anyone's standards—but then you look ahead and see where you're going—or, the real point, you see *the place you're never going to reach*—and you make a choice. You might decide you're content with the path ahead, even though it's less than you dreamed. Maybe you've had enough of new mountains to climb and greater successes ahead. But if not, if there is more Extreme You to develop, it's time to step off the bus. Time to give up the degree of success you've had until then and instead get really, *really* uncomfortable, because that's the only way to drive new growth. That's the ultimate act of personal imagination leadership: when you decide that you can't settle for what you see up ahead and so you set a new vision. Then you get to work inspiring yourself to go for it, through all the confusion, pain, and uncertainty of remaking yourself anew.


## NEW POTENTIAL

For almost twenty years, five or six mornings a week, I started the day with a five-mile run. I know that to some people that sounds impressive. "She's so Extreme, she runs five miles every day!" But for me, after so many years, it felt familiar, comforting in its way, but no longer a challenge. No longer Extreme. Repeating that old workout gave me no chance to make a difference that I could feel in my muscles or see in my personal-best times. All that running was just running in place.

When I started as president of Equinox, I decided that to understand what the company stood for and what it offered its members, I would use my own gym membership to let Equinox guide my fitness routines. I started working with an awesome personal trainer named Kevin Hernandez at the club near my home. I went into our first session feeling cocky about my morning runs and my impressive fitness level, but after the mortifying experience of that horrible weight-to-fat-ratio machine (*you* imagine being weighed by one of your coworkers!) and the famous "functional movement screen" where I scored 2 out of 3, my humility meter kicked into high gear and I was ready to listen. Kevin helped me understand what running could and couldn't do for me: although it had made my thighs very strong, my hamstrings were pitifully weak, and I was a complete wimp when it came to upper body strength. He suggested I drop a couple of runs a week and begin functional movement training instead—break my old habits to make room for new ones.

For the first month, it was serious pain training. I can remember doing foam rolling for the first time; it feels like some medieval form of torture when you're not used to it. Even the warm-ups for my training sessions were killers. I'd be doing all sorts of work with those evil little rubber bands around my legs, then go hobbling home at night and wake up with major muscle soreness.

Next I added Pilates to my routine, working with a fantastic instructor, Cheryl Tiles. If you've ever poked your head into a Pilates Reformer studio, you'll know that the machines look like bizarre torture racks, so it's intimidating, to say the least. And let me confirm for you: even though the session itself feels amazing, so much stretching and strengthening, you discover the teeniest micromuscles you never even knew existed, and they seem to hurt even more than the muscles you knew about already.

I also learned new methods of regeneration, such as better stretching, and much more consistent sleep practices, and I took major steps toward improving my nutrition. I decided to quit my twenty-year diet cola habit cold turkey (the headaches, the headaches!) as well as remove the stashes of candy from the drawers in my desk at work. My goal was to do for my body what I hoped to do for my career. In time I felt a giant difference, with heaps more energy to get me through the day. Though I weighed the same as I had back at Gatorade, my body fat was down by 3 percent. What's more, I made it across an entire set of monkey bars for the first time since I was a child. This new training reminded me that when you live Extreme You, there is *always* more potential to be released.

My experience at the gym has been borne out by research on improving cognitive ability. It turns out that the brain will improve with training, but it needs a serious challenge. Here's an example. The scientist Richard Haier asked study participants who had never played Tetris before to train on the game for several weeks. The subjects experienced an increase in cortical activity, glucose use, and cortical thickness—meaning more neural connections, or more new expertise. Once they reached mastery, however, they experienced a *decline* in cortical thickness and activity; their brains became more efficient, and cognitive energy was allocated elsewhere. Training worked, but only as long as there was a new, challenging task.

Summarizing his research on the *Scientific American* blog, Andrea Kuszewski explained, "Efficiency is *not* your friend when it comes to cognitive growth. In order to keep your brain making new connections and keeping them active, you need to keep moving on to another challenging activity *as soon as you reach the point of mastery* in the one you are engaging in. You want to be in a constant state of slight discomfort, struggling to barely achieve whatever it is you are trying to do." Growth starts, whether at the gym or in your career, whether physical or mental, with a willingness to break yourself down, try in new ways, and hurt so good again—to remake yourself even better.

## HOW TO FEEL RICH

Let me just say that it takes guts. Not just everyday courage—I'm talking giant cojones and deep resilience. I saw this in my great friend Amrita Sen. I met her because she was married to one of my closest colleagues from the days of my Virgin Megastores disaster and we'd developed a friendship beyond the walls of the office. Since the first day I'd met Amrita, I'd thought, *Wow, I want to be her.* She had a ridiculous intellect and creativity, combined with a no-bullshit, get-things-done approach. You might think that after my "Virgin suicide," all my Virgin Megastores colleagues would have been only too happy to see the back of me, but great friends are the ones who stick with you despite your royal fuckups. She and her husband, Ravi, never missed an opportunity to reach out and support me through my darkest unemployed days. So it was awesome for me as a friend to watch her take her career in a whole new direction—and reach unexpected success later in life.

Amrita's dream, all the way back to early childhood, was to use her natural gifts as a singer, musician, and visual artist. By the age of nine, growing up in New Jersey, she was already doing remarkable drawings and paintings, as well as studying Indian music on visits to Calcutta, where many of her relatives were singers. Her aunt was a celebrated performer in the classical Indian tradition. Amrita also studied Western classical singing, especially opera, making for a unique combination. She performed Bollywood songs at festivals and conferences and even made records. "I knew as a child I was a really good singer," she told me, "able to do things with my voice, naturally, that other people couldn't do. But I didn't know what that meant in terms of how you build a career. And I didn't have anyone in my family who knew the ins and out of the music business in America or anything about the music business for that matter."

What she had, instead, in her immigrant childhood in New Jersey, were two motivating factors: First, she grew up during the time of the "dot buster" movement, when Indian immigrants were targeted and bullied, often with extreme violence. Second, she had a father who was very focused on her academic achievements. "Now that I think about it, thankfully for me, I had a dad who was an Asian 'tiger mom' times one hundred. This allowed me to ignore the bullying that was going on in school and focus on making myself a better person. Otherwise, I would not have gotten through it as a young girl." Her parents pushed her to succeed academically, and even her music and art became an occasion to demonstrate mastery and avoid mistakes. "My singing, drawing, and everything I was doing became so much about perfection, about technical knowledge and details, that it became a job—technically remarkable but now, looking back, not creatively inspired."

By the time she got to college, she felt that her "most important mission was to make a lot of money. I had the dot buster thing in my mind and in my heart, and I always grew up with the fear that I would be sent back to India, as absurd as that sounds. I thought, if I make a lot of money, at least I don't have to live in NJ." She graduated with a bachelor of science in finance from the Wharton School, and after working for the investment firm Goldman Sachs and then in the office of the CEO at Columbia/Hospital Corporation of America, she applied to Harvard Business School. "I didn't really know why I wanted to go back to business school, particularly after Wharton, but my dad always wanted me to go to Harvard, and more than anything, I wanted to make my dad happy."

After Harvard, though, she decided to stop working in finance. "Money was always important to me, but I had to figure out a way to bridge my creative skills with my business background."

Ravi had a career opportunity working in the entertainment industry in Los Angeles, and Amrita decided that if she could not make art, she could at least work for others who did. In time she began to work for an agency that represented both visual artists and singers, including Beyoncé and Gwen Stefani. Then she went out on her own as a branding agent for stars such as 50 Cent and LL Cool J. Professionally she was a huge success, working with some of the top names in the business. Personally, though, working for others who were able to build the kind of creative, successful life she had given up, she was miserable.

"How did it feel to work so close to these artists? Horrible. Like being in jail for ten years." She focused on making her clients successful and on starting a family, but once her two kids got a little older, she felt "pretty awful, like dead almost. I couldn't get out of bed. I was sleeping eighteen, twenty hours a day—for months. My husband said, 'What the heck?' I knew if I continued I was going to affect my family and my kids."

Amrita found a psychiatrist who helped her begin to revive the artistic life she had abandoned. "He helped me unlock more creativity. In our house we had a side closet that was empty, and that's where I kept my harmonium. I started singing again and writing songs. I was practicing two hours a day in that closet. Ravi would come in and ask, 'Why are you practicing?' And I'd say, 'I don't know. I just have to.'"

Returning to music and drawing was like a medication for Amrita, a "pill" that let her function in the rest of her life. She would let others know she was a singer and musician only in small, private ways. When I first met her at a party at her house, I saw the piano, and I remember later that night she sang a couple of songs and I thought, "Woooow. I had no idea she was so talented!" Even though she was just riffing and singing at a party with her friends, the quality of her voice was better than anything any of us had ever heard.

By that time she had begun to jam a little with other players of Indian music. One day, through a music connection, she heard that the famous Indian composer A. R. Rahman was auditioning singers to perform songs from the sound track to the hit movie *Slumdog Millionaire*, which had been nominated for an Oscar. Amrita had been practicing her singing for two hours a day, and her voice was strong again. She was one of many at the audition, among a large group of men and women. Afterward, Rahman's manager called to say he had heard her tape.

"A.R. had only one question: Are you a professional singer?"

Amrita told him, "I used to be."

After so many years of performing only privately, Amrita was asked to sing at the Oscars for a global audience of 36 million people. Hooooooly shit! I mean, nothing like going from your living room to the biggest stage in the entire world. I simply had to know how it felt for her. Sweat bullets on the forehead? The need for many a nervous pee? Or were we talking full-on, grab-me-a-puke-bucket nervous—which I think is how I would feel?

She remembered feeling remarkably calm. "I knew in the back of my mind it was something significant. If I'd known how it would change my life, I probably would have been a lot more nervous. I just thought: I have to have really good technical skill when I go out there. Same as when I was a kid—I have to have really good technical skill and I'll get into trouble if I don't. It's hard to break those habits." But in this case, singing the music she wanted to sing, the old training that was so tedious now served her. Her Oscar performance went beautifully. And that success led to more performances with Rahman, including her favorite, a classical concert for an audience of twenty thousand in which Amrita sang Indian vocals while Rahman conducted the Los Angeles Philharmonic. "That was the best one."

Amrita had realized a long-denied ambition. She had reawakened the world-class singer she had been as a child. She had remade herself. And yet—it wasn't enough to change her life. Having that extraordinary talent and developing it through intense practice was not enough to remake her life. Getting Out of Line and giving a triumphant performance, even a string of triumphant performances, was not enough to remake her life. When the applause ended, she went back to her old way of living.

"Different people have different reactions to their fifteen minutes of fame," she told me. "On the Monday after the Oscars, I was scheduled to get on a plane and go to a major client, a retail chain. I called my client and I said, 'Listen, I just did the Oscars, I want to spend some time with my family and think about what just happened to me.' And the client said, 'Yeah—I saw you on the Oscars—whatever. So are you getting on the plane?' He didn't give a crap. It was horrible. And of course, I got on that flight, wearing my gray suit. I didn't have the nerve to quit my job."

A. R. Rahman had returned to India, and Amrita went back to her life representing other celebrities' brands. She had come far in remaking herself, but she hadn't yet found the courage to break down her old self. What was going wrong? Professor Jeff DeGraff of the Ross School of Business at the University of Michigan pointed out in his book *Innovation You: Four Steps to Becoming New and Improved* that people often assume, wrongly, that they can create a change in their lives by adding to their list of goals. The problem is that we all have long to-do lists already. Real change requires "creative destruction": taking things *off* your list to make room for something new. And that kind of choice—and change—comes with costs. You give something up, and that's painful.

It took time before Amrita looked ahead and admitted to herself that she couldn't go back to her old life permanently. To her, the old life felt like a kind of dying. She realized, "If I'm going to raise my children to be inspiring and to inspire others, I have to at least try to do the same."

With Rahman away on the other side of the world, Amrita set a new goal: to work with the producer Timbaland. "Timbaland here is like A.R. there, in India. So I hunted down his manager and pitched him that I wanted to work with him. It took six months. Finally I sang for Timbaland and he said, 'What are you doing tonight? I want you to be in the studio with me.' When we got there, he told his mixing guys: 'All that stuff I was sampling? We're not using it. This is the real thing. She's a real Indian singer.'" Timbaland helped Amrita get the chance to sing with Missy Elliott and Justin Timberlake, who wanted Indian-influenced melodies in their work. How completely badass is that!

Amrita's husband, Ravi, encouraged her to make music and art her career. He told her, "This is what you should be doing!" But she still couldn't imagine a way forward. She told him, "No one cares about Indian music." In a way, she was stuck back in the place she had gotten stuck in as a child artist—successful, full of inspiration to make music and to draw but convinced it would never succeed as a career, that people didn't really want her to do it. But now she came to understand that she needed to do it anyway. "You just have to do what you're good at even if nobody's listening. That's how I think—a lot of songs I write, I don't know if anyone will give a crap—and most of the time, they don't!"

Unlike in childhood, she had resources now to draw on for building a musical career and Extreme support close by. Amrita and Ravi had spent years working in the music and branding business, and they had skills and knowledge that helped her understand her artistic gifts and the practical opportunities for employing them. Ravi suggested, "Do your Indian music as part of your art, make it a character. If you don't want to go out as Amrita Sen, go out as Bolly-Doll, the alternate you."

Amrita's old firm had represented Gwen Stefani, the leader of the ska band No Doubt, who had branched out very successfully into fashion design and other commercial ventures. Then, for her first solo album, Stefani had imagined four characters she called the Harajuku Girls. She wrote songs about them and hired four backup singers to play them in concert. She marketed dolls that wore their fashions, which she had designed, and launched an animated television series in which the Harajuku Girls were superheroes fighting evil and pursuing careers in music. Amrita took Stefani's approach as her model. "I can't actually operate on big, grand strategic goals," she explained. "I have to think about what is realistic, what can I actually achieve without giving away the farm. For me, what seemed actually achievable was to create ten to twelve characters in the form of paintings and to write twelve songs. That I knew I could do. I went back through my notes on what deals Gwen had done and I replicated them. I put the style guide together, I put the CD together. I created the illustrations. I went on Lynda.com and learned the software I needed—Photoshop, Illustrator, InDesign, After Effects, Premiere Pro, Logic, Pro Tools. I was a living commercial for software tutorials. And when people in the business asked me to articulate my new project, I wouldn't go into the deep sources of BollyDoll in Indian mythology. I'd just say, 'This is an Indian Harajuku Girls.' I kept it extremely simple!" Amrita had found a way to pursue the art she needed to make but to present it to the music industry in the language of her marketing career.

Two years after her Oscar performance, she finally left her old job for good. She gave up the prestige and financial security that came from managing some of the biggest names in the business. For years, she had regretted many of the biggest decisions of her life: taking such a technical approach to her music as a young person, giving up music and going to business school, and working for other artists rather than living as an artist herself. But now, as she built her BollyDoll characters and brand, she was drawing on the technical discipline and the business training she had often questioned. She'd seen other recording artists give 25 to 50 percent of their earnings to their commercialization partners, but as she explained, "because of my work as an agent, because of my business skills, I didn't have to involve others. That's money I kept. That's a frigging big deal. I'm also married to someone who's right now very skilled at this kind of stuff, has the muscle memory for it, Ravi is doing deals every five minutes, so it's habitual for him—he knows how to navigate various aspects of the business."

Amrita's journey continued to evolve. Many of her retail partners suggested that she use her own name instead of BollyDoll for her next season. "I was scared. I didn't think Amrita Sen as a designer name would have any impact. And I'd kind of grown comfortable hiding behind BollyDoll." But she realized that in order to tell more stories, present different designs, and branch out into new types of music, she did need to brand her name. "I came up with the idea to do a story called *Cosmic and Eternal Love* by Amrita Sen, and then I came up with another idea to do *Awakened* by Amrita Sen, and then I thought I want to do *Diamonds and Flames* by Amrita Sen. I ended up writing and illustrating all of them!" Last year, Amrita showed a publisher all those new collections under her own name. "Well, believe it or not, the Amrita Sen brand, art books, gift items, and a CD, came out in fall 2016 through a five-hundred-store end cap in Barnes and Noble. And . . . it's of Indian influence. Who knew? This is a long way from the days of the dot busters!"

As she remade herself as a commercially sophisticated songwriter and visual artist, parts of her life that had seemed wasted now came together in new ways to serve Extreme Amrita. "All the parts of myself I'd perceived as my handicaps are now gifts! I was always so focused on making money, but I didn't feel rich. I make less money now, but I feel richer."

That's the reason to go through the pain of breaking yourself and the hard work of making yourself again: when you can combine more of your Extreme aspects in the service of your personal vision, you get to live more of who you are, and the parts that seemed mismatched and unfortunate can come to seem more like a perfect mosaic. For an Extremer, that's the ultimate personal success.

## THE EXTREMER CYCLE

For Condoleezza Rice and Amrita Sen, the need to break themselves came in response to profound disappointments. Condi saw that she could never be the pianist she'd dreamed of being. Amrita saw that a life that didn't make use of her gifts was more like death. But for many Extremers, the decision to break themselves comes not only when they smash into a wall of disappointment but also when they see a fresh opportunity to be Extreme. It may happen many times in a career or lifetime. That was the case for Mister Cartoon, whom we met in chapter 7. He first felt the necessity of breaking himself as a teenager, and he would feel it again repeatedly for decades, as he discovered the Extremer Cycle: success, plateau, new beginning, new success.

"People always told me I was gifted, blessed with being able to draw at a young age," he said. "At fourteen years old, I was the best artist in my class—bad at math, good at art. But the older I got, the more I realized a lot of people could draw. They were really good at it. I wasn't so special after all.

"My mom was like, 'You're a great artist, I love you, but you're lazy—go get a regular job. You need to know how hard regular people have to work. You need to learn the work ethic of a McDonald's employee.' But I was too lazy for that shit. I felt: I have to, have to, *have to* make art work."

Cartoon was fascinated with all the practical arts he could see around him in Los Angeles, but he didn't know if he would find what he needed in graffiti, airbrushing, tattoo, or something else. With each new artistic trade he set out to learn, he had to break himself down and become a beginner again. "I was already good at drawing with pencil and paper, but when I learned graffiti I had to start over. I had to be sloppy, learn my trade. Then I wanted to get into sign graphics. How many people now even know what that is? Back in the day, if you went to a jeweler or attorney or a business with class, they had their name painted in reverse gilded gold leaf in the window of their office. The only school on the West Coast that teaches sign graphics was LA Trade Tech, the famous trade school. So I started sign painting. And I sucked. It took me days, months, years to figure it out. I would get paint all over my fucking hands, my clothes. And then I thought, you know what? If I practice every day all my life I will never be as good as them. I know how to do that now, I understand and admire it, but maybe that's not what I want to do for a living.

"Then I went into designing apparel. I hadn't gone to fashion school, I just watched my friends. If these idiots can do it, I thought, then I can do it. I use that with everything—if I see my partners are really successful, I study them, mirror them, ask them questions:

'Hey, man, what time do you wake up? How do you get inspired this way?' In apparel, sign-painting technique became my secret weapon. I thought, what if I take that style of lettering from the signs and put it onto apparel—no one was doing that. I could stand out that way."

Cartoon built a unique and successful career over the decades by breaking himself down, learning different art forms, and then combining them in his own Extreme ways. It's a formula that has taken him from painting low-rider cars to making movies. As he put it, "I always end up starting over in anything I do. But it's hard to humble yourself when you're used to kicking ass." That's the formula right there! To remake yourself, you have to be willing to break yourself, to start over, and to be a beginner again. Each time, even though you've been used to kicking ass, you have to be messy and humble for a while.

If you're willing, the Extremer Cycle can carry you from success to success for decades. You have to Stay Stubbornly Humble, willing to struggle and to learn from others. Then you combine the new elements you've added with existing interests and skills until you find a new Specialist Game, maybe even a new chance to Change the Game entirely. And then, sometimes the hardest part, you have to be willing to acknowledge when you've gone as far (and kicked as much ass) as you can in one direction and start the cycle over again.

But that last part—the starting over, walking away from success back into uncertainty alone—too often gets edited out of most success stories. We don't realize how many of the steps that today in hindsight look inevitable might never have gotten taken at all. Angela Ahrendts, whom we met in chapter 1, went from Donna Karan to Liz Claiborne to Burberry to Apple, an astonishing run of brilliant moves. But her experience each time was of uncertainty and doubt.

"I fight my fate," she said. "Because I'm a fifty-fifty, half left brain analytical and half right brain intuitive in my approach to everything, it's often hard when I'm making a big decision to get my brain to just *shut up*. I'll get excited about a new opportunity, but then my left brain wants to start confusing me with 'the facts': *You can't do this and you don't know this and you don't know that. . . .* So with each move in my career, I always have this massive battle with myself. It took me almost a year to accept the job at Liz Claiborne, which ended up being one of the best moves I ever made. I learned so much about people, products, process, and most importantly leadership there. But when it was offered to me, I didn't want that job. My mind didn't want that job. I had come from Donna Karan, I had been in luxury, and my intuitive right brain had flourished. I knew it, I felt it, I lived it, I breathed it—I *was* one with that company. So when I was offered the position at Liz Clairborne, a role that was so perfect for my business left brain, my creative right brain said 'No, I don't want to do that.' But I'm sitting where I am today because I have had both the more right-brain experiences with DK, followed by a balance of a left brain/right brain role at Liz Claiborne—strategic planning, operational execution, acquiring businesses, all while dreaming with incredible founders and visionaries." That combination was what prepared her to become CEO of Burberry, but again, as she told me, it did not seem obvious or easy at the time. "I said no to Burberry for eighteen months. Because by that time I had a husband and three kids. I finally had a work-life balance, if that's possible in New York City with three kids. I loved my job! And I had built very close relationships with the amazing people there. My right brain said,

'Isn't that what's important in life?' We don't talk about leadership or loyalty in business. Professionally I felt, *I'm part of this! I've helped build this! How can I possibly leave and let everyone down? My personal life is also perfect—so please leave me alone! Life can't get any better than this.*"

Yet that more analytical side kept wondering what the probability was of getting another opportunity to become CEO of an exciting global luxury brand. Her left brain won the day. Once she took the position at Burberry, she discovered she could brilliantly combine everything she had learned in her previous jobs. "I could use every bit of experience I had gained along the way, and I was free to draw on all of that experience, collaborating with a right-brain creative partner and an incredible left-brain chairman I could be myself for once and trust myself with no fear of failure."

It's an awesome story, and I just had to know how she makes difficult decisions—to take the risk, break herself down, and do the precise thing she felt most afraid to do. She told me, "I have finally learned to turn off my head and let whatever you want to call it—the cosmos, the ether, the Holy Spirit—help me get out of my own way. I come from a pretty strong faith background, and believe everyone has a purpose. All I want to do while I'm on this planet is align with my higher purpose to ensure I make the dent I'm meant to make. Far be it from me to know what that is. In going to Burberry, I finally just gave it up. I asked, 'Lead me, guide me, show me.' I begged for signs of clarity. So I try to turn off my brain, and one day if something's meant to be, I'll wake up and it's as clear as day that I need to do this. I have tremendous faith, and that gives me the courage to let go in order to move forward and hopefully be able to make an even greater impact in my short time here. You might say it's my calling."

## A DREAM TUCKED AWAY

When I left Gatorade for Equinox, I was hoping to start a new round of that Extremer Cycle, both for myself and for the company. I was making a deliberate decision to disrupt myself by getting out of a products business and back into a services business—moving to a luxury gym to bring my career almost full circle by reconnecting with my experiences in luxury airlines all those years ago. I wanted to focus my personal growth on bringing out the Extreme in an entire company by playing one amazing Specialist Game. It was a big decision for the entire Robb O'Hagan family to relocate for the fourth time in eight years to yet another new city that we would all have to figure out and learn to love. I had high hopes that Equinox was going to be my home for a long, long time. I was ready to put down some roots both personally and professionally: to move into a house and a neighborhood and make friends I wouldn't have to say good-bye to in a few years, and to become a big part of the long-term future of a brilliant company.

Within a few years, though, it became clear that I was unlikely to reach my full potential at the Nox. Unlike Gatorade, which involved a complex and intense business turnaround, Equinox was an established, successful business looking to continue on its well-established path. I felt proud that we were well under way on our innovation journey, thanks to the kick-ass team of leaders working collaboratively together, and I thoroughly enjoyed the many great moments of helping others bring out the Extreme. But pretty soon, the team had momentum enough to continue the journey by itself without my pushing it—and without it pushing me to grow. My learning curve those first couple of years went from steep to average to flat—far quicker than at Gatorade—and there was no bigger job or role in the company for me to evolve into. I was aware that I was beginning to "run in place," just as I had experienced with my physical fitness when I first joined the company. I was feeling a little too *comfortable*.

Sometimes you realize, when you're halfway up a mountain, that you've given so much of your passion and energy to get there but it's not the mountain you thought you were climbing. That's a deeply sad, disorienting feeling. What should you do? Should you hold on in the hope that your feelings of frustration will pass? Should you settle for playing at less than your full potential?

Late in 2015, I made a trip home to New Zealand to visit my mother. Extreme Jenny is without a doubt my most inspiring original Extremer. My entire life she's been blazing amazing trails while telling dirty jokes and making embarrassing gaffes along the way. Mum was deeply intellectual and widely read, yet due to the era in which she grew up, she'd had to drop out of school at fifteen with no qualifications. Thanks to her sheer force of personality, she went on to an exciting working life as a bookings agent in New Zealand for BOAC, the airline that went on to become British Airways. For her, falling in love with my dad had meant that she had to make a choice: to get married or to continue with her career. The airline had wanted to promote her to a global traveling ambassador role— but only if she wasn't married. Mum made the really tough choice that so many women made in her day: to give up her flourishing career and go on to be the lead parent for our family. Attempting to do both or to share family responsibilities with my father just wasn't an option then. She was so excited when I started my career in the airline business, as she could see that I might realize opportunities that she never could.

You can imagine the profound impact it had on me when, at the age of thirteen, I watched as my mum Got Out of Line and proudly told us she was going to go back to university to get a degree and begin a new career. That meant she would have to study and pass exams just to prove that she had the intellectual capability to study at the undergrad level, let alone move forward with the actual course work. And picture this: by the time my older brother Olly rocked up for his first year of college—clearly wanting to enjoy the great feeling of independence from your parents—Extreme Jenny was just coming into her own among all the cool kids on campus. There she'd be, walking from one lecture to the next with our decidedly overweight black labrador on the end of a leash and calling out at the top of her voice "Hi, darlings!" to my brother and his friends, who were trying to mind their own business.

She went on to achieve her BA and then her master's in English language, write a book about grammar called *Punc Rocks: Foundation Stones for Precise Punctuation* (tell me that isn't awesome), and become a highly accomplished tutor for foreign-language master's students. And all that because she broke herself after twenty-five years as a full-time homemaker to remake herself at the age of fifty.

It was therefore a very tough experience for me to visit her new "home"—a nursing home in Auckland, where she will now live out the rest of her days due to her aggressively progressing Alzheimer's disease. I can't imagine that she ever contemplated that her time would be cut short by this horrible fucking degenerative disease, but I know if she could, she'd look back now and say that her years as a researcher and teacher were some of the most fulfilling of her life. (There's not a lot that she can remember in the short term these days—but it's remarkable how many of her favorite dirty jokes can still be told in all their glory.)

Returning from this trip triggered a painful period of self-reflection. Talk about a wake-up call that life is short and health is never guaranteed. I badly wanted to ask Mum what she would do in my position at the Nox, but I couldn't—so instead I turned to my siblings for advice. What I realized in the weeks that followed was that if I were able to let go of the comfort and the wonderful support system and life that I had created for myself at Equinox—and frankly let go of the future vision I had dreamed of for myself within the company—then gradually opportunities would reveal themselves to me that I could not otherwise see.

For example, here I was writing this book—becoming more inspired on a daily basis by the stories I have heard, the research I have read, and the amazing amount of potential that I believe is waiting to be unleashed in the world. I'd been viewing it as a side project, one I would squeeze in during late-night flights, vacations, and weekend breaks from my real job, but now I began to see it as a chance to lead global positive cultural change.

One of the discoveries you can make, when you allow yourself to break away from the life you're comfortable in and reconsider your goals and your vision, is that there may be a dream tucked away that you've never admitted. I always dreamed of building an entire idea or platform of my own and to create a brand from scratch, but with a career of as much momentum and intensity as mine, I'd never found the right moment or the deep courage to do it. And so I decided: the next step in bringing out the Extreme in myself and others would be not just to write a book but to see if I could turn the endeavor into a multifaceted platform that would enable Extremers the world over to bring out the best in themselves. Just as I'm sure my mum discovered in the second half of her life, the most fulfilling experience I ever have is seeing other people achieve more of their own potential. How might it feel to do that on a really large scale?

The magnitude of this decision was far scarier than any in my career before, but I realized that if I were going to "walk my talk," I needed to have the courage to break myself down, become that naive beginner again, and start over. You can't continue on in the safety of the "known" and get into position for new growth, so as sad as it is to let go of what you have loved, you have to believe in your potential to experience more and just make the leap.

## EXTREME MOVES

When is it time to Break Yourself to Make Yourself? When you find that you're looking ahead and the way forward no longer matches your vision. For Condoleezza and Amrita, the day came when continuing on their already successful paths was not going to be enough. They didn't want the future they could see ahead, so they looked for ways to step off the train, beginning again with uncertainty, discomfort, and hard work. For Mister Cartoon and me, in contrast, there wasn't one dramatic roadblock or heartbreak, but we could feel at different points in our lives that we were losing steam, that it was time for another round of the Extremer Cycle.

What we all had in common was that despite achieving success along the way, we realized we still had untapped potential—and that we would never be satisfied just to wash, rinse, and repeat. We looked around and asked ourselves: *Is there a chance up ahead to develop even more of Extreme You, or is it time to change course?* We chose to give up reliable success, to become beginners again, to get uncomfortable, unsure, confused, and messy. We chose to hurt again. If you do, the payoff is developing parts of yourself that you had ignored, combining elements of Extreme You more than you have ever done before, and releasing more potential and new possibility.

## 1. Refuse to Become Obsolete

Isn't it dangerous to break yourself and start again? Wouldn't it be safer to stick with what you already know? I can imagine someone thinking that it might have been all right for someone like Amrita to break herself, when she was so miserable living a life with no room for her Extreme Artist. Any risk has to be better than being so unhappy that you spend twenty hours a day sleeping! But what about the rest of us?

I put this question to the Strava guys, whom we met in chapter 7. Before they created their social media platform for athletes back in the 1990s, they had launched an enterprise software company, building it until, at one point, it had a market cap of $11 billion. Fifteen years later, when they set out to launch a new venture, wouldn't it have made more sense for them to launch a similar business, so they could repeat the playbook that had made them big winners?

True Extremers, they saw it the other way. To them, the real danger was that they would become too dependent on what they already knew. The world of business changes very fast, they figured, but at least if they went into something new, they would know that they *didn't* know how to do it! Their first experience together, they told me, taught them that exactly when they don't know how to do something, they make good decisions—by asking experts who do. Michael said, "We know we don't know, so we'll go learn. That way we are less apt to apply our own associations and make mistakes. It's also a lot more fun! We've enjoyed the adventure."

It's as true for an individual's career as it is of founding a business. Even if you get hired or promoted on the basis of your established expertise, there's a danger in thinking that your new responsibilities are exactly like something you've seen before. If you assume you can go with what made you successful the last time, you may miss the nuances of the new thing in front of you. Breaking yourself may seem risky at first, but it turns out to be almost a kind of insurance against becoming obsolete—instead of repeating yourself until the old way lets you down, you remake yourself and stay current.

So be willing to Break Yourself again—and though it will hurt at first, trust the process and look for the chance to enjoy the discoveries along the way. One thing that unites Extremers is their relentless curiosity. They're always looking for new things to figure out. They keep asking: Where's the next area I want to explore?

## 2. Rethink Your Stubborn Beliefs

I've talked about the importance of finding your Extreme Mates— those who can do what you can't. But as you Break Yourself to Make Yourself, you may find that the skills and interests that "weren't you" in the past are ones you can embrace today. Personally, I had always steered clear of finance because I freakin' hated it. I failed accounting in my first year of my commerce degree at university, and after that I built a giant mental block in my head: *I hate finance, and I will never understand it, let alone like it!* But once I got to Gatorade and I really cared about guiding a whole business, not just the marketing or innovation aspect, suddenly finance looked a whole lot more compelling. In my third year, I actually asked Massimo if I could take a finance course—and was blown away when he not only said yes but agreed to send me to Harvard Business School Executive Education. Holy shit! I jumped at the opportunity because now it was part of my new vision for myself, as the leader of a whole company. I remember calling home most nights and telling Liam,

"I think I'm becoming a total finance geek!" I mean, you know it's serious when on the flight home you choose to reread your case studies instead of *People* magazine.

Now, did I understand finance at the level of the chief financial officers who were there just to brush up on their skills? Ummm—yeah, not so much. But I came home knowing a hundred percent more than I had known before, and it made me a far more experienced and balanced executive than I'd been—not just because of what the course taught but because now finance didn't feel like a foreign language. When people around me "spoke" it, I no longer glazed over and tuned out. I joined in! And then, because I joined those finance conversations, I learned even more. I started asking questions I'd never known to ask before.

We all have things we've said we'll never freakin' do. Remaking yourself can mean choosing to try some again. And what happens if you let those "nevers" go? Good things! So why the hell not try?

### 3. Let It Go

I do want to be clear that Breaking Yourself down doesn't have to mean leaving your company or organization to find new growth, because in so many companies there is such a wonderful wealth of opportunity to stretch into new areas, participate in new experiences, and acquire new skills. But you do have to have a willingness to make sacrifices and let go of circumstances that are comfortable. And that is one of the hardest and most important things you need to do. Just as the decision I made in my twenties to jump at the career opportunity in the United States meant I had to let go of the close proximity to family and friends, every truly pivotal growth point in my life has required the courage to give up the safety net.

It's scary and daunting when you are looking out at a future that you do not know, yet it seems that every time an Extremer makes one of those bold moves, he or she never loses but always gains. The fact is, you don't lose the friendships you leave behind; they just evolve to form a new role in your life. You don't lose the skills you have honed in one area of expertise; they evolve when combined with new areas of knowledge. But you can't unleash new potential unless you are willing to let go of some of the comfort you have today.

And if you do, what will happen next? Where will it take you? You can find out only if you keep working to release more of Extreme You. So—this is it! I've taken you this far; now it's your turn. Go forth! Ride that Extremer Cycle as far as you can, bringing out the Extreme in yourself and in others. One thing you can be sure of: it's going to be a wild ride, full of unexpected possibilities and new successes. Enjoy it!

# EPILOGUE

In February 2016, I resigned from my position as the president of Equinox and threw myself full-time into exploring all of the possibilities of Extreme YOU. No matter how well prepared I was for the move, it turned out to be equal parts shit-your-pants scary and enormously invigorating. After twenty-three years of showing up to an office every day and having a back-to-back meeting schedule where I barely had time to eat lunch, suddenly I found myself sitting alone in my daughter's unambiguously pink bedroom (the quietest room in the house) staring at my laptop, trying to put lots of hopes, dreams, and ideas into words—specifically, into the eighty thousand words that would become this book. To quote my great mate Bode, "When you're in the start gate, you're by yourself—things get awful quiet."

In the first few months I felt total panic. The days, weeks, and months were flying by, and I still wasn't clear in my mind on where I was going or how I was going to bring my big idea to its full potential. Everyone I met with assumed I was starting some kind of tech company (isn't that what all start-up founders are doing these days?), and they were quick to want to help me secure outside funding. Meanwhile, I was thinking of Extreme YOU as a "platform" because I was more focused on starting a movement of positive cultural change than I was on getting a big financial windfall with my "exit." At first the discrepancy was quite distracting for me. Holy shit—am I wasting my talents and missing my potential? Am I thinking about this the wrong way? But with the benefit of the insanely inspiring conversations that I was having with all of the Extremers in this book, I was able to remind myself to keep following my passion in my own way by applying the pillars of Extremeness to my own new adventure. I knew I wanted to go slowly with this thing so as to do it the right way and to be as patient as necessary to let it find its own audience and place in the world.

With the unwavering support of my friend Lauren Schechtman, who had worked with me many moons ago at Atari (yes, we survived that shit storm together!), and my amazeballs writing partner Woodie (that's Greg Lichtenberg, for those not following along), we brainstormed every conceivable Extreme YOU content idea from podcasts to reality TV shows to training curriculum to friggin' insane live events complete with Friday-afternoon disco dance parties. We were also lucky enough to be able to recruit onto the team my trusty hubby, Liam, to build us our first website, tapping into his "before kids" work skills. I particularly loved spending a bunch of time thinking about the ways in which Extreme YOU might be able to pay it forward to those who don't have the same opportunities in life that I have had.

Along the way we hit the road and had heaps of exploratory meetings, and I am so enormously grateful for the incredible insight and support that so many people gave us as we pieced together the bones of a platform plan for our Extreme venture. I can assure you that there is no end to the possibilities we see to help people of all ages tap into their most Extreme version of themselves. It may take me a lifetime to have the kind of impact I dream of having, but I'm deeply committed to this cause.

During the enlightening process of Checking Myself Out, I realized how much I enjoy the process of "stripping down" to my naked ambition. It has been a long time since I had to pound the pavement to explain something that I am working on and to get such a wide swath of people excited about a vision that does not currently exist in the world. At the same time, I became aware of a slight nagging feeling: with all my focus on the teaching of Extreme YOU, I still missed the day-to-day experience of being in business and of continuing my own personal development as a business leader. The more time that passed, the more I began to acknowledge that I hadn't quite yet reached my goals as an executive, goals that I had been pursuing since that first Get Out of Line moment some twenty years before when I had landed a job at Air New Zealand. I just didn't feel ready to be a full-time "teacher," spending all my time on the speaking circuit, writing blog posts, and giving seminars.

At the end of the summer of 2016, just as I was finishing writing this book, I got an unexpected call for a job opportunity in the fitness field. My first reaction was nope, the timing is not right—I don't want to jump back into a full-time business role until after this book comes out. But thanks to the efforts of a very persuasive investor who I could tell had the very familiar characteristics of a great mentor, I decided to at least explore a great company called Flywheel Sports. For those of you who've not heard of it, it's an absolutely ass-kicking boutique fitness business. It features an indoor cycling workout that tracks your performance as you are riding (oh, yeaaaah!—for those ever so slightly competitive folk like me, it's so friggin' motivating to see in real time how you are performing compared to previous rides). Ultimately Flywheel is about inspiring people to push themselves to even greater levels of sweat-busting awesomeness whenever they ride, so that they can push themselves to high performance in their lives and in their work just the way they do when they get on that bike.

Unlike every other major job I have been offered in my life, this time there were a few additional things that made it even more compelling. I wasn't pregnant or having to relocate my family to a new city in order to take the job, and, most important, I was able to consider the opportunity with a stunningly clear filter. I knew that for me to take another role, it would have to be the most awesome manifestation of my specialist game so I could bring great value to the team and the business, and of course it needed to be something that exemplified and had the potential to amplify the ideas of Extreme YOU.

As you know by now, I made the decision to take the role of chief executive officer of Flywheel. So that's where you'll find me—still getting very sweaty and still trying to convince anyone and everyone around me to get their workout on. And, most important, I'm still Extreming FULL STEAM AHEAD! So I'd love to hear your feedback and your Extreme stories at www.Facebook.com/ExtremeSarah, or on Twitter @ExtremeSRO.

And please come visit us at www.extremeyou.com. You can sign up for Team Extreme and be kept up-to-date with news from the Extreme YOU community. We will not stop until we have unleashed the Extreme in every single one of you!

For now, go forth, find your mountain, and enjoy the amazing journey to the summit of your own potential.

# ACKNOWLEDGMENTS

Let me start by saying, it takes a friggin' village! I had *no idea* when I began this process how hard it would be, how long it would take, and how many people would give so much love, care, and support to me in getting it done. Given that I started my life as a stubborn little girl with an "I can do it, I can do it" attitude, it's never come easy to me to rely on so many others for help. But this process has been infinitely more rewarding because I fully let my guard down, and the proof that I am so much better with the help and input of others is demonstrated in these pages.

I want to start by thanking the brilliant architect, the incredible mind, and the tireless engine behind this entire process, my dear friend and writing partner Greg Lichtenberg (aka Woodie) without whom this book simply would not exist. Woodie, I thank you for betting your time on me, for getting the concept so deeply, for caring so much about it, and for your incredible stamina through thick and thin to get this thing written. You've taught me more than you will ever know and helped me focus my crazy messy brain to turn my ideas into something real and digestible. You are truly one of a kind, and I'm honored to have you as my co-driver on this journey.

Thanks to Carol Franco, my wonderful agent, and her fantastic partner in crime Kent Lineback. I didn't quite know what I was getting into when you asked me to fly to New Mexico to sit around your kitchen table and "find my book," but I thank you both for that day and the many months that came after it. Even if this book had never been published, I'd be so grateful to you both for helping me make sense of the turning point that I was at in my life.

To Hollis Heimbouch, the legendary woman from HarperCollins: I heart you more than you will know. You "got" this book the minute you saw it; you fought for it, you championed me and our cause, and you made the book infinitely better with your feedback and input. And to the rest of your Extreme Team, Tina Andreadis, Leslie Cohen, Stephanie Hitchcock, and Brian Perrin, for the enthusiasm you have all shown and the care to help launch this revolution the right way, I'm forever thankful that I landed with such the perfect team to nurture this baby to enter the world.

To Sara Lucian and Gretchen Gavett, my amazing, ever-curious, utterly supportive research team: You've helped me see that being Extreme is the proven method I hoped it was—and with the amazing research you've dug up, you've taught me so much and made me even more passionate about this cause.

To Lauren Schechtman, my wonderful, Extreme partner from the shit tunnel right through to the Ritz Carlton spa: I owe you a giant amount for your never-ending belief in this movement. Every time I have doubted myself and my ability to take this on, you've pushed me, you've laughed with me and at me in the most rewarding way(!), and you've ensured that I didn't give up.

To Gordon Thompson, who has long been my strategic sparring partner and was there to help me turn this crazy idea into something I could *see*, which is what kicked off all the momentum to get it going. That trip to the MOMA bookstore was a huge turning point, and your guidance to get this thing looking and feeling like *me* was instrumental in building my confidence.

To Darryn Lochead from Oomph in New Zealand, who did all the design work for our branding and the book: It fully KICKS ASS. You're a magician in the way you put up with all my insane noodling and still turned it in to something great.

To Adam Grant—or should I say "the" Adam Grant (I'm still convinced there must be clones of you out there in the world for how much you do!): You are beyond generous with your intellect, your cheerleading, your belief in me, and your connections that helped get this project off the ground. I aspire to be as much of a giver as you. And to Reb Rebele and Dena Gromet and Laura Zarrow from the Wharton People Analytics team, for helping me think about how to measure someone's Extremeness!

To Susan Cain and Paul Scibetta, for showing me the road map and being such relentlessly positive cheerleaders and givers: I aspire to have the kind of impact that you've had, and I'm honored to be a passionate follower of the Quiet Revolution.

To Nilofer Merchant, for kicking my ass many years ago and telling me I needed to write a book and getting me going on the process.

And now to my amazing, inspiring, ass-kicking, game-changing team of Extremers (starring in alphabetical order): Angela Ahrendts, Mister Cartoon, Will Dean, Angela Duckworth, Mark Gainey, Michael Horvath, Sam Kass, Dan Keyserling, Liz Miersch, Bode Miller, Francisco Nunez, Mary O'Hagan, Alberto Pearlman, Beto Pérez, Condoleezza Rice, Bozoma Saint John, Amrita Sen, Janet Shamlian, Sage Steele, Laura Wolf Stein, Gordon Thompson, Casey Wasserman, and Alli Webb.

I just don't know where to start to thank you all for the gift you have given me and the world by sharing your stories. The minute I explained the premise of this book—that I wanted to shine a light on the vulnerable parts of your incredible success stories to help others learn what it takes to become the best version of themselves—you all immediately said "I'm in." It speaks volume about your commitment to helping others grow that you have been so willing to support this project in all the many ways that you have. I thought I knew your stories before I spoke to you, but you have given me new insights that have taken my love and respect for you to a whole new level. As my editor Hollis agreed, you made us laugh, you made us cry, and you made us learn a hell of a lot. All I can say from the bottom of my heart is THANK YOU.

Writing a book is an incredibly humbling experience, as it forces you to look back on the most important moments of your life and reflect on the people who were there, guiding, shaping, and pushing you the most. I want to start by thanking my Whanau. I couldn't have possibly been luckier to have been born into the family that I was. I want to thank my mum, Extreme Jenny, for *always* telling me that every dog has its day, and my dad, JBB, for teaching me how important it was to never let the side down. You both set the standards very high, and as a result I've always felt compelled to push myself hard to hold my place as the junior member of our brilliant team.

To Anna: You've always been such a rock, from picking my major at university to picking me up off the floor when my heart was smashed into pieces. You and Shane have provided such incredible guidance *every* step of the way, and it's your wisdom that has always helped push me to find my own steam.

To Rach, the world's most committed supporter, always cheering and waving the flag for me, believing that I can and should do more and *always* there in the audience with giant proud Jenny-style, tear-filled eyes when I'm doing my thing: You have been instrumental in boosting my confidence when I needed it most—and reminding me to never give up.

To Ol: From the days when you made me play goalie to today, when you're always there for advice when I need it, you've always pushed me in just the same kind of way JBB would have, and even though I don't say it to you often enough, you are a big reason I've gotten to where I have. Thank you for telling me not to move back home to end up leading the Dalgety Women's Country Association and for always letting me know when the boots are too much.

To my dear Master Randa, the one we adopted into the Whanau: "Help me, Randa, help, help me, Randa!" I still can't believe how lucky I was the day Extreme Jenny picked you out from the crowd to be my new best friend, but I just can't imagine what the last thirty-five years would have been like without you. You are truly the ultimate Extremer. Your sheer love for life inspires me *every* time I hear your voice, and I thank you for knowing me as well as pretty much anyone and always guiding me expertly in my biggest decisions.

To darling PerkySam: You taught me more in your thirty-three years than I will ever fully grasp in my lifetime. I never stop working toward being a human being instead of a human doing thanks to you. "Today is a gift—that's why we call it the present." I will always appreciate your #BlueSkiesForever and feel so blessed with the gift you gave me of Jill, Tones, Simon, and Oli as Whanau.

To my bridesmaids Dee Gourlay and Meg Matthews, who've been there cheering since those embarrassing days at O'Rorke Hall through to my first half marathon in Huntley blaring "Don't Stop Me Now" from the speakers in my car, and my modern family sisters, Nic Parton and Ferrell McDonald, who keep it real with annual half marathons and constant life analysis sessions on WhatsApp.

To Glenn Foulds and Craig Oram, the two men in my life who

would have been bridesmaids if they were chicks: I stopped short of asking you to cross-dress for me at my wedding, but you've both been such amazing, caring, hilarious friends—there for all the important occasions from weddings to funerals to American road trips and SuperCheese parties. I love you both like brothers.

To Mark and Deb D'arcy: You lent me $100 when I had run out of money to eat, and you adopted me into your family when I had *no* solid ground around me. Mark, you were the mastermind behind the "Shaglantic" breakthrough that pushed my career to the next level.

To Christina Jelesky and Susan Calvi: There is no greater gift than the gift you give of loving my kids as if they were your own. You two will always be like sisters to me, and I am bursting with pride watching you chart your own Extreme paths with your own families.

To the Marshfielders and my amazing Larchies—you know who you are: You are the global family that we have adopted and who have adopted us. The journey is imminently more fun with all of you guys—lip sync battles, ghetto block parties, and everything in between. I love you *all*!

To my adopted parents, Norm and Jenny Thompson: I'll never be able to thank you enough for making the bet on the crazy kid with the American dream. Normie, it was one thing to be such an amazing boss, but for you and Jenny to take me in as your third daughter was a whole new level of support, even if it meant the awkwardness of my undies getting mixed up in the boss's laundry.

There are also the other incredible mentors that have made such an impact on my life and career and haven't been too put off by the fact that I have clung on to you all like a dog with a bone.

Tony Marks, the biggest cheese, who actually took the time to meet with me when I was a first-year trainee and you never stopped supporting me from that day forward.

Gary De Stefano, who believed in my dream to get beyond marketing: You once told me that I was lucky that I had the ability to work both very entrepreneurially and at scale and I should continue to develop both sides. I never lost sight of that advice, and it has served me so well.

Joaque Hidalgo: You were more instrumental than you know in helping me rebuild my confidence as I stepped into the big leagues at Nike HQ.

Eric Sprunk: You took me under your wing and showed me how to get confident with the stuff I didn't know—and you let me go from the Nike nest with exactly the right tone to force me to succeed.

Adam Helfant: You were instrumental in helping me make the single biggest career decision of my life (twice!). I've adored getting to know you and Sheila as friends and value your advice and support so very much.

Massimo D'Amore: I adore you for pushing me harder than anyone ever has before and bringing out the true Extreme in me as I learned to become fierce as well as determined.

Dr. Pheeel Sanfilippo: You were the ultimate rock of support, arriving in my life when I needed it most and always sorting the bullshitters from the straight shooters for me.

Jim Lynch: I never even knew what a supply chain was until I met you; you taught me so much and contributed more to my ideas and therefore my confidence than you probably even know.

Scott Rosen: I thank you for your tireless counsel, your belief in me and your friendship, and the never-ending excited texts about Bruce Springsteen.

Larry Segall: for your care and willingness to let me ask questions and be painfully vulnerable when I was the big leader still trying to learn.

Greg Hill: for the hours and hours of support you gave me pre, during, and post my time at the Nox.

Carlos Becil: for inspiring me to have courage in creativity and never stop fighting for what's right.

Renee Durocher: you are equal parts rock of incredible support and wonderful reminder that life is for living. #LifeByRenee!

And to the brilliant John Young, for your incredible mentoring afternoon tea sessions.

To Lew Frankfort: for having the patience to let me see for myself that the next amazing mountain range was right in front of me, and the extraordinary will to set me up to go for it.

Anthony Salemi: You *are* my secret weapon! You've never let me back away from the hard work of trying to be a better me, but with your giant long arms that give the world's greatest hugs to your brilliant one-liners (MAKE THE DECISION RIGHT!), I move through the world with confidence whenever I think of your words.

Debbie Moss: You are extraordinary at what you do. Thank you for helping me drop the baggage whenever it was needed and helping me see that I should not buy shoes that are a size too small—no matter how cute they are!

And then to the insanely inspiring teams that I've had the great pleasure of being a part of:

- At Air NZ—my dear bestie James Boyd—who led me into dancing one on one with the governor of California when I had no idea who he was. You helped me find my American dream.
- At Virgin—Amy Curtis: Thank you for hiring me, you incredible woman, you! David Tait and Tim Claydon: You gave me the greatest break of my life. Ravi Ahuja and Amrita Sen: You became like family to me, and you stuck with me through the toughest of times. LJ Gutierrez, Michael Pendleton, Nic York Bogen, and Amy Molina: I'll never, *ever* forget your kindness and your love in peel-

ing me off the bottom of the canyon of despair after I let you all down and got fired. You stuck by me and helped me move forward. I will always love you for that.

- At Atari—Alyssa Padia Walles: You are a wonderful, insanely fun ball of crazy energy, and I thank you for bringing me into the greatest springboard opportunity of my life. Tracy Magnuson: You believed in me even when I was utterly clueless. I will forever be a lamer gamer with you both!

- At Nike—Jason Cohn, Darla Vaughn, and Drew Greer: You helped me find my inner Extremer again, and, Nancy Monsarrat, you helped me blow it out. Awesome Orson Porter and generous Gina Warren: You taught me so much about turning my passion to doing good in the world, and I'm still trying to do good on that lesson.

- At Gatorade—it was a cast of literally hundreds of people who had the passion and commitment to chart such a bold new course. It is one of the most epic turnaround stories in consumer product history, and I feel so honored that I got to be a part of it. I'm grateful for absolutely every member of the G team past and present for having the courage and tenacity to make it all happen. I want to especially thank those who worked most closely with me and gave so much invaluable support and counsel: Opokua Kwapong, Heather Smith, Morgan Flatley, Carla Hassan, Andrea Fairchild, Mary Doherty, Scotty Paddock, Pete Brace, Randall Brown, Xavi Cortadellas, Joanne Hogan, Robert Lewis, Susie Cruz, Gordon Thompson, David Heath, Stanley Hainsworth, Jonah Disend, Lee Clow, Jimmy Smith, Jayanta Jenkins, Nick Drake, Brent Anderson, and Steve Howard. And last, Indra Nooyi: Thank you so much for supporting our Specialist Game and for sticking with us until it finally paid off.

And then the amazing Noxies who inspired me every day and in every way to push myself out of my own comfort zone, both in my fitness and in my life. Thank you to Harvey Spevak, who gave me the opportunity to join amazing Equinox in the first place. I also want to thank those who charted an even bolder course than I could imagine and humored me by willingly participating in all those karaoke nights: Jeff Weinhaus, Samir Desai, Barry Holmes, David Harris, Gian Pozzolini, Jack Gannon, Griff Long, Cathy Cassidy, Judy Taylor, Patrik Hellstrand, Liz Nolan, Liz Henning, Caitlin Schneider, Jay Blahnik, Nicole Smith, and Hazel Betancourt. Thank you for the inspiration to really learn how to bring out the Extreme in others. Such a brilliantly talented, high-energy team—you allowed me to feel what it was like to tap into the real power of my Specialist Game.

And last but most certainly not least, I want to thank Liam, the incredible rock of support who stepped into my life when it was a total shit sandwich and somehow helped me find my full power. I can't imagine how hard it is to be married to someone as stubborn, as drawn to the fire, and as determined as me, but somehow you put up with it all—the wonderful highs and the crashing lows—and you remind me that, no matter what, you're there for me. Without you, I would never have the greatest wonderful joys of my life—the great formation that is team Robb O'Hagan. Sam, Joe, and Gabby: You are my inspiration and my pride. All I want for the three of you is that you become the happiest, most fulfilled, most Extreme versions of yourselves—leaving a wonderful positive mark wherever you go.

# NOTES

**Introduction**

xxi **He didn't need a selfie:** Mike White, "Me! Me! Me! Are We Raising a Generation of Self-Obsessed Brats?" *North & South*, July 2016: 41.

xxii **"not engaged":** Amy Adkins, "Employee Engagement in U.S. Stagnant in 2015," Gallup, January 13, 2016, http://www.gallup.com /poll/188144/employee-engagement-stagnant-2015.aspx.

**Chapter 1: Check Yourself Out**

7 **"When it comes":** Drake Baer, "Success Is Random, So Court Serendipity," *Fast Company*, August 30, 2012, https://www.fastcompany. com/3000910/success-random-so-court-serendipity.

15 **The term "random walk":** "Random walk," Wikipedia, https:// en.wikipedia.org/wiki/Random_walk.

18 **"Our brains, wired":** Kevin Evers, "Unleash Your Inner Odysseus," *Harvard Business Review*, October 2012, https://hbr.org/2012/10/un leash-your-inner-odysseus.

18 **"If we could predict":** Baer, "Success Is Random, So Court Serendipity."

**Chapter 2: Ignite Your Magic Drive**

28 **"This is good news!":** Carmen Noble, "How Small Wins Unleash Creativity," *Working Knowledge*, September 6, 2011, http://hbswk.hbs .edu/item/how-small-wins-unleash-creativity.

30 **"Nonstop recognition":** Ashley Merryman, "Losing Is Good for

You," *New York Times*, September 24, 2013, http://www.nytimes
.com/2013/09/25/opinion/losing-is-good-for-you.html.

30 **"You're going to lose":** Ibid.

31 **Every college student's a winner!:** Sita Slavov, "How to Fix College
Grade Inflation," *U.S. News & World Report*, December 26, 2013, http://
www.usnews.com/opinion/blogs/economic-intelligence/2013/12/26
/why-college-grade-inflation-is-a-real-problem-and-how-to-fix-it.

31 **Linkagoal's Fear Factor Index 2015:** "What Scares Us Most: Spiders
or Failing? Linkagoal's Fear Factor Index Clears the Cobwebs," Linkagoal, October 2015, https://www.linkagoal.com/blog/2015/10/research
-reveals-fear-of-failure-has-us-all-shaking-in-our-boots-this-halloween
-1-in-3-admit-they-are-terrified-of-failure/.

31 **That number is up:** Donna J. Kelley et al., "2014 United States Report," Global Entrepreneurship Monitor, 2015, http://www.babson
.edu/Academics/centers/blank-center/global-research/gem/Documents
/GEM%20USA%202014.pdf.

43 **"harmonious passion":** Robert J. Vallerand et al., "Les Passions de
l'Âme: on Obsessive and Harmonious Passion," *Journal of Personality
and Social Psychology* 85, no. 4 (October 2003): 756–67, https://self
determinationtheory.org/SDT/documents/2003_VallerancBlanchard
MageauKoesnterRatelleLeonardGagneMacolais_JPSP.pdf.

44 **If you're just doing:** Laird J. Rawsthorne and Andrew J. Elliot, "Achievement Goals and Intrinsic Motivation: A Meta-Analytic Review," *Personality and Social Psychology Review* 3, no. 4 (1999): 326–44, http://
selfdeterminationtheory.org/SDT/documents/1999_RawsthorneElliot
_PSPR.pdf.

44 **three things motivate us effectively:** Daniel H. Pink, *Drive: The Surprising Truth About What Motivates Us* (New York: Riverhead Books,
2009), 10.

52 **"whisker goals":** Dan and Chip Heath, "Set Smaller Goals, Get Bigger Results," *Fast Company*, March 1, 2009, http://www.fastcompany
.com/1150180/set-smaller-goals-get-bigger-results.

## Chapter 3: Get Out of Line

69 **"contribute big on day one":** Liz Wiseman, "3 Ways to Get Noticed at Work," *Fortune*, February 8, 2015, http://fortune.com/2015/02/08/3 -ways-to-get-noticed-at-work/.

74 **According to a number of studies:** Frank Belschak and Deanne Den Hartog, "Being Proactive at Work: Blessing or Bane?," British Psychological Society, November 2010, https://thepsychologist.bps.org.uk /volume-23/edition-11/being-proactive-work-%E2%80%93-blessing-or -bane.

75 **"America is the land":** Matt O'Brien, "Poor Kids Who Do Everything Right Don't Do Better than Rich Kids Who Do Everything Wrong," *Washington Post*, October 18, 2014, https://www.washingtonpost.com /news/wonk/wp/2014/10/18/poor-kids-who-do-everything-right-dont -do-better-than-rich-kids-who-do-everything-wrong/.

81 **"initiative paradox":** Belschak and Den Hartog, "Being Proactive at Work."

## Chapter 4: Get Over Yourself

92 **"Although individuals":** Tom Rath and Barry Conchie, *Strengths Based Leadership: Great Leaders, Teams, and Why People Follow* (Washington, DC: Gallup Press, 2008): 23–24.

100 **Notice what you're avoiding:** Gwen Moran, "The Importance of Finding (and Facing) Your Weaknesses," *Fast Company*, February 10, 2014, http://www.fastcompany.com/3026105/dialed/the-importance-of-finding -and-facing-your-weaknesses.

## Chapter 5: Pain Training

121 **"the deeper we will wade":** Martin A. Schwartz, "The Importance of Stupidity in Scientific Research," *Journal of Cell Science*, no. 121 (2008): 1771, http://jcs.biologists.org/content/121/11/1771.

122 **the difference that journaling makes:** Sonja Lyubomirsky and Matthew D. Della Porta, "Boosting Happiness, Buttressing Resilience: Results from Cognitive and Behavioral Interventions," in *Handbook of Adult*

*Resilience*, ed. John W. Reich et al. (New York: Guilford Press, 2010): 450–64.

128 **"Retrenchment is the wrong response":** Dan and Chip Heath, "Set Smaller Goals, Get Bigger Results," *Fast Company*, March 1, 2009, http://www.fastcompany.com/1150180/set-smaller-goals-get-bigger -results.


**Chapter 6: Stay Stubbornly Humble**

133 **the difference between power and status:** Adam Grant, *Originals: How Non-Conformists Move the World* (New York: Viking, 2016).

137 *Humility was the strongest predictor*: Bradley P. Owens et al., "Expressed Humility in Organizations: Implications for Performance, Teams, and Leadership," *Organization Science* 24, no. 5 (September–October 2013): 1517–38, http://faculty.washington.edu/mdj3/Humility%20and%20per formance.pdf.

140 **a survey by the Forum Corporation:** "Driving Business Results by Building Trust: Findings from 2013 Forum Global Leadership Pulse Survey," Forum Corporation, 2013, http://www.forum.com/wp-content /uploads/2015/10/Driving-Business-Results-by-Building-Trust_2013 .pdf.

142 **it is impossible:** Deborah Ancona et al., "In Praise of the Incom- plete Leader," *Harvard Business Review*, February 2007, https://hbr .org/2007/02/in-praise-of-the-incomplete-leader.

146 **"If a leader starts":** Erika Andersen, "Admitting You Don't Know, When You're the CEO," *Harvard Business Review*, August 17, 2015, https://hbr .org/2015/08/admitting-you-dont-know-when-youre-the-ceo.

147 **"Inconsistency is surprising":** Dave Murphy, "Believe Me, I Have No Idea What I'm Talking About," Insights by Stanford Business, April 1, 2010, https://www.gsb.stanford.edu/insights/believe-me-i-have-no-idea-what -im-talking-about.

149 **"Every time we need":** Andersen, "Admitting You Don't Know, When You're the CEO."

## Chapter 7: Play Your Specialist Game

157 **"Crawl into the skin"**: Carmen Nobel, "Clay Christensen's Milkshake Marketing," Harvard Business School Working Knowledge, February 14, 2011, http://hbswk.hbs.edu/item/clay-christensens-milkshake-marketing.

172 **"The difference between successful"**: Adam Grant, "8 Ways to Say No Without Hurting Your Image," LinkedIn, March 11, 2014, https://www.linkedin.com/pulse/20140311110227-69244073-8-ways-to-say-no-without-hurting-your-image.

173 **"8 Ways to Say No"**: Ibid.

## Chapter 8: Change the Game

194 **"blue ocean strategy"**: W. Chan Kim and Renée Mauborgne, "Blue Ocean Strategy," *Harvard Business Review*, October 2004, https://hbr.org/2004/10/blue-ocean-strategy.

206 **"field independence"**: "Herman Witkin," Wikipedia, accessed September 10, 2016, https://en.wikipedia.org/wiki/Herman_Witkin.

208 **Michelle Greenwald's list**: Michelle Greenwald, "The Power of Benchmarking Nature and Other Industries to Generate Breakthrough Innovation Ideas," *Forbes*, June 24, 2014, http://www.forbes.com/sites/michellegreenwald/2014/06/24/the-power-of-benchmarking-nature-and-other-industries-to-generate-breakthrough-innovation-ideas/#2bdee3dc2242.

## Chapter 9: Calling All Extremers

223 **"The center of gravity"**: Peter F. Drucker, "The Coming of the New Organization," *Harvard Business Review*, January 1988, https://hbr.org/1988/01/the-coming-of-the-new-organization.

229 **"stop talking about work-life balance"**: Anne-Marie Slaughter, *Unfinished Business: Women Men Work Family* (New York: Random House, 2016), 90.

230 **"first follower"**: Derek Sivers, "How to Start a Movement," TED2010, February 2010, https://www.ted.com/talks/derek_sivers_how_to_start_a_movement.

### Chapter 10: Break Yourself to Make Yourself

239 **"Efficiency is *not* your friend":** Andrea Kuszewski, "You can increase your intelligence: 5 ways to maximize your cognitive potential," *Scientific American*, March 7, 2011, http://blogs.scientificamerican.com/guest-blog/you-can-increase-your-intelligence-5-ways-to-maximize-your-cognitive-potential/.

244 **people often assume:** Jeff DeGraff, *Innovation You: Four Steps to Becoming New and Improved* (New York: Ballantine Books, 2011), 88–91.

# INDEX

# ABOUT THE AUTHOR

SARAH ROBB O'HAGAN is an executive, activist, and entrepreneur, and the founder of Extreme YOU, a movement to unleash high performance. As the global president of Gatorade, she led its reinvention and turnaround, and she is the former president of Equinox Fitness Clubs. Named one of *Forbes*'s "Most Powerful Women in Sports" and one of *Fast Company*'s "Most Creative People in Business," she has also held leadership positions at Nike and Virgin Atlantic Airways. She is now the CEO of the fitness company Flywheel Sports. A sought-after expert on innovation, brand reinvention, health, fitness, and inspiring human performance, Sarah lives with her family in New York.